Legal System
Between
Order and Disorder

Legal System Between Order and Disorder

MICHEL van de KERCHOVE
FRANÇOIS OST

Translated by
IAIN STEWART

OXFORD UNIVERSITY PRESS
1994

Oxford University Press, Walton Street, Oxford OX2 6DP
Oxford New York
Athens Auckland Bangkok Bombay
Calcutta Cape Town Dar es Salaam Delhi
Florence Hong Kong Istanbul Karachi
Kuala Lumpur Madras Madrid Melbourne
Mexico City Nairobi Paris Singapore
Taipei Tokyo Toronto
and associated companies in
Berlin Ibadan

Oxford is a trade mark of Oxford University Press

Published in the the United States
by Oxford University Press Inc., New York

British Library Cataloguing in Publication Data
Data available

Library of Congress Cataloging in Publication Data
Kerchove, Michel van de.
[Système juridique entre ordre et désordre. English]
Legal system between order and disorder/Michel van de Kerchove, François Ost; translated by Iain Stewart.
p. cm.
Includes bibliographical references and index.
1. Law—Methodology. 2. Justice, Administration of. 3. Law—Philosophy. I. Ost, François, 1952– . II. Title.
K213.K4713 1993
340′.1—dc20 *93-4411*
ISBN 0-19-825692-2

1 3 5 7 9 10 8 6 4 2

Typeset by Create Ltd, Bath, Avon
Printed in Great Britain
on acid-free paper by
Bookcraft Ltd, Midsomer Norton, Avon

Acknowledgements

Translation of this book has been made possible through the generous support of the Fonds de la Recherche Fondamentale Collective.

The translator wishes to thank the authors for their considerable assistance. A few misprints in the French edition have been silently corrected. Any errors of translation that remain are, of course, the translator's responsibility.

I.S.

Contents

Preface to the French Edition

The starting point of this essay will be the obvious fact that law—at least, modern Western law—takes the form of a system. The central question throughout will be: in exactly what sense is law a system?

There is no shortage of models claiming to explain the systematicity of law: the geometrical model of a system as 'calculation' which Leibniz recommended to jurists, the model of a system as 'mechanism' in terms of which Bentham conceived law,[1] the vitalist model of a system as 'organism' which, according to Savigny and the Historical School of Law, was to renew legal science; while, today, discussions in legal theory appear to be seized by the 'new paradigm' of 'general system theory',[2] or investigation of systems, which has developed at the intersection of biology, cybernetics, and mathematical communication theory, following in particular the works of von Bertalanffy. Although it is not yet possible to unify the countless studies emerging in the field that this new paradigm has opened up, one can none the less make out, among them, two dominant theses. The first concerns the unity of knowledge: investigation of systems begins from the idea that the models the investigation develops are capable of application in every field of knowledge, even if—since it is sometimes unable to provide mathematical constructions, for example in the social sciences—it is limited to operating as a 'guiding idea'.[1] The second thesis involved in the concept of system concerns the idea of complexity: that idea supposes abandoning the classical definition of a system as a 'set of elements', which still conveys an analytical and classificatory perspective, in favour of a firmly interactionist conception, which would stress the exchanges that develop among those elements.

From this new angle, a system is less a collection of elements than a network of processes generating emergent properties which the com-

[1] Bentham 1970: 236.

[2] Von Bertalanffy 1973: xv, 'The system viewpoint ... represents a novel 'paradigm' in scientific thinking'; Laszlo 1972. [Von Bertalanffy speaks of 'system' in this paradigmatic sense, and of 'systems theory', 'systems philosophy', and so on when referring to specific approaches within the paradigm. This distinction is maintained here, although it is absent from the French translation, used by the authors. Tr.]

[3] Von Bertalanffy 1973: 22.

ponents, seen in isolation, did not possess. In this logic, simple relations of a linear kind (deduction, causality, and so on) tend to be replaced by recursive exchanges (retroactive loops), while the image of a principle of external command (great watchmaker of the universe or sovereign legislator) is replaced by the description of a self-regulated system, capable of guaranteeing its own autonomy and permanence simply because of its control over its own programme.

What better chance of becoming central to legal thought does this paradigm have than its predecessors did? Should one share the optimism on this of Krawietz[4] or Le Moigne?[5] One point is definitely established: legal dogmatics conceives itself in the categories of a system; it was not yesterday that jurists began to indulge in 'apologies for system builders'.[6] But, again: what system?

To answer that question, one might refer to the irresistible movement of rationalization of law, so well demonstrated by Weber. If it be granted that Roman law was more casuistic than systematic, despite such astonishing anticipations as the *Institutes* of Gaius—with their logical classification of persons, things, and actions[7]—on the other hand, in our part of the world the very process of systematization appears to begin from the twelfth century with the double rediscovery of Aristotelian logic and Roman law. Under the combined action of canonists anxious to harmonize the Roman heritage and canon law, court jurists employed to consolidate the Prince's *imperium*, and practitioners concerned with systematizing commercial practices, the formal, conceptual, and systematic rationalization of law progressed rapidly, further encouraged by the requirements of university teaching of legal subjects. Since in the classical age the model of a *mathesis universalis* predominated, the ground was fertile for its application to law. The theoreticians of modern natural law were busy proposing ambitious syntheses of an ideal law, which would be fully rational. The baton would soon be taken up by the great civilists (Loysel, Pothier, and Domat), who tried to carry this ideal over into arranging the civil laws 'in their natural order'. When eventually the Revolution completed the pro-

[4] Krawietz 1986: 282 ff. Krawietz sees in 'modern systems theory' (largely inspired by the works of Luhmann) the framework of a realist theory of law, of a 'post-positivist' kind (1986: 305), capable of producing a 'fusion' between legal and sociological theories of systems (1986: 303). Compare the more prudent responses of Friedmann (1986: 311) and Vullierme (1986: 353 ff.).

[5] Le Moigne 1985: 155 ff.

[6] Rivero 1951: 99 ff.

[7] Gaudemet 1986: 11 ff.

cess of liquidating the old law and the bourgeoisie succeeded in imposing a political régime and legal frameworks corresponding to the economic weight that it represented, the law took the centralized and codified form with which we are still familiar today.[8]

The most varied theories of law contributed to this movement of progressive systematization: iusnaturalism, utilitarianism, and analytical positivism. Even the Historical School of Law participated in the general movement: although it rejected the French-style universalist and rationalist codifications, this was the better to exalt positive law issuing from the traditions and customs of the Germanic nation, and we know how this legal romanticism soon led to the Pandectist movement, which undoubtedly represented one of the most extreme forms of formalism applied to law. Although, of course, the Common Law countries took different paths from the countries of Continental law, the need for systematization cannot be said to have been unimportant there; for one thing, the bindingness of precedent, linked with important work of doctrinal synthesis, contributed very effectively to the stability and generality of the solutions adopted.[9]

It was as if, in its diverse forms (codification, custom, cases, and doctrine), modern law had necessarily to take the form of a system. Moreover, this phenomenon probably extends beyond the legal sphere itself: it shares the rationalist and systematized form adopted by Western thought since the advent of modernity. This may explain the almost total absence of resolutely anti-systematic types of legal thought. Of course, excesses of conceptualism and formalism have been denounced at regular intervals—'professors' law' has been denounced in the name of 'living law'—but the ordered and systematic nature of the solutions was never really placed in question. And, although from these confrontations legal systematization sometimes emerged in more flexible form, that only made it more effective. It was as if the graft of an anti-systematic paradigm onto the legal tree had no chance of taking.

Some examples will help to show this. One might have thought that, in Germany at the beginning of this century, the questioning of *Professorenrecht* and *Begriffsjurisprudenz* by the adherents of sociological or 'free' law (the *Freies Recht* movement), could have given birth to a genuinely alternative model. But it is sufficient to note the verdict of Geny, well known to have been very sympathetic to these

8 See, especially, Varga 1979.

9 Similarly, Varga 1979: 300–1.

efforts to open legal science up, in order to understand why the attempt had small chance of success: 'without a fully interconnected system, able to harmonize all efforts toward a single aim', this movement 'aroused mistrust' rather than 'encouraged reform'.[10]

In the same period, on the other side of the Atlantic, there developed an intellectual movement whose inspiration was much akin—the School of Sociological Jurisprudence and the American Legal Realist Movement. Their rejection of pre-established laws in favour of judicial decisions led to a decisionism situated at the antipodes of legal axiomatics. The realism of the writers participating in this tendency, several of whom were judges of the US Supreme Court, generally kept them from any excessive conclusion and led them rather to take into account the thousand factors capable of guaranteeing the homogeneity of case law: they invoked by turns 'the immemorial traditions of professional technique', a common approach to reading precedents (despite the multiplicity of States and jurisdictions), a particular language, and particular values and ways of thinking.[11] This number of conditions, even in the absence of a strict principle of fidelity to statute and of a Court of Cassation to enforce that principle, led to certainty and systematicity comparable, and even superior, to those prevailing in the families of codified law. As can be seen on the canvases of the pointillist masters, extreme multiplication of points of reference is by no means incompatible with the emergence of an extremely rigorous wholeness of form.

Closer to home, in the post-war francophonic universe, there has been a very clear return to Aristotle, which too has tended to shake up the classical modes of legal reasoning and description. One thinks of Viehweg, with the reintroduction of the 'topic', Villey, apostle of classical natural law, and Perelman, theoretician of the 'new rhetoric'. Though Viehweg does not have words strong enough to exorcize the ideals of axiomatization and formalization—which in his judgement bear no relation to legal practice, which is essentially casuistic—he none the less appears never to attack the idea of system itself.[12] It may therefore still be supposed that topics (which are points of view, 'common places' for argumentation) are in their turn

[10] Geny 1919: ii. 391; see also 701, 'None of them has managed to discover the objective criterion that could transform "free law" into the instrument of social certainty that the very notion of positive law energetically postulates'.

[11] Similarly, Michaut 1985: 203–8.

[12] Viehweg 1969: *passim*, esp. 27, 61–6.

capable of constituting an axiological or teleological kind of ordering.

In the same way, although Villey stresses that 'law is not a logical system nor, in the strict sense, rational'[13] and, against the deductivist illusions of the moderns, claims inspiration from a 'completely different conception of law', that of a natural law which is 'outside and independent of our minds, in external reality—in the last analysis, hidden in nature', he does not hesitate to define the latter as 'an order, a harmony, a set of logical relations, for', he adds, 'there is a reason within things'.[14] He means that, if legal reasoning does not pertain to the logic of the rational, at least it tends, through dialectic and debate, to attain the logic of the reasonable, which makes do with 'pieces of system' or with 'open systems'.[15]

Perelman's perspective is barely different. Here, too, it is a question of opening the system rather than of rejecting it. Enjoining the judge to 'adapt rules to the result sought' by introducing 'into the legal system considerations of appropriateness, justice and the general interest',[16] Perelman is content in the end to recommend making the system more flexible by infusing into its structure 'elements of indeterminacy'.[17]

The convergence of these observations is significant in more than one way: it teaches us both that modern law does not escape from the model of a system and that this model is actually less formalistic than the ideal imagined by classical legal dogmatics might lead one to believe. Ambiguously, the model simultaneously lays claim to the most rigorous order and puts up with a definite dose of disorder.

We now have, if not an answer, at least the beginning of an answer to the question we formulated at the beginning: 'what system for law?'. A very clear awareness of the ambiguity of legal discourse and practice, a taking into account of the 'in-between' or 'double game' which seems to be its chosen territory, ought to save us from taking at face value the various models that some have wanted to impose on law from the outside: of system as 'calculation', 'mechanism', or 'organism'.

Are legal systems, in the final analysis, open or closed, self- or hetero-regulated, static or evolving? To try to answer these questions, we need to multiply the directions of approach rather than

13 Villey 1978: 9. 14 1978: 7. 15 1978: 8–9.
16 Perelman 1984: 73. 17 1984: 71.

adopt a single paradigm from the start, which would be bound to bias the investigation. We shall investigate:

1. the elements of a system: norms, for sure, but also concepts, institutions, values, and so on;
2. the relations that develop among those elements: whether they configure a static or dynamic, formal or substantive, linear or circular systematicity; and how the systematizations effected respectively by the legislator, doctrine, and cases are joined together;
3. the relations that the system maintains with its environment: whether control, dependence, or indifference; and whether the answer will remain invariable according to whether one envisages successively exchanges between legal system and social order, between legal system and ethical system, or, again, between different legal orders; and
4. the specific temporality of legal systems: whether one can pinpoint their conditions of emergence, transformation, and survival.

Dealing with these different questions will progressively confirm our initial intuition: legal systems will appear plainly to be characterized by a curious entanglement of order and disorder, rather like a Borromean knot. The limits of the formalization of legal discourse appear on all sides; yet, despite these denials inflicted on the 'logician's ideals' that dogmatics claims to pursue, there persist a style of reasoning and an institutional ordering that bear the stamp of deductive verticality. There are ceaseless changes of register from formal logic to ethical considerations, from spirit to letter, and from the useful to the legal, without tearing the web of a discourse whose form is Protean.

This appears to be because, far from opposing one term to another, as one is led to think by binary logic—the logic of true and false, of permitted and forbidden—order and disorder secretly complement each other, multiplying their exchanges according to a rationality whose nature has still to be described. Just as theoreticians of living forms have recently introduced the principle of 'order through noise',[18] jurists too will no doubt be led to recognize the determinative part played by exterior disorder (from the modest fact produced in court to the hypothesis of revolutionary change) in legal systematization. It appears, indeed, that, without

[18] Atlan 1983: 97.

this element of indeterminacy introduced into its heart, a legal order condemns itself to ineffectiveness and immobility.[19]

In this way, if at least one wishes to get free from dogmatic description without in the process falling into a nihilistic scepticism, one must learn to think in terms of a logic of paradox:[20] is not a legal system in fact *simultaneously* static and dynamic, formal and substantive, open and closed, autonomous and dependent?

There emerges a plural and graduated rationality—one writer has referred in this regard to 'fuzziness of law'[19]—which prevents one from remaining content with a monological (yes/no) answer to the most basic legal questions. To know whether this particular rule envisages this exact case, whether this particular norm belongs to this particular legal order, or whether this particular solution is purely legal, most often supposes an estimation expressed in degree of belonging rather than a categorical judgement, which would actually be bound to damage the flexibility and, overall, the fluidity of that legal system. Thus it is not only legal language that presents an 'open texture', as the English have taught us, but a legal system as a whole, whose borders always appear uncertain. At the limits of law, politics, ethics, economics, and society loom spaces of confrontation and exchange whose moving outline constantly produces reorganization of the systems concerned.

Is this a congenital weakness of law? Yes, probably, if one continues to cultivate the ideal of a legal certainty derived from strictly deductive logic and rigorous autonomy. But not if one becomes aware once and for all of the illusoriness of such certainty: for, on the contrary, it is because it is able to multiply its relations with society and, when need be, soften the rigour of its deductions that law is able to espouse the peculiarities of facts and so offer a reasonable degree of foreseeability. Moreover, the effectiveness of the values that the law means to promote is obtained at the same price: it is, for example, the flexibility and adaptiveness of a general principle like that of the accused's right of reply that has allowed its application to ever broader areas.

19 Le Moigne 1985: 168, refers in this connection to 'the capacity that legal systems should have, to tolerate—and even create—some ambiguities and equivocations, some redundancies and even some disorders within their internal as well as external articulations, so as to facilitate the conditions for some innovative moments of self-organization'.

20 See Barel 1979.

21 Delmas-Marty 1986.

Far from appearing as the antithesis of order, or at least as its fallen image, disorder operates rather as a condition of order—of an 'other' order, a new direction guaranteeing the system's indispensable adaptation. For, after all, disorder may well be only the emergent form of a rationality that, though it still escapes us today, may well become clear tomorrow.[22]

These therefore will be the plan followed and the thesis developed. The method of this book will be quite firmly pedagogical. Refraining from the extreme sophistication and, sometimes, trendy language that characterize certain debates of systemic enquiry, we have tried to stick as closely as possible to the classic questions of legal theory, the better to make out, on the obverse of the arguments exchanged, the kind of systematicity that each supposes. Rather than hunt in the legal arsenal for some easy and momentary confirmation of such-and-such a hypothesis borrowed from systems theory, we have made ourselves search through the problematic of legal system in most of its essential dimensions, without sheering away from what seem the most traditional questions—for example, those of interpretation, validity, the functions of law, and the relation between law and morality. It seems to us that it is only at the end of this journey, where jurists will be able easily to recognize themselves, that we shall be in a position to formulate some hypotheses about the kind of systematicity evident in the functioning of legal discourse and practice. We believe that we can thus avoid the 'wild' transdisciplinarity that imports into the legal field, without clearing them through customs, concepts, and theories forged in quite different domains. Conversely, this scrupulous taking account of the 'jurists' internal point of view' should, we hope, make the fruitfulness of these external instruments of investigation more evident. Such, at least, is the desire for a critical interdisciplinarity that we shall attempt to put into practice.

The introduction to this book would not be complete if we failed to mention, at least in brief, the initial impulse to which it is indebted. As it happens, the present essay owes its existence to a both friendly and insistent suggestion from André-Jean Arnaud. In anticipation of the World Congress of Sociology of Law held at Aix-en-

22 See, similarly, the fine observation by one of the editors of the *Dictionnaire Lalande*: Parodi, after defining the concept of order by the idea of 'intelligible relation' and in this context opposing order to disorder, adds, 'Perhaps, besides, there is here only an illusion, and all disorder is at base only confused knowledge or absence of knowledge' (Lalande 1962:, at '*Ordre*' 720).

Provence in August 1985, Arnaud asked us to present a summary report explaining the concept of a legal system. In the light of experience, this anodyne suggestion proved fearsome; as question followed question, the summary report finished by occupying a volume. Probably thanks to the many comments from which it benefited both at the time of its presentation at Aix in 1985 and, in an already more fleshed-out form, at Éguilles in May 1986, in the 'Cercle de Cordialité' of which Arnaud is the prime mover. A large number of the original insights that may be contained here are also owed to the stimulating observations generously provided by, especially, Jacques Commaille, Vicenzo Ferrari, Sheldon Leader, Jean-François Perrin, Michel Troper, and Jerzy Wróblewski.

Beyond that, the authors would also like to express their gratitude to Mireille Delmas-Marty and Gérard Timsit, who edit the series in which our study appears.[23] Their support and penetrating comments have helped to give the manuscript its final form. Thanks to them, we are particularly pleased to be able to present the outcome of our researches to the public in a series whose declared object is 'the opening up of a discipline long closed in on itself' by introducing 'models deriving from a different form of coherence: mobile, multidimensional, and risky'. In such convergences, surely, lies the charm of research.

23 ['Les voies du droit' (Presses Universitaires de France). Tr.]

I
General Problematic

Before looking at the main questions raised by the investigation of law as system, it seems useful to mention some preliminary problems. How can the concept of system interest the study of law? What different epistemological orientations might that investigation follow and, in particular, which orientation will this book adopt? What general perspectives opened up by the investigation of systems explain the choice of the various problems dealt with in this book? On the fringe of general system theory, indeed, may one not see in writers such as Kelsen and Hart true precursors of a theory of legal system?

1.1. INTEREST OF THE CONCEPT OF SYSTEM FOR THE STUDY OF LAW

Although legal phenomena probably are never readily amenable to the complete and rigorous systematic treatment that nowadays can be envisaged in terms of 'general system theory', it is undeniable that the idea of system and the ideal of systematization directly characterize modern Western law. The proof of this is that one hardly ever sees major questions concerning modern Western law that can now be handled without recourse to that idea.

1.1.1. *Definition of Law*

In beginning with the basic problem of the *definition* of law, one may take it that highly fruitful perspectives on this level have been opened up by an approach stressing the features or specific structure of a legal system, rather than the distinctive properties of its elements. Thus, believing that traditional legal thought had committed the error of 'looking at the tree and not the forest',[1] Bobbio noted that a

[1] Bobbio 1960: 7. See also Troper *1986: 30*. On the links noticeable between this change of perspective and renewed questioning of the classical definition of law in terms of common genus and specific difference, see, especially, Ost and van de Kerchove 1987: 152 ff.

satisfactory definition of law can be formulated only from the standpoint of 'the legal order' and not from the standpoint of 'legal norms' considered in isolation.[2] In an identical perspective, one can also cite Romano: 'If one wishes to define a legal order as a whole, one must not look only at what one believes to be its different parts—that is, the norms that it contains—and then say that it is the sum of those parts. On the contrary, it is indispensable to grasp the specific nature of that set, that totality.'[3]

1.1.2. *Validity in Law*

It is not difficult to see that the problematic of the *validity* of legal norms can no longer be approached correctly by abstracting from the concept of system. While there are of course some tendencies in legal theory that have privileged criteria of validity—whether empirical or axiological—criteria that are thought to permit abstraction from any form of reference to the existence of a given legal system—it is plain that these 'radical' conceptions generally do not manage to avoid, at the heart of their claims, the return of a third 'formal' or 'systemic' criterion, understood as the conformity of a legal norm to the conditions of membership posited by a particular legal system.[4]

In this context, one seems inevitably limited to a 'moderate' conception of the validity, whether axiological or empirical, of legal norms which combines the criteria of systemic validity with the earlier criteria.[5] One may even propose without difficulty that the most central meaning of the concept of validity indicates precisely that the norm envisaged belongs to the system from which it claims to come, without however having to neglect its other dimensions.

1.1.3. *Interpretation in Law*

Analogous considerations concern the problematic of *interpretation* in law. One cannot pass over the lessons of modern theories of language, which have shown clearly that the meaning of a term or proposition is very largely determined by the use made of it within a lexicon or a given body of propositions.

[2] Bobbio 1960: 7. [3] Romano 1975: 7.
[4] See, especially, Ost and van de Kerchove 1987: 292.
[5] See, especially, Wróblewski 1987: 136–7.

Following these theories, it is necessary, in law, to supersede both theories in which the accent is placed on the constraints arising from the will of the author of the norm interpreted or on the norm's literal meaning, and theories emphasizing the interpreter's subjective freedom which arises from the inherent limits of such constraints. Thus one may begin from the idea that, basically, what polarizes interpretation in law is the interpreter's concern to maintain or restore the rationality of the legal system as a whole.[6] Likewise, one may also consider so-called 'systematic' interpretation as occupying a position that is both privileged and in some way grounding, in relation to the different particular methods of interpretation.

To these different central questions may be added the equally traditional question of the *relations between law and morality*. In this regard we shall confine ourselves to mentioning Hart's opinion, according to which a satisfactory and complete answer to this question depends on grasping it not at the level of each norm in particular but at the level of the legal system overall.[7]

The same idea may be extended to many other problematics, such as the rôle of sanctions in law and the relations between law and coercion or between State and law. It reveals, through the different 'decentrings' that have been suggested—from investigation of the norm to investigation of the system—the evident interest that the concept of system can acquire for the study of law.[8]

1.1.4. *General Features of the Concept of System*

That clarified, it still seems necessary to distinguish, if not a true definition of the notion of system—which might not be discoverable—at least a certain number of general features that appear to be recurrently associated with that notion and which will serve as backdrop to our later arguments.

A preliminary question of terminology must however be mentioned. In legal language the term 'order (*ordre*)', or 'ordering' (*ordonnancement*), (compare *Ordnung*, *ordinamento*) is often found beside or in place of the term 'system'.[6] One may also suppose that it

[6] See, especially, Ost and van de Kerchove 1987: 442.
[7] See below, Sect. 4.5.
[8] On the importance of the concept of system in law teaching (at least in the countries of Continental law), see Cousy 1983: 3–22.
[9] On the emergence and historical evolution of these different terms, Tarello 1979: 91 ff. may usefully be consulted.

is probably not accidental that the term 'legal order' derives from a more traditional usage than that of 'legal system'; for, in contrast with the latter, it obviously bears a double meaning: that of ordering or system and that of command or norm.[10] Now, there can be no doubt that 'law is . . . an order both in that it is "systematic" and in that it is "normative"' and that 'the concept of legal order expresses that conjunction and crossover of two dimensions, the systematicity and the normativity of law'.[11]

Independently of this duality of meanings, there is still the problem of knowing whether the term 'order', understood in its first dimension, may be considered to be strictly synonymous with 'system'.

In this regard, it is possible to distinguish two categories of writer. Some, such as Kelsen,[12] Romano,[13] Raz,[10] Troper,[15] and Alchourrón and Bulygin,[16] take these two expressions to be synonyms, while, however, generally giving preference to the one or the other of them.[17] Other writers, on the contrary, give these terms different meanings, even if they do not necessarily mean to oppose them to each other.[18]

Three types of distinction, in particular, are proposed. On a first distinguishing criterion, some writers characterize the concept of legal order by the existence of a type—particularly a hierarchical type—of unity among its elements, while they characterize the concept of legal system by the existence of a type of consistency among them.[19] On a second criterion, some associate the concept of legal order with a voluntary mode of organization, while the concept of legal system involves the existence of an involuntary or spontaneous mode of organization.[20] Lastly, on a third criterion, the concept of normative order is considered to be broader than that of normative

10 See, especially, Chevallier 1983: 7; Goyard-Fabre 1986: 25 ff.

11 Chevallier 1983: 8.

12 Kelsen 1967: 195.

13 Romano 1975: 7, 31.

14 Raz 1970.

15 Troper 1986: 30.

16 Alchourrón and Bulygin 1971: 4.

17 Thus the term 'order (*ordinamento*)' occupies a central place in the work of Romano, while conversely that of 'system' predominates in the work of Raz, Troper, Alchourrón, and Bulygin—while Kelsen employs now one, now the other.

18 See, e.g. Arnaud 1981: 22, 'Order cannot be opposed to system. It is a question of two different levels of approach.'

19 See Bobbio 1960: 23; Arnaud 1981: 21.

20 Similarly, especially, Combacau 1986: 78. This distinction is itself very close to that developed by Hayek between *taxis* and *cosmos*, the one defined as 'constructed' or 'artificial' order, the other as 'grown' or 'spontaneous' order (1982: 35 ff.).

system, in that the latter covers only so-called 'static' orders, while the former also covers so-called 'dynamic' orders.[21]

While admitting that distinctions of this kind may throw some light on the different levels on which legal phenomena may be investigated, it does not seem useful here to adopt terminological conventions that not only are far from being generally accepted but also risk placing exclusive stress on one or the other dimension of the problem, according to the term employed. Although we have chosen to privilege the concept of legal system, we do so by taking it to be a synonym of legal order, in the first sense of that term. On the other hand, the fact that within the framework of this book we have approached legal phenomena in terms specifically of system obviously implies, on our part, a desire to supersede the 'trite' meaning that many jurists give indifferently to the terms 'order' or 'system', meaning thereby only a simple body or collection of norms.[22]

In order to go beyond such an approach, it seems necessary to grasp that—in a sense which, although more technical, is nevertheless current—the notion of system supposes the uniting of at least three general features.

At the minimal level, the notion of system appears at first to require the uniting—the Greek term *σνστημα* (systēma) meaning assemblage[23]—of a set of elements, according to the expression used in set theory, or of components,[24] according to the expression often used in systems theory. These elements may be not only of a very different nature, between one system and another, but also of a different nature within a single system. Moreover, it is perfectly possible for these elements themselves to constitute subsystems,[25] uniting in their turn more elementary entities. The first idea met with at this level is therefore that of a *set* (*ensemble*).

The notion of system therefore appears to imply the existence of specific *relations* between these elements and not their simple jux-

21 On this see, especially, Jori 1984: 349. Beyond its terminological dimension, this question is taken up below at Sect. 2.1.1.

22 See, especially, Tarello 1979: 91; Bobbio 1960: 19.

23 See, especially, Lalande 1962, at '*Système*'. See also Gardies 1987: 173, 'In Greek, *σννιστημι* (synistēmi) means to put together (*mettre ensemble*) and the noun *σνστημα* (systēma) covers any kind of set (*ensemble*): a *troop* of soldiers, a *herd* of animals, a *strophe* of verse, a *constitution* of political principles, a *system* of philosophical ideas.'

24 See, especially, Churchman 1968: 39; Ladrière 1985: 586.

25 Ibid. See also Walliser 1977: 39 ff.

taposition; it supposes, in other words, the existence of an ordered or organized totality:[26] that is, the existence of bonds of interdependence,[27] interaction,[28] and solidarity[29] among the system's components. Thus, at this level the central idea is that of *order* or *organization*.

Finally, the notion of system appears to imply a certain unity,[30] and not merely a play of interactions among different elements.[31] This unity of a system involves both a negative aspect of differentiation from the exterior and a positive aspect of identity,[32] which makes it possible to determine both the elements that belong and those that do not belong to the system. This unity, sometimes presented in the form of a cohesion,[33] is based in particular on one or more principles governing the relations among the various constitutive elements[34] and determining the system's structure.[26] The essential idea to add here is therefore that of *structure*.

1.2. EPISTEMOLOGICAL ORIENTATIONS

After constructing a minimal delimitation of the general notion of system and noting that notion's interest for the study of law, the next step must be to determine the different epistemological perspectives in which it can be studied, particularly when that is to be done within a specifically legal framework.

1.2.1. *Distinction Between Internal and External Points of View*

It seems useful here to turn to an epistemological model taken particularly from Hart, which consists of distinguishing two different points of view—characterized as internal and external—from which legal phenomena may be apprehended.[36] While the internal view operates, as it were, 'in a mirror'—that is, by adhering to the discourse that legal institutions use about themselves and

[26] Lalande 1962, at '*Système*'; Canaris 1969: 12.
[27] Thinès and Lempereur 1975: 935.
[28] Chevallier 1983: 9; Gassin 1981: 356.
[29] Lalande 1962, at '*Système*'; Gardies 1973: 173.
[30] Canaris 1969: 12. [31] Ibid. [32] Chevallier 1983: 14.
[33] Ibid. [34] 1983: 15.
[35] Gassin 1981: 362; Arnaud 1981: 22.
[36] On this see, especially, Ost and van de Kerchove 1987: 27 ff.

sharing the 'pre-understanding' underlying it—the external point of view, in contrast, supposes an 'epistemological break' or theoretical distancing that consists either of giving an account, in descriptive and explanatory terms, of the internal point of view adopted by the actors in the legal system ('moderate' external point of view) or of making a theoretical reconstruction that would abstract completely from the existence of that internal point of view ('radical' external point of view).

1.2.2. *Adoption of an Internal Point of View*

Starting from the internal point of view, there seems to be no doubt, at least with reference to contemporary Western societies, that 'the requirement of systematicity' is found 'written in the hearts of legal phenomena',[37] whether this is seen in terms of a substantive cohesion, on the level of the contents and purposes of rules, or in terms of formal properties, such as decidability, independence, completeness, or consistency—on which we shall have more to say later. However, it is not difficult to perceive at the same time that these requirements are actually far from being completely satisfied and that, failing perfect systematicity of law, one can speak only of a recurrent intrinsic tendency toward systematization.

This idea is important, for, if one accepts that the enterprise of systematizing legal orders is always uncompleted, the problem arises of knowing to what extent it is legal science's job to pursue it.

On this level there appears to be a risk of basic confusion. There can be no doubt that the requirement of systematicity inheres equally in thought in general and particularly in the development of scientific thought, of which it forms one of the postulates or major presuppositions.[38]

At this point, one might easily be tempted to believe that, when attempting to develop a science of law, the requirements of scientific and legal systematicity coincide. And that is indeed how doctrine[39] and especially legal dogmatics have conceived their rôle: by pursuing the systematization of a particular legal order, these disciplines have traditionally claimed to do scientific work, in appearing to develop a systematic body of knowledge of their object.

37 Chevallier 1983: 11; Canaris 1969: 16.
38 Canaris 1969: 14; Ladrière 1985: 586.
39 See, especially, Rivero 1951: 99 ff.

As is well known, when general theory of law has laid claim to being scientific it often has not managed to evade this confusion.

Kelsen's pure theory of law illustrates this excellently when it sets up the principle that 'the cognition of law, like any cognition, seeks to understand its subject as a meaningful whole and to describe it in noncontradictory statements'.[40] The requirement of scientific systematicity readily leads Kelsen, as it happens, to satisfying requirements of systematicity that really belong to the point of view internal to the object that he is studying. Amselek has pointed out this confusion clearly, in remarking that there is obviously no logical contradiction in describing a contradiction that is internal to the legal order being studied.[41] A lack of systematicity in the object studied thus in no way affects the systematicity of the theory developed in relation to that object.

Some theoreticians of legal systems, such as Alchourrón and Bulygin, appear to suffer from the same kind of confusion. Although they appear not to consider it legal science's job to eliminate gaps and contradictions within its object, for that would be to modify the system in force,[42] these writers none the less suppose that its function of systematization involves eliminating certain faults of the system,[43] such as redundancies and excess of casuistry,[44] as well as formulating general principles underlying the norms in force.[45]

Thus, in such a perspective, the point of view adopted seems, once more, close to coinciding with the internal point of view, even if limits are imposed on it.

Contrary to appearances, it seems that many idealist theories of law, in basing themselves on axiological considerations, do not go so far as to break with the internal requirements of law but seek simply to provide them with a rational legitimation. An example of such an outlook may be found in the theory of legal systems developed by Canaris, who presents systematicity as a postulate inherent in the idea of law, answering to the ethical requirements of justice and legal certainty.[46] The perspective adopted by such a theory thus, far from breaking with the internal point of view, tends to provide it with an ultimate justification.

If one now accepts that a truly scientific attitude cannot limit itself

[40] Kelsen 1967: 206. [41] Amselek 1964: 187.
[42] Alchourrón and Bulygin 1971: 79.
[43] Ibid. [44] 1971: 80. [45] 1971: 81 ff.
[46] Canaris 1969: 16–17.

to adopting this internal point of view, but supposes what Hart has called the adoption of an external point of view, it is nevertheless still important to determine whether this point of view should adopt a 'radical' or 'moderate' form.

1.2.3. *Adoption of a Radical External Point of View*

The break of perspective involved in the radical external point of view consists of studying legal phenomena by taking absolutely no account of the internal point of view. In the present case, it would consist of developing a theory that would completely neglect the requirements of systematicity that are internal to law, by dissolving systematicity, as for example Marxist theory does, into a social system of which 'the legal order would only be a mere reflection'[47] or that would deny any form of legal or social systematicity by reducing law to a body of momentary decisions, as American realist theories, in particular, would suggest.

Such theories, however, are in danger of no longer accounting for the specificity of their object. What they claim to gain in explanatory power, they lose in power of comprehension.

1.2.4. *Adoption of a Moderate External Point of View*

In our view, the only perspective that makes it possible both to understand the object 'law' in its specificity and to provide a theory that can explain it is that which adopts a moderate external point of view consisting, as Hart has said, of taking account of the point of view internal to law without adopting it. In relation to the present problem, this attitude consists of providing the most comprehensive possible account both of the requirements of systematicity that are inherent in law and of the limits to such systematicity, without taking upon itself the job of pursuing that systematization. It involves, moreover, the job of laying out, in an explanatory perspective, a set of relations between the phenomenon so characterized and other phenomena that are coextensive with it.

While the development of such an explanatory theory evidently itself supposes some degree of systematicity, it is essential to grasp that this systematization of cognitions is of a different nature from systematization of the object being studied.

[47] Chevallier 1983: 11.

If, moreover, in our view, such a perspective would make the science of law interdisciplinary, it goes without saying that the completion of such a task goes beyond our own limited skills. Consequently, we can only begin to construct research perspectives—our aim being only to break down the isolation from which the study of legal systems suffers through generally being undertaken in a purely internal and dogmatic perspective.

1.3. PERSPECTIVES OPENED UP BY INVESTIGATION OF SYSTEMS

Can the study of legal systems benefit right away from the achievements of systemic enquiry? It must be recognized that, despite the ambitious titles of some works of systemic enquiry—such as Le Moigne's *La théorie du système général* (1977) and *La théorie générale des systèmes* (1978)—systems theory is still in a largely programmatic state. None the less, there has been progress in formulating certain recurrent questions, which have produced some attempts at conceptual elaboration in which the study of legal systems can already find inspiration.

A first series of questions concerns the components or constitutive elements of a system. In this regard, anything can make up a system, so far as a principle of integration ensures the unity of the set. A system may be formed out of natural entities, such as the cells of a living organism, material entities, such as the pieces of a motor, or social and symbolic entities. In this respect one can build up systems of observational and/or normative propositions, of values, of practices, of rôles and attitudes, and of institutions. While Kelsen or Hart grasp a legal system as a set of norms, Romano presents it as 'legal order' corresponding to the ideas of institution and organization.

A second series of questions concerns the kinds of relation that can be developed among a system's constitutive elements. This point is important, since in principle a system possesses properties that are not reducible to those characterizing its elements. Among the multiple modes of ordering that might be thought to exist among these elements, one can distinguish static and dynamic, formal and substantive, and linear and circular modes of structuration. These will be considered throughout the rest of this book.

The third series of questions arising from systemic enquiry concerns a system's relations with its environment. Here the initial question is that of identifying the system: what degree of internal structuration is required for a set of elements to differentiate itself sufficiently from its environment to be apprehended as a system? After answering that question, one needs to determine the nature of the system's environment: is it disorder, the undifferentiated, or, on the contrary, an area that is equally, and perhaps better, systematized? This operation requires, in its turn, discovering the kinds of exchange that occur between the system and its exterior: does it integrate or repel the surrounding disorder? Does it form relations of co-ordination with other systems of the same level, or relations of subordination with regard to a more encompassing system, or does it perhaps integrate into itself a series of subordinate subsystems?

These questions can be answered only after determining the degree of openness of the system being studied. In this regard, one can distinguish closed systems, folded back on themselves and insensitive to pressures from outside, and open systems, turned towards the exterior and broadly receptive to the promptings of the surroundings.[48] This classification, in its turn, assumes that one has been able to answer the question of the type of regulation that is characteristic of the system being studied: is it a cybernetic type of system that can claim to regulate itself—even, like living systems, to produce itself by itself, a central mechanism taking it upon itself to adapt the system's programme to encountered needs—or is it rather a hetero-regulated system, whose functioning supposes the intervention of exterior agents? Writers like Crozier and Friedberg, in *L'acteur et le système* (1977), present social systems and subsystems as 'open and concrete action systems', open to strategies developed by the actors; these strategies, though lying within the constraints inherent in the various social games, none the less assume that there remains a degree of irreducible unpredictability.[49]

Finally, one of the most fruitful perspectives opened up by systemic enquiry concerns the study of systems' evolution. At each moment in time, a system is characterized by a given state expressed in the configuration of the set of its elements. But, in the course of time, and apart from the exceptional case of an absolutely static system, these states may alter, either in response to internal modifications which might affect its components or through the interactions that might take place with its environment. This evolution

[48] 1983: 19. [49] Crozier and Friedberg 1977: 207–12.

may occur as much in the form of a stability constantly recovered through mechanisms of adaptation to changes as in the direction of greater internal integration linked to processes of annexing the environment, or finally in the direction of gradual disintegration, the system being unable to resist the entropy affecting it.[50]

1.4. TWO PRECURSORS: KELSEN AND HART

1.4.1. *Kelsen*

Although Kelsen is the theoretician *par excellence* of legal system, he was not, of course, the first writer to emphasize its importance for legal science. As he recognized himself, he had often only developed in a rigorous way ideas already established in nineteenth-century German dogmatics: here one could mention the names of Jhering, Savigny, Windscheid and many others.

We shall attempt to synthesize Kelsen's conception of legal system by examining in succession the answers he gives to four problematics already mentioned, concerning respectively: the elements of a system, how those elements are ordered, the relations that a system forms with its environment and a system's characteristic evolution.

(*a*) *Elements of a Legal System*. For Kelsen, a legal system is composed exclusively of a set of legal norms and a supposed basic norm which ensures their unity and validity. Since, moreover, a legal system is held to be identical with the legal community grounded in that order (in the case of a relatively centralized legal order, the State),[51] a legal system may also be presented as a set of organs creating law.

(*b*) *Relations Among These Elements*. As to the mode of ordering that ensures these norms' articulation, Kelsen distinguishes two principles of unity:[52] a static and a dynamic principle. According to the first, norms are derived from each other by a deductive operation; from a higher norm may be deduced the content of a lower norm, as the particular is deduced from the general. In such a hypothesis, which may characterize moral normative systems, the basic norm determines not only the validity but also the content of the norms derived: in that sense, the system may be called static. On the other hand, legal systems generally follow a principle of dynamic structuration: their basic norm is limited to authorizing the supreme

[50] See Ladrière 1985: 587. [51] Kelsen 1967: 286. [52] 1967: 195.

authority of the system to create law. This has two main consequences: negatively, 'any kind of content might be law',[53] the ordering among the system's elements being purely formal; and, positively, law has the essential characteristic that it 'regulates its own creation and application'[54]—in just this lies its systemic nature. Kelsen is assuredly one of the first writers to have clearly distinguished the characteristic inherent in the idea of system that is the system's capacity for self-organization. For Kelsen, this capacity operates in a linear and hierarchical mode: the lower being always grounded or authorized by the higher.

'The norms of a legal order', Kelsen writes, 'are not a complex of valid norms standing coordinatedly side by side, but form a hierarchical structure of super- and subordinate norms.'[55] Thus the creation of general legal norms by legislation and custom takes place through application of the Constitution; then, in applying those general norms, individual norms are created by the decisions of courts and administrative bodies.[56]

For Kelsen, however, this articulation of norms, or these relations of authorization between organs, do not rest on any empirical observation or consideration of practical convenience; the articulation really corresponds to epistemological postulates. The first of these is that all knowledge postulates the unity of its object; the second lies in the irreducible distinction between is and ought. By virtue of the postulate of unity, says Kelsen, it is necessary 'to understand all law in onc system—that is, from one and the same standpoint—as one closed whole':[57] it follows that all legal norms considered simultaneously valid must necessarily be articulated in one system; and Kelsen adds that that system cannot contain persistent contradictions, a sign negating unity.[58] In addition, the separation of *Sein* and *Sollen* leads to the idea that a norm's basis of validity can only be another norm and not a fact of *Sein*—for example, the will of its author or the recognition accorded to its author by lower organs.

In Kelsen's thought, of course, it is the *basic norm*, authorizing the supreme authority to create law, which ensures that those postulates come into operation, in that it simultaneously confers on the set of norms under consideration unity, non-contradiction and a basis of validity. The reason why any legal norm belongs to a given legal

53 1967: 198. 54 1967: 71, 197–8. 55 1967: 201.
56 1967: 234–5. 57 1967: 328. 58 1967: 205.

order and consequently is considered valid is that it has been created in conformity with a higher norm and, in the last instance, in conformity with the basic norm of that system. The basic norm thus guarantees both a norm's membership in a system and its validity within that system.[59] Conversely, what ensures the identity of a legal system and thus guarantees the unity of the plurality of the norms composing it is the fact that all these norms are derived from a single basic norm. With the basic norm, legal systems, already endowed with a hierarchical and dynamic mode of organization, are further assured of a single principle of differentiation, unity, and validity which guarantees, in the literal sense of the word, their autonomy. This autonomy, however, even in Kelsen's thought, is not absolute: on the one hand, because a legal system exists only if it is accompanied by a minimum of effectiveness; on the other, because a legal order's dynamic development makes room, at each stage of the process of individualization of law, for a margin of indeterminacy which the organs applying law utilize in order to reinforce political choices or ethical values. In this sense, each act applying a higher norm is at the same time partly a creation of new law, the lower norm not being purely and simply 'deduced' from the preceding norm. The higher norm appears, rather, as a framework open to several possibilities of determination, all equally admissible from the standpoint of legal knowledge and among which it is the interpreter's rôle to choose through an act of will inspired by extra-legal considerations. From this point of view, the situations of judge and administrator are not essentially different from that of a legislator adopting a general norm in conformity with the Constitution. However, the study of these extra-legal choices is in no way within the competence of legal science as Kelsen conceives it.

(*c*) *A Legal System and Its Environment.* The ideas just reviewed make it possible to understand how Kelsen conceives the relations between legal order and moral order on one side, and between separate legal systems on the other. Regarding the first question, Kelsen defends the postulate of the separation of law and morality, which, although it does not prohibit evaluating the content of law from the standpoint of any particular morality, none the less entails that the validity of positive legal orders is independent of their conformity to a moral system.[60] A legal system and a moral system do not derive

[59] 1967: 194. [60] 1967: 66.

from one and the same basic norm; accordingly, conflicts may arise between the prescriptions of these two orders and, in that event, one has to make a choice that will lead to maintaining the validity of only one of the two normative orders under consideration.[61]

The same principles guide Kelsen in elucidating relations between legal orders, both as to relations between national law and international law and as to those between national law and corporative law as well as the law of decentralized entities. The dominant idea is that the same persons cannot be subjected at the same time to two or more legal orders that are considered to be both valid and separate. 'No one can serve two masters,' Kelsen reminds us.[62] If two legal orders are simultaneously valid, that is because, far from being separate from each other, they stand in a relation of inclusion, one of them being derived from the other, its organs being authorized by those of the higher order and its norms finding the basis of their validity in the basic norm of the latter, with a further consequence that no antimony can persist between systems articulated in this way. This rigorous monism leads therefore to a new pyramid. This pyramid includes, at its base, the corporative legal orders whose organs have been delegated and the statutes enacted by the state legal order, presented from this point of view as a total legal order encompassing the multiple partial legal orders,[63] which may also include decentralized public communities.[64] The same monism must equally prevail at the top of the scale in the relations subsisting between national law and international law, these two systems being unable to impose themselves simultaneously and independently. Here, however, Kelsen offers an alternative between two versions of the monist theory, a choice that can be justified only by considerations of legal politics: either international law is conceived as a legal order delegated by state law and consequently incorporated in the latter, or it is considered as a total legal order that delegates the state legal orders and includes them all as partial orders.[65] Here one sees that a strictly autonomistic conception of legal orders—to which, on the institutional plane, the idea of the sovereignty of encompassing and supreme legal communities corresponds—leads Kelsen to conceive only two kinds of possible relation between legal orders: either independence and even indifference, or integration. There is no place for any form of co-ordination or co-operation—therefore, no place

[61] 1967: 329. [62] Ibid. [63] 1967: 177. [64] 1967: 314.
[65] 1967: 333, 346.

for any pluralism of legal orders. In Kelsen's view, sovereign legal orders are definitely exclusive and, in their own eyes, unique.[66]

(*d*) *Legal System and Temporality*. Finally, as to the *problematic of the evolution of legal systems*, it can be seen, on one side, that the dynamic conception of the creation of a system makes it possible to think of a constant process of effecting and adapting, while, in addition, the operation of the principle of effectiveness makes it possible to take account of more radical changes, of a revolutionary kind. When a revolution is successful, when officials who are not authorized by the earlier constitution take over and norms are applied that are not derived from that constitution, one is compelled to modify the basic norm so that henceforth it will delegate legal authority to the organs that are effectively obeyed.[67]

1.4.2. *Hart*

In Hart's theory of law, as with Kelsen, the notion of legal system undoubtedly occupies a central place—in relation to the problems of defining law, of the validity of a legal norm or of legal interpretation.[66] In particular (to summarize), one of the essential causes to which Hart attributes classical legal theory's failure to define its object is that it has always claimed to find, in the different norms composing a legal order, common characteristics that allow one both to determine their legal character and to differentiate them from non-legal entities. Now, as Romano, for example, had suggested earlier, though in a somewhat different perspective, Hart stresses both the diversity of legal norms and that the most satisfactory characterization of legal phenomena lies rather in the specific articulation possible among norms of different kinds within a single system. Hart thus effects a fundamental decentring at the level of the definition of law by displacing the accent traditionally put upon norms, as constitutive elements of a legal system, towards the legal system itself and the specific relations existing among its elements.

What, then, are the main ideas to be found in Hart's thought concerning the notion of legal system?

(*a*) *Elements of a Legal System*. Firstly, as to a system's *components*, Hart evidently privileges in his theory the concept of *rule*

66 Kelsen 1925: 102 ff.; 1926: 263 ff.; Romano 1975: 106 n. 1.
67 Kelsen 1967: 210. 68 Hart 1961.

rather than those of institution, order, principle, or value. However, the essential differentiation that he introduces among these rules lies in the famous distinction between primary and secondary rules. As many writers have emphasized, this distinction is far from univocal, for it depends on partially different criteria. One writer has even managed to distinguish eight of them.[69] We shall confine ourselves here to reviewing the three most important: primary rules impose duties or obligations, while secondary rules confer powers; primary rules refer to behaviour, while secondary rules refer to other rules; and, lastly, primary rules concern physical actions while secondary rules concern the creation of duties and obligations, that is, legal acts.

The first distinguishing criterion is plainly the weakest, since several secondary rules cited by Hart himself do not appear solely to confer powers but just as much to impose obligations[69] or even, in certain respects, to confer neither powers nor obligations.[71] Conversely, it seems certain that the primary rules are capable not solely of imposing obligations but also of creating rights.[72]

The way to the most satisfactory differentiation seems, rather, to be to reconcile the other two criteria. If one accepts the Kelsenian theory that a legal act is an act creating a legal norm—that is, creating rights and obligations, as distinct from what jurists see as a merely 'factual' (*matériel*) act (one that does not create rights or obligations)—it appears that the two criteria very broadly coincide, in the sense that a rule referring to a legal act necessarily concerns the norm created by that act. The converse, however, appears not necessarily to be true, particularly in so far as one can maintain that a norm, such as a custom or a general principle of law, does not necessarily find its source in a legal act in the strict sense of the term. It therefore seems that a secondary rule may be defined as a rule referring to other rules, including in this the legal act by which the first rule may have been created; a primary rule, on the other hand, is a rule referring to behaviour, understanding by that only factual acts, that is, acts that do not create legal effects.

(b) *Relations Among These Elements*. The interest of this distinction obviously concerns simply the specific *relations* that can be discovered between primary and secondary norms.

[69] Tapper 1973: 248–9. [70] Raz 1970: 199–200; Sartorius 1971: 136.
[71] Tapper 1973: 252; Bulygin 1976: 39. [72] Tapper 1973: 249.

From a purely formal point of view, one could be tempted to say, as some writers have, that between these norms there is the same relation as between an object-language and a meta-language—that is, that primary norms would stand to secondary norms in a relation of object-norms to meta-norms. It would then be easy to understand how the articulation of these two kinds of norm is essential to the formation of a legal system,[73] since, in specific respects, each secondary rule helps to confer on the set of primary norms certain properties of formal systematicity. We shall come back to this later.

However, Hart appears to have been at least equally aware of the social functions[74] fulfilled by the introduction of secondary rules. This appears clearly in the way that Hart presents his classification of secondary rules. It is only after describing the specific social conditions in which one can conceive that a community might be able to live under the governance of exclusively primary rules (kinship relations, beliefs, common feelings, stable environment) that he points out the defects that such a régime would indubitably show under different social conditions. These defects are, he says: *uncertainty* on the level of identifying rules, the *static* nature of rules and the *ineffectiveness* of the diffuse social pressure that ensures the maintenance of rules.[75] Hart introduces the three categories of secondary rules precisely as remedies to each of these defects. To uncertainty corresponds the rule of recognition, which makes it possible to identify the rules belonging to the system, by determining their conditions of validity. To the static nature of primary rules correspond the rules of change, which authorize an individual or a body of persons to introduce new rules and repeal old ones. Lastly, to the ineffectiveness of social pressure correspond rules of decision authorizing individuals to resolve authoritatively the question of knowing whether a primary rule has been broken and determining the sanctions to be applied. These rules of decision also involve the authorized individuals remedying the indeterminacy that can affect the meanings of primary rules, as well as the uncertainty by which the rule of recognition itself may be affected.

In these three perspectives, secondary rules stand in a relation of 'supplementation'[76] with respect to primary rules; that supplementation takes the form of three specific social functions. It is also in this

73 Also asserted by Hart (1961: 89, 91).

74 Raz 1979: 178.

75 Hart 1961: 89–91.

76 1961: 91.

sense, Hart says, that the 'union of primary and secondary rules is at the centre of a legal system'[77] and that 'all three remedies together are enough to convert the régime of primary rules into what is indisputably a legal system'.[78]

(*c*) *A Legal System and Its Environment.* Beyond the relations that Hart discovers between a system's components, one may mention briefly the relations that he sees between a legal system and other normative systems, whether legal or otherwise.

As to relations between a legal system and other normative orders that are not legal, we shall look first at the relations between law and morality as Hart conceives them.

Although he rejects the iusnaturalist idea that the validity of legal norms is owed to their conformity to certain moral principles,[79] which would somehow suppose that law loses all autonomy of morality, Hart just as strongly rejects the positivist idea that 'law may have any content', which supposes, on the contrary, that morality is completely irrelevant to law and that law is completely autonomous of morality.

Midway between these two extreme positions, Hart states two kinds of close relation between these two normative orders.

The first is a relation of 'natural necessity'[80] between assigning a certain minimum moral content to legal rules and achieving the minimal programme of forbearance and compromise that men form by associating,[81] having regard to what they are and what is their natural environment. This first zone of overlap between law and morality lies in what Hart has called the *minimum content of natural law*, whose existence constitutes, in Hart's eyes, not a condition inherent in the very definition of a legal system but a condition inherent in its successful functioning.

The second relation between law and morality, moreover, is one no longer of strict necessity but of what might be called auxiliarity. It rests on the basic idea that a legal system's stability is not only founded on strict obedience to rules by the citizens but also supposes voluntary acceptance on their part.[82] Hart spends much time in demonstrating that this acceptance is largely dependent on law conforming to conventional morality, whether at the level of its elaboration or at that of its interpretation. And so it seems to him, again,

[77] 1961: 96. [78] 1961: 91. [79] 1961: 205 ff. [80] 1961: 195.
[81] 1961: 189. [82] 1961: 196.

that, although such conformity is not necessary to the existence of a legal system, it is bound up with the development of a 'good legal system'[83] enjoying sufficiently broad support from the citizens and a satisfactory degree of stability.

As to relations between different legal systems, Hart has had occasion, in the course of criticizing Kelsen's views on the unity of law, to propose two essential ideas which will now be considered briefly.

The first of these essentially concerns the relations between state law and international law, but it seems possible to extend it to relations between state law and sub-state law. This idea asserts, against Kelsen, that one legal system's claim to ground the validity of another is not sufficient to reduce these two systems to unity. It is also necessary, Hart says, that the courts or other organs for identifying law that belong to that legal system recognize the rule formulating that claim and consider it a reason to recognize the legal rules that it claims to validate.[84]

The second idea concerns the relations between different state legal systems and allows Hart to refine the first. It asserts that the application of a foreign law by a national court does not amount to reducing the two legal systems concerned to unity, albeit that that application supposes, in a certain sense, recognition of the foreign law. The reason, Hart says, is that in this case the recognition has a 'derived' character, in the sense that the reasons on which that recognition is grounded consist, at least partly, of the fact that these rules are or would be recognized by the foreign country's courts. Conversely, to reduce the two legal systems to unity would suppose, on the part of the courts of the State being considered, an 'original' recognition, that is, a recognition that would not be based in any way on that attested by the courts belonging to the other legal system.[85]

(*d*) *Legal System and Temporality*. A final problem in Hart's work on theory of legal systems is that of their evolution. Three ideas may be considered here.

The first is that the formation of a legal system may be achieved gradually, the introduction of each type of secondary rule constituting, as Hart puts it, a step taken from a pre-legal into a legal world.[86] In this respect, the existence of certain primitive societies,

[83] 1961: 201. [84] 1983: 337. [85] 1983: 342. [86] 1961: 91.

as well as the current state of development of international society, provide examples of societies where a legal system certainly exists only in a very embryonic way, but which are capable of moving gradually towards the model referred to. Consequently, this idea makes it possible to envisage stages of development that are completed to a greater or lesser extent and corresponding systems of greater or lesser complexity.[87]

The second idea, as has been seen, is that legal systems, in the full sense in which Hart conceives them, are dynamic systems, since they comprise rules of change ensuring that essential social function.

The third and last idea is of the transformations, including misadventures, that a legal system may undergo in the course of its existence. Unity and continuity of a legal system suppose, according to Hart, the conjunction of two conditions: on one side, that the rules of behaviour that are valid according to the system's ultimate criteria of validity are generally obeyed; on the other, that its secondary rules are effectively accepted by the system's agents.[88] A legal system may therefore become 'pathological', unstable in a particular way, from the moment when one of these two conditions is no longer conjoined. Ultimately, this situation will lead to the emergence of a new legal system, beginning from the old.

87 Bobbio 1971: 115. 88 Hart 1961: 113–14.

2
Elements of a Legal System

2.1. LEGAL NORMS

Common to the theories of Kelsen and Hart is a reduction of the elements of a legal system to rules or to norms. To privilege this level of enquiry is understandable, since norms are clearly 'a legal system's most prominent element'.[1] As Jhering suggests, 'what the human mind perceives first are the prominent, exterior and practical parts of law, the parts whose action strikes it immediately: the legal rules'.[2] Moreover, by retaining only this element it is possible to satisfy both a requirement of homogeneity inherent in the existence of what has been called a 'system of synthesis'[3] and a requirement of rigorous unity of object that some writers such as Kelsen have erected as a basic epistemological postulate.

Whatever the interest of such a choice, it also appears both to be fraught with difficulties and not to be the only choice conceivable.

The first such difficulty lies in the problem of the '*individuation* of laws',[4] that is, of determining what constitutes a complete legal rule, as an element of a legal system. The example given by Bentham is particularly symptomatic in this respect, in that he 'offers us no less than four models of a complete law'.[5] One of these models has been developed particularly by Kelsen in his theory of 'dependent legal norms',[6] in terms of which 'norms that do not themselves stipulate coercive acts . . . are dependent norms, valid only in connection with norms that *do* stipulate coercive acts' and hence incomplete.[7]

A fortiori one can accept, in a general way, that a legal rule or legal norm does not necessarily coincide with a statutory provision, understood as 'an editorial unit of the legislative text'.[8] Thus, if 'a statutory provision does not always include each of the elements that

1 Orianne 1982: 32. 2 Jhering 1969: 28.
3 Grzegorczyk 1986: 288.
4 Raz 1979: 80. 5 See Brito 1972: 463; Hart 1982: 120ff.
6 Kelsen 1967: 54.
7 1967: 58. 8 Pleszka and Gizbert-Studnicki 1986: 112.

constitute a norm, it can also happen that a single provision may contain the elements of several norms'.[9]

To these difficulties of identifying the exact kind of unity to be considered under the term legal 'rule' or 'norm', one can also add those inherent in the *diversity* of the phenomena that these terms may cover. Apart from the specific problem of knowing whether these terms indicate 'principles', or whether it is important to distinguish them from 'legal rules' properly so called,[10] it has also to be asked whether these terms indicate only norms of general scope or also norms whose scope is individual;[11] whether they indicate only rules of behaviour (which Hart calls primary) or also other rules that 'refer to these' (which Hart calls secondary and which might be thought of as 'meta-rules'); and whether they indicate only rules embodying 'commands' or also rules containing 'recommendations'.[12]

Aside from these various difficulties involved in the choice of rules or norms as elements of a legal system, it is also important to grasp that that is not the only choice conceivable. For it is possible, from the start, to privilege other elements, even if that choice may appear to be at least as reductive, if not more so, as an exclusively normativist approach to law.

2.2. CONCEPTS, INSTITUTIONS, BRANCHES OF LAW, GENERAL PRINCIPLES, OR VALUES

One can first bring into the picture elements of an order below that of norms, such as the concepts or classes of concept that constitute in some way a 'basic subsystem' by which the rules themselves are sustained.[13] The conception of law as a 'system of concepts' may itself take different forms: there may be a system of purely formal concepts, of which every legal order is reckoned to be composed,[14] as there may be a system of concepts loaded with a particular content within a particular legal order.[15] The systematic nature of the set of concepts considered lies, in either case, in a form of unity that binds them together and which has sometimes been conceived

[9] Ibid. [10] See, especially, Dworkin 1978: 35ff.

[11] See, especially, Kelsen 1967: 19.

[12] See, especially, Amselek 1986: 156. [13] Gassin 1981: 361.

[14] On this, see Canaris 1969: 20. [15] 1969: 49.

'organically'—as, for example, by Schelling, Hegel, or Savigny—and sometimes 'logically'—as by Puchta in his celebrated 'genealogy of concepts', in which concepts are ordered like a pyramid from the more general to the more particular.[16] Among these concepts, certainly, that of a right enjoys a privileged position in the history—at least, the recent history—of legal thought and has allowed certain iusnaturalist writers in particular to conceive law as a set of individual prerogatives that it is possible to 'deduce' from a small number of fundamental rights.

One can also take into consideration, however, elements of an order higher than that of norms, by which rules are sustained in their turn. Among these, one may first mention *institutions*. These are not, actually, limited to uniting a body of rules around a single directive idea. As Dabin has quite rightly argued, they 'can themselves be grouped into broader syntheses',[17] which may be considered in their turn as 'systems of institutions'.[18] Different ordering criteria may be applied to them: the logical criterion of subsumption ('thus, the institution "sale", as contract, depends on the institution "contract", which itself depends on the institution "legal act"'[19]); the hierarchical criterion of subordination (thus the institution 'family' prevails over the institution of 'individual rights of spouses or children'—or the converse, according to the legal orders under consideration and the different phases of their evolution); and the axiological criterion of relation between principle and exception (thus institutions, whose recognition involves a derogation from principles, 'look like separate branches' of those principles, yet, 'by the same token, their places are marked within the logical complex of the law'[20]).

As well as institutions there are *branches of law*, which, likewise, can perfectly well be considered not only as subsystems grouping different norms together but also as elements of a particular legal system.[21] The ordering of these different elements may be achieved in its turn according to different relations, such as the traditionally recognized hierarchical relation between public law and private law, the relation between principle and exception often also accepted as

[16] On this, see, especially, Larenz 1969: 17ff.
[17] Dabin 1969: 104 (also 1950: 287).
[18] Canaris 1969: 50; Pleszka and Gizbert-Studnicki 1986: 110; Lachmayer 1975: 106.
[19] Dabin 1969: 104 (also 1950: 287).
[20] 1969: 104 (also 1950: 288).
[21] Pleszka and Gizbert-Studnicki 1986: 111.

subsisting between civil law and social law, or the functional relation between principal and secondary factors sometimes declared to exist between certain branches of law such as civil law or administrative law and others such as criminal law, when the last is thought of as a kind of 'accompaniment' to them.

Finally, some other writers prefer to consider a legal system either as a system of *general principles*[22] or as a system of *values*.[23]

Moreover, it is certainly possible to consider elements of an order comparable to that of norms, although distinct from them. Among such elements may be noted decisions, actions regulated by norms,[24] organs, statutory provisions (so far as distinct from the norms that they contain), normative acts[25] and so on.

2.3. HETEROGENEITY OF THE ELEMENTS OF A LEGAL SYSTEM

With these different conceptions, which exclusively privilege one or other of these elements in turn, may, however, be contrasted a different conception, which accepts and tries to describe the heterogeneity of the elements composing a legal system. Thus it is proposed that a 'normative system is not to be identified purely and simply with a system of norms',[26] in the sense that it embodies not only normative propositions but also 'mixed' propositions that are 'half norms, half information'.[27] This conception has also been proposed by Romano, for whom norms 'are or may be part of a legal order, yet are far from exhausting it'.[28] Assimilating the concepts of legal order and institution,[29] he refers especially, among the elements that ensure for this entity a 'stable and permanent unity', to 'the persons taking part in it, as well as its patrimony, resources, interests, beneficiaries, rules, and so on'.[30] Subscribing to the same perspective, Orianne has more recently proposed the idea that one should 'take into consideration not only norms themselves and the relations that they maintain among themselves, but also the *totality of the space in which law is deployed*, according to its function, and observe especially the various *activities* to which the execution, application and

[22] Canaris 1969: 46 ff. [23] 1969: 51; Grzegorczyk 1986: 291–2.
[24] Grzegorczyk 1986: 290.
[25] Pleszka and Gizbert-Studnicki 1986: 112. [26] Gardies 1974: 81.
[27] 1974: 83, 85. [28] Romano 1975: 15.
[29] 1975: 29. [30] 1975: 28.

control of norms give rise'.[31] This leads to considering in its turn every kind of activity possessing 'a visible point of attachment to the world of norms',[32] such as the authors of such activities.[33]

While being ourselves won over by this last conception, in the following discussion we shall be compelled to place the stress on one or other of these elements, according to the nature of the problem to be dealt with.

[31] Orianne 1982: 130. [32] 1982: 131. [33] 1982: 134.

3
Relations Among the Elements of a Legal System

It has already been noted that study of the relations among elements of a legal system may be envisaged *a priori* in two different perspectives: either these relations are seen as inherent in the object studied, 'law', so that one could speak of a system *per concreto*[1] or an 'objective' system,[2] or they are seen as inherent in theory developed in relation to that object, so that one could speak in that case of a system *per abstracto*[3] or a 'scientific' system.[4]

Subject to the specific problems raised by the existence of doctrine or legal dogmatics, which are distinguished by appearing simultaneously as a scientific discourse about law and as forming 'part of the phenomenon "law"',[5] we intend here to study these relations only in the first perspective.

At this level, however, a new distinction becomes important. The relations inherent in the object 'law' that make it possible to present it, at least within certain limits, as a 'system' are both *diverse* and *variable* in their intensity.

It is therefore necessary first to distinguish from an analytical point of view different *types of systematicity*. Although other distinctions might be equally possible, we shall consider three that seem essential for studying legal phenomena: static and dynamic systematicity; formal and substantive systematicity; linear and circular systematicity.

Secondly, however, given that this systematicity never appears in law as a finished and stable property, but rather as a dynamic and tendential phenomenon, it seems important to deal with the *processes of systematization*[6] and to identify the specific rôles of the main actors taking part in it: the legislator through codification, the jurist through doctrine, and the judge through case law. System-

1 Grzegorczyk 1986: 285. 2 Canaris 1969: 13.
3 Grzegorczyk 1986: 285.
4 Canaris 1969: 13. 5 Grzegorczyk 1986: 286.
6 On the terminological distinction between systematicity and systematization, see, especially, Rials 1986: 71.

aticity, in its different forms and to various degrees, thus appears either as the *terminus a quo* or as the *terminus ad quem*[7] of an activity running through every part of the creation and application of law.

3.1. THE DIFFERENT TYPES OF SYSTEMATICITY

3.1.1. *Static and Dynamic Systematicity*

(*a*) *Weaknesses of Kelsen's Distinction*. The distinction between dynamic and static systems occupies, as has been seen, a central place in Kelsen's thought, and, moreover, is the only typology in terms of which he attempts to characterize a legal system, from the standpoint of the relations among its norms.

We have seen that Kelsen defines a *static* system as one in which norms 'are valid on the strength of their content: because their validity can be traced back to a norm under whose content the content of the norms in question can be subsumed as the particular under the general'.[8] He defines a *dynamic* system as one in which a given norm belongs to such a system 'because it was created in a fashion determined by the basic norm—and not because it has a certain content'.[9]

Apparently simple, this distinction gives rise to a number of difficulties, of which we shall look only at those that are directly internal to Kelsen's own thought.

Although we are dealing here with ideal types, the conception of normative systems belonging exclusively to one of these two categories appears to be fundamentally problematical in the light of certain presuppositions that Kelsen accepts.

On one side, the existence of a purely static system seems to him to be utterly indefensible. When writing *Pure Theory of Law*, Kelsen considered such a system to be conceivable only if the content of its basic norm were considered to be 'directly evident':[10] that is, that the basic norm 'is immanent in, or emanates from, reason',[11] which 'presupposes the concept of a practical reason, that is, a norm-creating reason'.[12]

Postulating, however, the existence of a radical dualism between reason and will, Kelsen holds the concept of practical reason to be

[7] Troper 1986: 29. [8] Kelsen 1967: 195. [9] 1967: 197.
[10] 1967: 196.
[11] Ibid. [12] Ibid.

'indefensible' and consequently believes that 'there can be no such things as norms which are valid only in virtue of their directly evident content'.[13] Now, according to Kelsen, a norm can appear to be directly evident only 'because it is believed that it is created by the will of God or another superhuman authority or because it was created by custom'. The upshot is that the ultimate basis of validity of norms belonging to such a system necessarily lies, in Kelsen's view, in 'a presupposed norm which prescribes that one ought to behave according to the commands of the norm-creating authority or according to the norms created by custom'.[14] It thus appears that these norms 'constitute a dynamic system of norms'[15] and not a static system.

To this first objection may be added a second, which, as will be seen, is still more radical, in that it leads logically to denying the very idea of a normative system. It must be remembered that Kelsen's thought developed towards the end of his life and that in his *General Theory of Norms*[16] the Austrian legal theorist came to deny the applicability of logic, and in particular rules of inference and the principle of non-contradiction, to the domain of norms. Such a presupposition is obviously difficult to reconcile with the idea of a static system, for 'it is impossible to maintain at the same time on the one hand that, in a static system, the content of the lower norm can be deduced from the content of the higher norm and on the other hand that a norm cannot be deduced from another norm'.[17]

As to the existence of purely dynamic systems, on the other hand, although at first sight it appears to have the support of the arguments above, it has rightly been remarked that it too finds itself weakened—not, to be sure, in its dynamic aspect but, more radically, in its very nature as 'system'. It appears that the idea of a system is incompatible not only with abandoning the principle of non-contradiction between norms[18] but also with the way in which Kelsen conceives the adoption of a norm by the competent organ. That is, one can judge that such a decision has been taken within the limits of the organ's competence only by comparing 'the consistency of this decision with the content of the power-conferring norm, and this presupposes a logical relation between the two norms in question'.[19] This allows Wróblewski to suggest that Kelsen's conception of law

[13] Ibid. [14] Ibid. [15] Ibid. [16] Kelsen 1991: 232ff.
[17] Troper 1986: 39. Similarly, Wróblewski 1984: 326.
[18] Wróblewski 1984: 327. [19] Ibid.

breaks completely with any form of 'systemism' and accepts a form of 'decisionism',[20] in the sense that law will consist of a 'set of decisions not related by any links of consistency'.[21]

If this typology, then, seems to be logically condemned in Kelsen's thought, must one suppose that it will have to be abandoned, even if one disregards those of its presuppositions that are plainly debatable?

(*b*) *Other Interpretations of this Distinction.* Some writers, such as Timsit, have tried to overcome these difficulties by taking the view, contrary to what Kelsen suggests, that it is important not to speak of 'duality of normative system*s* but of duality of *a* normative system considered as to its *two* constitutive elements: a normative order strictly so called (NO), which is a hierarchized system for creating norms based on the existence of a hierarchical relation or a relation of order between norms, and a normative space (NS), a system in which norms belong to or are included in a non-hierarchized set'.[22]

Interesting though this interpretation may be, it only exploits another distinction introduced by Kelsen, between a static and a dynamic *approach* to law[23]—a distinction which, though not unrelated to the first, seems to lie on a fundamentally different level, in Kelsen's thought as well as independently of it. In itself, it does not provide any particularly new light on the typology we are now discussing.[24]

The problem, therefore, can be approached correctly only by stripping this typology of the presuppositions that accompany it in Kelsen's thought.

Wróblewski, especially, appears to do this when he defines a dynamic normative system as having a 'formal' character, in the sense that it 'is characterized by the lack of the relations of content of the norm[s] belonging to that system'[25] while a static normative system is characterized by the fact that it includes 'a special norm of validity' that is 'bound by determined content in such a way that all the norms belonging to this system can be inferred from it according to the accepted rules of inference'.[26]

In the same way, Troper has proposed a new formulation of Ke-

[20] Ibid. [21] Ibid. [22] Timsit 1986: 25.

[23] 1986: 95, 'The opposition between static and dynamic in law corresponds fairly closely to that between NO and NS'.

[24] It should, however, be emphasized that Timsit also proposes a new typology on the basis of this distinction (1986: 125ff.).

[25] Wróblewski 1972: 226. [26] Ibid.

lsen's typology. In his view, an exclusively dynamic system 'would be a system of delegation',[27] in which 'the content of decisions is not prescribed' and in which 'in this regard officials enjoy a totally discretionary power'.[28] This system does not however exclude prescribing a particular 'procedure'[29] for making such decisions. Considering, moreover, that 'the problem of the applicability of logic to law does not arise',[30] he thinks that 'an exclusively static system would be a system, like morality or natural law, in which a statement would have the meaning of a norm solely because it is accepted, in a particular society, that it has been derived from another statement'.[31]

Before attempting to relate legal systems to this typology, it may be useful to establish parallels with some other classifications that have been proposed, which partially enrich it.

Firstly, Hart's contrast, following his celebrated distinction between primary and secondary rules, between the 'simplest form of social structure', which would involve only a 'régime of primary rules',[32] and a developed social structure, which ensures the 'combination of primary rules of obligation with the secondary rules of recognition, change and adjudication'.[33] Spontaneously, one could be tempted to associate the first régime with a static system and the second with a dynamic system.

That distinction, however, does not coincide completely with Hart's. On the one hand, his 'régime of primary rules' does not form a 'system',[34] given that it 'will simply be a set of separate standards, without any identifying or common mark'.[35] Neither is it obvious that the régime of primary rules is purely static in the sense defined earlier, since it is not certain that these models can be 'deduced' from each other or from a common and more general norm. On the other hand, the secondary rules, in Hart's second régime, are not exclusively rules of authorization or procedure, in terms of which some individuals would possess a discretionary power to determine the content of norms or of decisions to be adopted. It is sufficient to note that, in Hart's view, such a system's 'rule of recognition' can include multiple criteria of identification[36] and does not necessarily involve the existence of an '*unlimited* legislative power',[37] which is attested by the frequent existence of constitutional limitations.[38] The same goes for 'rules of change', in which the powers conferred 'may be . . .

[27] Troper 1986: 42. [28] 1986: 43. [29] 1986: 41. [30] Ibid.
[31] 1986: 43. [32] Hart 1961: 91. [33] 1961: 95. [34] 1961: 90.
[35] Ibid. [36] 1961: 92. [37] 1961: 103. [38] Ibid.

limited in various ways',[39] and also for 'rules of adjudication', which are not limited to 'identifying the individuals who are to adjudicate' and what is 'the procedure to be followed'[40] but, rather, the primary rules that they apply are 'something which they are not free to disregard'.[41]

The régime combining primary and secondary rules is therefore not necessarily a purely dynamic system. It would be so, apparently, only on the hypothesis of the 'imaginary kingdom of Rex I', as Hart fictionally conceives it, where 'the rule of recognition would simply be that whatever Rex I enacts is law'.[42]

This parallel between the typology of systems and Hart's theory reveals, in particular, that the existence of a dynamic system does not suppose merely the presence of secondary rules, for without these there could be no system; it also presupposes the existence of secondary rules of a specific type, that is, rules that 'confer powers, public or private',[43] to the exclusion of any other type.[44]

In the same line as Hart's theory is Bobbio's contrast between 'simple' and 'complex' normative systems:[45] the first are 'uniquely composed of primary norms and the norm or norms for identifying the system (which are in some way preliminary to the very formation of the system and without which it would be impossible to speak of a normative system)';[46] the second comprise, in addition to primary norms, both norms as to sanctions and norms as to legal production.[47]

Although Bobbio's distinction fails to clarify in any way what a purely dynamic system would look like, it might shed new light on the notion of a purely static system. Differing from Hart, Bobbio holds that a primitive society's set of rules, or a set of rules of etiquette, forms such a system,[48] owing to the presence of membership

[39] 1961: 93. [40] 1961: 94. [41] 1961: 142. [42] 1961: 93.

[43] 1961: 79.

[44] Although Hart had defined the notion of a secondary rule broadly as being that which specifies 'the ways in which the primary rules may be conclusively ascertained, introduced, eliminated, varied, and the fact of their violation conclusively determined' (1961: 92)—thus apparently embracing rules that are neither of authorization nor of procedure—he sometimes also, however, identifies secondary rules with this last type of rule (1961: 79). For criticism of such a restriction, see in particular Bobbio: 'It is hard to understand why Hart, after having clearly individualized what characterizes the relationship between primary and secondary norms throughout his book, produces arguments in a more debatable direction, by conceiving primary norms as those that ground obligations and secondary norms as norms attributing powers' (1971: 112 n. 4).

[45] Bobbio 1971: 115. [46] Ibid. [47] 1971: 117. [48] Ibid.

criteria, probably implicit, whose existence Hart seems to deny.[49] This is why, contrary to Hart, Bobbio thinks of these sets as 'systems' which he chooses to call 'simple'. Given the absence, in such systems, of rules about the production of norms, it is tempting to identify them with 'static' systems. However, as we have already remarked concerning Hart's conception of a régime of primary rules, such identification is not required *a priori*, since the existence of a deductive relation between the different norms belonging to such systems is not inherent in their definition.

This is why it seems useful to introduce a more basic distinction, such as Troper proposes, between a system that he calls 'non-hierarchized' or 'horizontal', in which 'the norms are all located on the same level' and where 'statements are not justified by each other',[50] and a 'hierarchized' or 'vertical' system, in which 'there is a hierarchy among the norms' and where 'a statement appears as a norm if its author justifies it by referring to a statement made by somebody else and that statement's application is the object of the author's own statement'.[51] Although, as Troper emphasizes, the distinction between a static and a dynamic system concerns only vertical and not horizontal systems.[52]

It thus seems possible to assert that 'simple' normative systems, in Bobbio's terminology, are sometimes 'vertical' and sometimes 'horizontal'. The first hypothesis—thinking particularly of systems of morality or of natural law developed *more geometrico*—would refer to 'static' systems. The second hypothesis—thinking, for example, of rules of etiquette or the rules of a primitive society—would concern systems that could not be called either static or dynamic, since, as horizontal systems, they do not fall within such a classification.

To the various parallels already drawn may be added one last, the distinction that Perelman makes between two extreme normative systems—corresponding, in his view, to two opposite utopias found throughout philosophical thought: 'the calculable', which 'presupposes the development of rules making it possible to avoid any power of decision'—a system of 'legislation without judges'—and 'the political', where 'the power of decision would be unlimited and arbitrary' and would be exercised 'without pre-existing rules'—a

49 Hart 1961: 90; Hart admits here, however, that such models of behaviour have in common the obvious fact 'that they are the rules which a particular group of human beings accepts'.

50 Troper 1986: 41. 51 Ibid. 52 Ibid.

system of 'adjudication without a legislator'.[53] The first hypothesis would correspond to a 'rationalist' utopia, the second to a 'voluntarist' utopia.[54]

Such a distinction appears to cut right across our typology: the order of the calculable aims to reduce every particular norm to a deduction commencing from the smallest possible number of general principles, whose content would be held to be rationally self-evident; the order of the political, in contrast, aims to justify the validity of any decision by the sole fact that it is made by a competent organ, without its content being limited by pre-existing rules. The first thus coincides closely with the existence of a 'static' system, the second with a purely 'dynamic' system.

If one abstracts from such utopian ideas, the construction of this typology seems interesting much less for placing the legal system within one or other of these categories than for emphasizing the essentially 'mixed' nature of such a system.

On this, the writers we have reviewed are almost unanimous. Even Kelsen, if one abstracts from the difficulties involved in typology itself, is content to hold that a legal order 'has *essentially* a dynamic character',[55] in the sense that 'Determining the organ is the *minimum* that must be accomplished in the relation between higher and lower norm.'[56] Although he appears not to exclude the hypothesis that 'the higher norm only determines the organ',[57] Kelsen nevertheless recognizes that higher norms may not only 'determine the organ by whom and the procedure by which the lower norm is to be created', but also 'the content of that norm'.[58] It clearly follows that, in Kelsen's view, legal systems may be of a mixed nature, although they need not necessarily be so.

The other writers we have referred to seem to have even less doubt of this necessity. Wróblewski—albeit that he has in mind only written legal orders[59]—holds that they belong to the category of 'complex dynamic-static' systems,[60] in which the different types of relation inherent in each of the other normative systems are found in combination. Troper, likewise, thinks that 'the positive law of modern societies is a system that is both static and dynamic, since all decisions are always justified both by their conformity to the content

53 Perelman 1961: 42. 54 Ibid.

55 Kelsen 1967: 198 (our emphasis).

56 1967: 235 (our emphasis). 57 Ibid. 58 Ibid.

59 Wróblewski 1972: 237.

60 Ibid.

of another statement *and* by the authorization conferred on their author'.[61]

While Bobbio's proposal, in which 'a legal order may be thought of as a typical example of a complex normative system',[62] seems not to be able to reach any firm conclusion on the level concerned here—since, as has been seen, it deals with a partly different problem—Perelman's position, in contrast, is much more clear-cut. Perelman maintains that 'law exists, as a technically autonomous discipline, only in societies that make room—between the calculable . . . and the political . . . for an order to whose construction a multiplicity of human wills contribute' and where 'one finds a constant dialectic of reason and will'.[63]

In other words, there can be a legal system only where there exist both general rules that ground the content of individual decisions and judges authorized to remedy authoritatively the imperfections inherent in those rules; that is, where the normative system is neither purely dynamic nor purely static.

3.1.2. *Formal and Substantive Systematicity*

(*a*) *Some Preliminary Points*. The opposition noted in Sect. 3.1.1 between static and dynamic systematicity concerned essentially the connection that might be established between different legal *norms* as to their *validity*, where the validity derives from a particular relation of conformity of some of these norms sometimes to the content, and sometimes to the mode of elaboration, defined by the others.

Independently of these links of 'grounding' visible between certain elements of the system, it is also important to distinguish two modes in which its elements may be ordered, to which correspond two possible types of *structuration* of a legal system. The first case envisages a purely 'formal' ordering, understood as 'a logical relation, characterizable independently of the meaning contained in the propositions that it links',[64] so that the system in which the propositions

61 Troper 1986: 43. 62 Bobbio 1971: 119. 63 Perelman 1962: 42.

64 Ladrière 1985: at '*Système (épistémologie)*', 586. The expression 'formal system' is therefore not used here in the sense referred to above, of a purely dynamic normative system, in which the validity of each norm finds its exclusive basis in a norm authorizing an organ to enact it, without there being any relation of content between the norms belonging to that system. It is, however, certain that one may also call such a system

are united by such a relation can be called a 'formal system'.[65] The second case envisages a 'material' or 'substantive' ordering, that is, an organic or teleological relation which cannot be characterized satisfactorily by abstracting from the content of the elements that it unites. In this sense one might speak of 'substantive' systematicity.

For the avoidance of confusion, however, it is important to note firstly that this distinction touches the nature of the relations that emerge among the system's elements and not the nature of the elements themselves, even if the latter is not totally indifferent. It might be tempting to think, as is usual, that formal systematicity concerns only the relations that can be established between norms, while substantive systematicity would concern other elements, such, for example, as institutions, principles, or values. Although these latter elements undoubtedly possess, by their very nature, a more evident teleological or organic dimension than is the case with norms, it is no less certain that that dimension may—at least up to a certain point—be made explicit so far as concerns norms and that, conversely, the existence of logical relations is not inconceivable *a priori* so far as concerns the other elements. This point is the more important because, on the terminological plane, expressions like 'value system', 'axiological system', or 'teleological system' are often used indiscriminately, without the user always noticing whether those labels characterize the nature of the elements belonging to the system—values or ends, in this case—or whether they characterize the nature of the relation—axiological or teleological—that unites them.[66]

A second remark is also required. The very distinction proposed here supposes understanding the notion of system broadly. In the eyes of one important current of thought, the notion of system can be understood only in a narrow, formal-logical sense.[67] We shall mention only Klug, for whom 'the very concept of system is a specifically logical term' and 'only logic can determine where a true system exists in a general way and what is meant by the fact that a domain of

'formal', but then by taking the expression in a sense partly different from that in which we are using it. On this, see Wróblewski 1972: 226. See also Battifol 1956: 49, speaking of a system that is 'formal in the Kelsenian sense'.

[65] Ladrière 1985: at *'Système (épistémologie)'*, 586.

[66] On this, see, especially, Peine 1983: 107. Following Engisch, Peine distinguishes three ways in which the aims pursued by legal rules may be linked to each other, which leads him to distinguish three kinds of system which he calls axiomatic, axiological, and teleological.

[67] See, especially, the various writers referred to by Canaris, 1969: 41.

knowledge may have been systematized'.[68] Against such a conception, we would accept that a system's mode of organization is not necessarily reducible to a formal-logical structure and that it follows that the notion of system can be understood in a different sense. The only concession that seems to be needed here lies in the fact that the very ideas of organization, unity, and cohesion that characterize the general concept of system seem inseparable from a certain formal—yet not necessarily logical—character, in whose absence one could not speak of systematicity in any sense at all.[69]

It can also be noticed that the two types of systematicity distinguished here are not necessarily mutually exclusive. Although many writers often place exclusive stress on one or the other of them, according to the philosophical conception of law that they subscribe to, it seems (as will be seen later) that these two modes of structuration of law are not only compatible but also complementary and partially interdependent.

Finally, whether under one or the other of these two forms, it is important to notice both the significance of the ideal of systematicity in the concrete functioning of contemporary Western legal orders, the extent to which it is actually realized and the limits that that realization encounters.

(*b*) *Formal Systematicity*. Although this first type of systematicity goes by a variety of names—'formal system',[70] 'formal-logical system',[71] 'axiomatic system',[72] 'logical system',[73] 'deductive system',[74] 'deductive-axiomatic system',[75] or 'calculative system'[76]—nobody has any doubt that the most complete model of such systematicity is to be found in logical systems, whose nature is simultaneously deductive, axiomatized, and formalized.[77] Moreover, such systems possess, in their most complete form, a certain number of formal properties, such as independence, completeness, decidability, and consistency.[78]

Without going into detailed analysis of these different notions,

68 Klug 1966: 5. 69 Likewise, especially, Canaris 1969: 45.
70 See, especially, Perelman 1984: 74.
71 See, especially, Canaris 1969: 20.
72 See, especially, Peine 1983: 108; Perelman 1963*b*: 207.
73 See, especially, Gardies 1987: 174.
74 See, especially, Heck 1948: 213; Bobbio 1960: 76.
75 See, especially, Varga 1979: 295. 76 Grzegorczyk 1986: 284.
77 See, especially, Kalinowski 1965: 30.
78 1965: 35.

which would go beyond our purpose, we shall summarize their significance here in order to assess how far they are capable of characterizing a legal system.

1. *Deductiveness.* It appears firstly that the deductiveness of a formal system is its principal constitutive feature,[79] in the sense that it characterizes in an essential way the kind of linkage existing among its elements. Thus, following Tarski, Alchourrón and Bulygin define a deductive system as 'any set of sentences which contains all its consequences',[80] that is, which includes the propositions deriving from those propositions in the light of rules of inference accepted within that system.[81]

How far is a legal system, or ought it to be, of such a nature? Even though law is now at the end of a long historical evolution, in the course of which Western laws have undergone a process of 'formal rationalization' and have gradually been adapted to the requirements of 'calculability',[82] it is clear that law has effectively been conceived on the model of a deductive system and that such a model has been able effectively to play a far from negligible rôle in the real functioning of law. As Blanché has suggested, even though over the past century the situation has been reversed, it appears that in Leibniz's time this model probably had a greater impact among jurists than among mathematicians.[83]

On the theoretical plane, it is certain that the conception of law as a deductive system first appears within the framework of rationalist systems of natural law developed during the seventeenth and eighteenth centuries;[84] these systems formed, as Arnaud puts it, 'the genesis of modern axiomatic systematism' in law.[85] Probably one of the first decisive manifestations of such a conception can be found in the work of Leibniz, who in 1667, in the *Nova Methodus Discendae Docendaeque Jurisprudentiae*, sets himself to criticize the classical conception of the tripartite division of the Roman *Institutes* and

79 See Alchourrón and Bulygin 1971: 48, 'The concept of system is based on that of deductive consequence'. See also Gardies 1987: 174, understanding by 'logical system' a 'system ordered by commencing from some of its parts posited as principles, from which its other parts are deduced'.

80 Alchourrón and Bulygin 1971: 49.

81 1971: 48.

82 On this, see, especially, Weber 1978: 809 ff.; Varga 1979: 297 ff.

83 Blanché 1967: 14, 'It is well known that mathematicians are unaccustomed to reasoning by *Barbara Celarent*, while that mode of reasoning was probably much more commonly used in legal matters.'

84 Perelman 1984: 69; Alchourrón and Bulygin 1971: 51.

85 Arnaud 1969: 125.

'wishes to reconstruct an order corresponding to nature, and that order can only be geometrical: commencing from first truths, to draw their direct consequences and, from consequence to consequence, arrive in the most logical way possible at an axiomatic system'.[86] This conception is also found in Pufendorf, who in 1672, in *Le droit de la nature et des gens, ou Système général des principes les plus importants de la morale, de la jurisprudence et de la politique*, 'was the first to try to construct a true system of natural law'.[87]

The application of such a model, inspired by the systems of natural law, to civil laws, finds typical expression in Domat, in 1689, in *Les loix civiles dans leur ordre naturel*. Domat's justification for his project of 'putting the civil laws in order' is that it is in the nature of the 'truths that compose a science' that,

> owing to the relationships and connections between them, they can enter the mind only through each other: that some that should be understood by themselves, and which are the sources of others, ought to precede those others; that the others ought to follow, according to their dependence on those that are understood by themselves, that those are linked together, and that the mind, having thus to connect some with others, should see them in order; and it is this order which forms the arrangement of definitions, principles and details.[88]

While these writers have thus helped to conceptualize the task of legislation on the basis of a deductive model, there are others, such as Montesquieu in 1748, in *De l'esprit des lois*, and Beccaria in 1764, in *Dei delitti e delle pene*, who have helped to transpose this same model into the framework of adjudication.

Montesquieu's conception of the judge's powers is well known. Although he believes that 'the power of judging' should be 'separate from legislative power and from executive power',[89] he at once adds that 'Among the three powers . . . that of judging is, in some fashion, null'.[90] Now, the judiciary's power can be reduced to nothing only by conceiving the act of judging in a purely deductive way and by thinking of judges as 'only the mouth that pronounces the words of the law, inanimate beings who can moderate neither its force nor its rigour'.[91] Still more explicit, although confined to the criminal area, Beccaria's thought culminates in conceiving the judgement on any offence in the rigorous form of a syllogism: 'The judge ought to make

[86] 1969: 132. See also Villey 1968: 99 ff. [87] Arnaud 1969: 136.
[88] Domat, Preface to *Les loix civiles*, p. xxiv; quoted, Arnaud 1969: 143.
[89] Montesquieu 1989: 157. [90] 1989: 160. [91] 1989: 163.

a perfect *syllogism*. The *major premiss* should be the general statute; the *minor premiss*, the action conforming or not conforming to the statute; the *conclusion*, release or punishment.'[92]

These different theoretical conceptions have, of course, had some practical consequences. Although the French Civil Code of 1804 finally obliterated any trace of Domat's proposed arrangement of the civil laws,[93] the success of his method[92] moved Cousin to observe that '*Les lois civiles dans leur ordre naturel* is like a preface to the Code Napoléon'.[95] It has been noted particularly, in this respect, that the general plan on which the Code is based 'is descended directly from the axiomatic plans discovered by the rationalist movement'.[96] It has also been remarked that the Civil Code does not abandon 'attention to deduction'[97] exclusively to the interpreter and that in many cases the Code itself sets out 'links between principle and conclusion', employing this 'logical relationship between a general idea and its applications ... in order to give its work a cohesion, a solidity, containing no sporadic solutions'.[98]

This adoption of a deductive model was not, however, reserved exclusively to the legislative task of codification. Beginning with the French Revolution, it was also extended to organizing the function of adjudication. The debates on organizing the judicial power show very clearly the Constituents' adherence to a syllogistic conception of the act of judging. Duport, for example, maintains that 'a trial judgement is nothing other than a syllogism of which the major premiss is a fact, the minor premiss a statute and the judgement the conclusion'.[99] Garat l'Aîné is content to rectify this arrangement by inverting the premisses' content and holding that

> for a syllogism to be good, it should: (1) in the major premiss, recount a general truth accepted by everybody, and consequently the statute in the judgement syllogism; for here there is no generally accepted truth except the law; (2) in the minor premiss, specify the singular relationship between the subject in dispute and the general truth and, consequently, in the judgement syllogism, the relationship between that subject, or the fact in dispute, and the statute; for here there is no other truth than that determined by the law;

[92] Beccaria 1979: 53; quoting what the translator identifies as the original text (n. 3).

[93] Arnaud 1969: 147.

[94] 1969: 146.

[95] Quoted, Ray 1926: 3. [The French Civil Code, or Code Napoléon, was also adopted by Belgium. It will be referred to in that sense as the Civil Code. Tr.]

[96] Arnaud 1969: 218.

[97] Ray 1926: 169.

[98] 1926: 170.

[99] Duport 1790: 20.

and (3), in the conclusion, declare how the statute shall govern the case; for here too, in the major and the minor premisses, the law alone is a supreme truth ruling all.[100]

The essential institutional consequences arising from such a conception[101] have lain first in a strict 'autonomization' of the judicial power with the aims of avoiding any form of judicial interference in the functions of legislation and administration, and of limiting judicial intervention to the strict application of statute, that is, to deducing the particular conclusions derivable from a general norm. Further consequences have been a reorganization of the courts, intended to unify the legal process, and the institution of reference to the legislature (*référé législatif*) and a Court of Cassation in order to keep the process under effective control. Finally, this conception of adjudication found its high point in the development of the Exegetical School, whose method of interpreting statute was 'essentially deductive'[102]—whether that was 'logically to deduce from a statute all the conclusions implicit in it'[103] or, beginning 'from a statute or the legal rules drawn from it', to attempt to 'reach back to the higher principle and then deduce conclusions from it'.[104] Thus, to the question 'What is law?' Laurent replied: 'It is a series of principles that can be drawn from statute or deduced from it',[105] and he added that the Court of Cassation 'has not hesitated to apply these principles, while remaining faithful to statute, in cases where, as the best writers have it, a literal interpretation leads to absurd conclusions'.[106]

Although this 'deductivist' conception of a legal system has not lost all its power of fascination on the theoretical plane, nor part of its impact from a practical point of view,[107] the limits of such a model are generally accepted.

Even resolutely rationalist writers like Kalinowski maintain that 'a system of moral norms' (in the broad sense, including legal norms) 'is comparable *from a distance* to a deductive system, because the

100 *Opinion de M. Garat l'Aîné, Député du Pays de Labour, sur les plans présentés par MM. Duport et Sieyès à l'Assemblée nationale pour l'organisation du pouvoir judiciaire*, Paris, l'an premier de la liberté, p. 30.

101 On this, see, especially, Lenoble and Ost 1980: 33 ff.

102 Husson 1972: 120.

103 Geny 1919: I. 44. 104 1919: I. 45. 105 Laurent 1881: 121.

106 1881: 18.

107 Particularly in the recent tendency of some writers—who have been called the 'new exegetes'—to advocate restoring an exegetical conception of interpretation that had been believed to have been finally abandoned. See Coipel 1980: 39.

normative propositions composing it divide ... into first and second, the latter being *partially* linked to the former ... by deductive modes of reasoning'.[108] Kalinowski makes it clear that, while 'the first norms are justified by their analytical self-evidence and some of the second norms by the normative syllogism ... which attaches them to the self-evident norms', on the other hand 'the other second norms (called 'complementary norms') are united with the first norms by a specific bond of a partially *extra-logical* nature',[109] which is the fact that they are 'enacted by the person on whom a legal norm confers legislative power which that person uses according to the content of the delegation received'.[110] This concession, moreover, confirms the conclusions reached in Sect. 3.1.1, by stressing that a legal system cannot be conceived as purely 'static', which would be the case if the content of all of its 'second' norms could be deduced from the content of its 'first' norms.

While these considerations clarify the limits of the deductive model in the creation of law, Kalinowski readily extends them to the application of law. Although maintaining that 'a legal syllogism is an *element* of' the application of law 'and, what is more, a *necessary* element',[111] he recognizes that 'the application of law is an *action* which includes *evaluation* and *decision*'[112] and that 'while the intuitive application of the corresponding rule of logic is in fact easy, considerable difficulties attach on one side to choosing the major premiss—that is, the legal norm to be applied—and on the other to choosing the minor premiss, in other words to establishing the facts that decide the application of a particular legal norm'.[113] To the extent that the choice of major premiss poses especially the problem of interpreting the rule to be applied, it is also noteworthy that Kalinowski is not going back to conceiving this operation as a purely logical activity, but rather as an activity 'governed by *two* groups of rules: extra-logical and logical rules', the application of the latter being feasible only *after* the former have been brought into operation.[114]

Other limits to the deductive character of a legal system are the following.

As to the deductive link uniting certain 'second' norms to 'first' norms, the latter's 'analytically self-evident' nature must now be doubted. First, the most general norms involve a basic indeter-

[108] Kalinowski 1967: 244. [109] Ibid. [110] Kalinowski 1965: 156.
[111] 1965: 174. [112] Ibid. [113] 1965: 175. [114] 1965: 170.

minacy of meaning which, even when they are enacted explicitly by a legislator, authorize the stating of a deductive link with more particular norms only by means of a previous interpretation which, as already said, cannot itself be reduced to a purely deductive operation. Moreover, as Geny has justly claimed, it is rare for statutes to express such 'first' norms—which he calls 'principles'—and it is far more common for them 'to contain, themselves, only conclusions, created by principles situated above and beyond them'.[115] Reconstruction of a principle then requires an operation arising more from 'intuition', 'legal instinct', and 'tradition' than from a strictly logical form of reasoning.[116]

Finally, even when a legislator seems itself to deduce certain particular conclusions explicitly from a general principle that it has previously formulated, Ray has rightly doubted whether the legislator is really proceeding to a strict deduction, understood as the fact that 'in passing from principle to conclusions, in a sense one is only passing from the same to the same'.[117] In using deduction, seen as a 'way of presenting ideas',[118] the legislator often 'constructs', rather than simply deduces, the conclusions that it adopts: 'the links from principle to conclusion are partially the legislator's work'.[119] We shall cite just one of Ray's examples. After positing the principle that 'in order to succeed, it is necessary to exist at the moment when the succession is opened', Article 725 of the Civil Code adds, '*thus* the following are incapable of succeeding: (1) someone who has not yet been conceived; (2) a child incapable of viable life; (3) someone who is civilly dead'. Now, as Ray has commented, it is clear that the legislator 'might very well regard a child incapable of viable life as having existed'.[120] *A fortiori*, obviously, the legislator could have regarded as existing someone who is civilly dead.

There are also comparable limits to the 'syllogistic' conception of the act of judging. In addition to the above difficulties involved in the problems of interpretation that arise in selecting a major premiss, there is also, more basically, the fact that, before interpreting that premiss, it is important to identify the norm appropriate to the concrete situation in the case. As F. Rigaux has suggested, 'in strict logic, a result could be attained only by inserting all existing legal rules, in succession, under the major premiss, in order to choose the

115 Geny 1919: i. 45. 116 Ibid. 117 Ray 1926: 168.
118 1926: 169. 119 Ibid. 120 1926: 170.

rule corresponding to the fact situation given in the minor premiss'.[121]

One may consider in the same light the complexity of the minor premiss and the idea that the established facts to which it refers 'are in no way pure facts', given that 'establishing of facts is subject to the rules of procedure and proof, which the judge may not break'.[122]

To these comments, some writers have added that 'the form of the syllogism is hardly appropriate to the natural movement of judicial reasoning'.[123] This argument can have two aspects. On the one hand, it may be supposed that 'the order of the premisses leads from the abstract to the concrete, from the general rule to the particular application, while the direction of the judge's thought is more naturally the converse'.[124] Reality, however, is presumably more nuanced and rather reveals 'the deep *unity* of fact and law' in judicial reasoning. If knowledge of the facts partly conditions the choice of rule, it is no less true that, conversely, 'the description of fact is necessarily subject to attraction by the concept through whose mediation *this* legal rule indicates the hypothesis to which it applies'.[125] The reason for the partial inadequacy here of the syllogistic form is therefore that it logically suggests that the premisses are independent of each other, while in law there is usually a close interdependence between them. On the other hand, it has also been suggested that there can be in law a form of retroaction from the conclusion to reasoning about the premisses, in the sense that 'when, for one reason or another, the result is unacceptable', 'the jurist is led to introduce a distinction that may have been omitted in establishing the premisses of the jurist's reasoning'.[126] This is the same idea that other writers have formulated in speaking of a 'method of *tempered deduction*' which prohibits going 'to the extreme of strictly logical deductions' when these come up against 'equitable or practical considerations'.[127] The same limits are suggested by the Mazeauds: 'In a chain of logical deduction there is always a moment at which one must stop, on penalty of reaching an unacceptable result. The jurist should know to give up on deduc-

[121] F. Rigaux 1966: 43. For the same reason, it has been held that the possible discovery of a gap in law supposes that 'the jurist must, before being able to assert without too much risk that a provision does not exist, consult all the texts in which the provision might be found' (Gardies 1979: 296).

[122] Perelman 1961: 271. [123] F. Rigaux 1966: 72. [124] 1966: 73.

[125] 1966: 80. [126] Perelman 1976: 9. [127] Geny 1919: i. 47.

tions as soon as they no longer tally with the necessities of social life and justice'.[128]

Must one then speak of 'judicial alogic', as some have done,[129] and conclude that in law 'deduction from premisses is quite unimportant'?[130] Such an absolute response seems, in its turn, reductive. While it is true that the deductive model does not take account of the overall operation of a concrete legal system, it does correspond to a real part of judicial activity. And, even if it can be maintained that the legislator or judge seems content to put forward 'solutions worked out beforehand in the mould of logical reasoning',[131] one cannot ignore the fact that such a picture continually recurs in legal thinking and fulfils functions at least as important as the axiological considerations that are supposed to temper its rigour. To take up an idea developed elsewhere, it can be said that, while deduction as 'logician's technique' plays a rôle in legal reasoning that is at once 'certain, yet limited', the deductive form of a legal system belongs to 'logician's ideals' which, 'in contrast, preponderantly determine jurists' approaches'.[132]

Although we have examined the problem of the deductive form of a legal system at some length, we still need to mention briefly the problem of its axiomatization and formalization.

2. *Formalization.* Although, logically, the problem of the formalization of law seems best treated after that of its axiomatization,[133] since it will be mentioned only briefly it will be dealt with first.

A system may be thought of as formalized when the operations of its construction are determined 'by specifying solely the graphical forms of the linguistic signs used and their distribution in space'.[134] In this respect, it seems to be unanimously accepted that law 'is not a formalized system',[135] for the double reason that 'the norms forming a system of law ... are not defined by their syntactic structure alone',[136] and that 'the plasticity of legal concepts ... is not amenable to sharp-edged formalization'.[137]

While these objections are not an obstacle to a certain degree of formalization in the 'representation' of legal data, as is shown by the

128 Mazeaud 1972: 42. 129 Miaille 1976: 201.
130 F. Rigaux 1966: 43.
131 1966: 42. 132 Lenoble and Ost 1980: 217.
133 See, especially, Blanché 1967: 22.
134 Kalinowski 1965: 31. 135 1965: 62. 136 Ibid.
137 Hébraud 1968: 36.

developing application of computer science to law, it must be accepted that the equivalence of that transposition is never guaranteed[138] and that one can speak at the most of a formalization '*in* law', understood as formalization of certain aspects of legal phenomena, and not as formalization '*of* law' as a whole.[139]

3. *Axiomatization.* As for the problem of axiomatization, a deductive system can be considered as axiomatized only so far as 'one states explicitly, from the beginning, by way of axioms, all the propositions that one will later call upon to support one's demonstrations'.[140] Axiomatization thus supposes 'avoiding appeals to intuitive self-evidence by requiring that all the principles that are relied on are made explicit'[141]—that is, the system's axioms, its basic terms, and its rules of construction.

Connected still more directly with the process of axiomatization are two specific formal properties: the decidability of the system and the independence of the axioms. A system possesses the property of decidability 'when, as to each expression that can be formulated in its language and that has the syntactic structure of a thesis, one can decide, by applying an appropriate technique, whether it is or is not a thesis of the system'.[142] Decidability therefore supposes the existence of rules for admitting axioms and for demonstrating theorems, in either case formulated expressly and rigorously—and this in fact forms one of the conditions for axiomatization.

Moreover, the independence of axioms consists of 'reducing so far as possible the number of basic terms and propositions', in such a way that it would not be possible to demonstrate one postulate by beginning from another.[143] While it is generally accepted that 'the independence of the postulates of a single system is not logically indispensable to its validity', the ideal of axiomatics is certainly to 'achieve such an outcome'.[144]

How far are these different properties applicable to law?

While some contemporary logicians do not exclude the possibility of a complete axiomatization of law,[145] thus keeping alive the dream already entertained, as has been seen, by many rationalist philosophers of the seventeenth and eighteenth centuries, they at least recognize that the practical difficulties that this dream comes up

[138] Bauer-Bernet 1986: 40. [139] Reisinger 1975: 24.
[140] Blanché 1967: 19.
[141] 1967: 21. [142] Kalinowski 1965: 35. [143] Blanché 1970: 52.
[144] Ibid. [145] See, especially, Klug 1966: 176.

against are considerable[146] and that law functions 'quasi-axiomatically'[147] at most.

We shall summarize the major difficulties, which other writers, however, readily identify as insurmountable obstacles.[148]

As Blanché, a logician who is not a jurist, has rightly noted, the first difficulty is that in concrete legal systems there is 'much that is implicit and in need of being made explicit . . . beginning with those "moral principles" that guide the legislator as much as the judge, often without them realizing it, and probably also, though perhaps in a more conscious way, the jurist'.[149] Now, the fact that such principles might not be formulated expressly in writing and might often be considered 'too obvious to need stating' seems not to constitute a simple problem of 'presentation' of a normative content that, were it made explicit, would remain completely unchanged. In the same way as the passage from oral to written language more or less deeply affects the message conveyed,[150] it may be supposed that to make an implicit message explicit will inevitably have repercussions for its content. As Ducrot has rightly remarked, recourse to the implicit makes it possible in particular 'to find . . . a means of expression that does not put it on display, that does not turn it into an object that can be earmarked and thus contested'.[151] Consequently, making a principle explicit 'is the first and the decisive step towards placing it in question',[152] in so far as it deprives the principle both of its status of self-evidence and of the specific fluidity of the unsaid.

This first difficulty leads to another, which is to determine the legal status of such principles and their exact relationships to other legal norms.

An abundant legal literature displays the wide variety of views on the problem of such principles' membership of a legal system (although today, however, that question has generally been resolved in the affirmative), the precise conditions under which a particular principle may be considered to belong to such a system and these principles' degree of autonomy in relation to other modes of law creation such as statute, custom, and case law.[153]

[146] Ibid. [147] Ibid. [148] See, especially, Canaris 1969: 26.

[149] Blanché 1967: 22.

[150] See, especially, Ricœur 1976: 28, 'Human discourse is not merely preserved from destruction by being fixed in writing, but . . . is deeply affected in its communicative function.'

[151] Ducrot 1972: 6. [152] Ibid.

[153] On this, see, especially, Jeanneau 1954; Gérard 1981.

There are equally important controversies over the logical relations to be established between these principles and the other norms belonging to the same legal system.

On one side, the formulation of such principles seems not to correspond in any general way to the idea developed by Alchourrón and Bulygin that 'it is possible to modify the basis of a system without modifying the system itself', in the sense that it provides a basis that is 'normatively equivalent to the original one'.[154] It seems, on the contrary, that such a formulation, even when it rests on a number of particular norms in force, does not boil down to a task of 'simple' or 'complete' induction,[155] but is rather of the nature of an 'amplificatory' induction[156] which, hypothetically, gives the conclusions a significance that is 'not logically equivalent to the premisses' but possesses a 'greater generality' and 'thus essentially enriches the legal system's content'.[157] That this mode of reasoning is in fact usually employed to fill a legal gap underlines such an operation's partially creative nature.

On the other side, if it is possible to establish a deductive link between a general principle and a number of particular norms that appear to follow logically from it, one can also note the importance in law of the principle *lex specialis generali derogat*, which is often cited against such a possibility. And the idea that the specificity of a particular situation may require a derogation from general principles is obviously scarcely compatible with the very idea of axiomatization.[158]

A last difficulty concerned with the choice of a legal system's axioms—arising partly from the foregoing—is that 'the number of explicitly given propositions' on which the system is based 'is incomparably higher than that of the axioms on whose basis a normal logico-mathematical system establishes the deduction of its theorems'.[159] The upshot is 'an axiomatics so concrete and teeming that the observer generally forgets that it is an axiomatics',[160] and it may also be thought no longer to correspond to the 'principle of

[154] Alchourrón and Bulygin 1971: 80.
[155] Kalinowski 1965: 149.
[156] Silance 1968: 489 ff.
[157] Opałek and Woleński 1975: 60.
[158] 1975: 63.
[159] Gardies 1979: 287. See also Opałek and Woleński 1975: 64.
[160] Gardies 1979: 287. See also Gardies 1987: 175, 'Although legislative texts may, in a legal system, be assimilated to an axiomatics, it must be recognized that such an axiomatics is *excessive*, the legislator multiplying provisions without much concern to reduce them to a minimum.'

economy'[161] generally associated with the very idea of axiomatization.

Finally, the difficulties of axiomatization concern the determination not only of axioms but also of the rules of inference accepted within the system. Such determination is difficult not only because legal systems 'are careful not to state all of the provisions necessary to the operations that their application entails'[162] but also because these systems 'presuppose almost all the resources of logic'[163] without establishing any true hierarchy among them. Hence also the importance of the organ charged with such inferences, which is connected with the at least partially dynamic nature of every legal system. Therefore there does not seem to be a way to make the rules of construction explicit in an exhaustive, consistent, and rigorous manner without at least partially altering the content of the concrete legal systems to which they are supposed to apply.

4. *Decidability*. This last difficulty makes it possible to connect the problem of the *decidability* of legal systems, with which it partially intersects, in that it highlights the impossibility of deciding with complete certainty whether particular legal conclusions that one could be tempted to infer from the 'axioms' of a particular legal system belong to that system. The limits inherent in the decidability of a legal system do not, however, derive solely from the impossibility of identifying the accepted rules of inference rigorously; they also derive from the difficulty of identifying precisely the rules for accepting the 'axioms' themselves. It is known that, while such rules for acceptance can be formulated explicitly within a legal system, particularly in the form of legal rules of competence, this is not necessarily the case. As Hart in particular has stressed, what he calls the 'rule of recognition' of a legal system 'For the most part . . . is not stated, but its existence is *shown*'[164] in 'a complex, but normally concordant, practice of the courts, officials, and private persons in identifying the law by reference to certain criteria'.[165] Again we discover the difficulties involved in making such rules explicit. It is also important that the rules of recognition belonging to most concrete legal systems are 'fuzzy'[166] in the sense that they formulate

161 Blanché 1970: 52; Alchourrón and Bulygin 1971: 78.

162 Gardies 1979: 286. So far as a legal system thus presupposes that a set of rules is 'already given', it has been called a 'post-grounding' system' (*système 'postfondateur'*) (Gardies 1987: 176). On these so-called rules 'of experience', see Sect. 4.5.1.

163 Ibid. 164 Hart 1961: 98. 165 1961: 107.

166 Wróblewski 1983*b*: 327.

criteria that make it possible to decide without hesitation whether certain rules are valid or not, while leaving the question in a state of uncertainty for other rules.[167] In Hart's terms, one can say that the rule of recognition possesses an 'open texture' making it possible 'to distinguish clear central cases, where it certainly applies and others where there are reasons for both asserting and denying that it applies'.[168]

For these differing reasons, the decidability of a legal system is far from perfect.

5. *Independence*. The same goes for the property of *independence*. While such a property supposes the absence of any 'normative redundancy', in the sense that several norms belonging to the same system would attach, wholly or partly, identical legal consequences to identical fact situations,[169] it is undeniable that, whatever might be the legislator's actual concern in this respect, as well as the presumption of rationality that the legislator enjoys in the interpretation of norms actually in force, reality rarely corresponds to such an ideal. This situation cannot be explained solely by the pragmatic functions of communication that redundancy can fulfil, according to the saying *bis repetita placent*. It is also and more basically to be explained by the impossibility of determining *a priori* and with certainty the respective fields of application of the different norms and principles in force, including the 'precise borderline between what may and may not be deduced from such and such a provision'.[170]

This impossibility is often due, for one thing, to the fact that often a particular provision may *a priori* be the object of an interpretation that is either analogical or *a contrario*—in the same way as a general principle may be thought of *a priori* equally as applying to the whole set of particular cases that it covers or as being the object of derogations justified by the specific nature of some of those cases. It thus clearly appears that at least partial redundancy, whether among a number of particular norms or between a general principle and specific particular norms, is far from being useless in the sense of excluding all interpretation in terms of reasoning *a contrario* or of derogation.

Fairly similar conclusions can be reached about the other formal

167 Ibid. 168 Hart 1961: 119.
169 On this, see Alchourrón and Bulygin 1971: 62.
170 Gardies 1979: 296.

properties of a legal system—in this context, consistency and completeness.

6. *Consistency.* As to *consistency* firstly, one cannot deny the importance of such a property, whether on the level of the general ideals that permanently polarize legal action and legal thought[171] or on the level of more specific definition of the very notion of legal system.[172] None the less, the consistency of a legal system exhibits both special features and limits in relation to that of a formal system. A first such feature may be found in its very definition: while a lack of consistency lies, generally, in 'perceiving a contradiction—the result of simultaneously affirming the truth of a proposition and of its negation',[173] in law it consists of perceiving 'two incompatible directives, to which it is not possible to conform at the same time, either because they impose two obligations pointing in opposite directions or because one of them prohibits what the other permits and there is therefore no way to conform to one of them without breaching the other'.[174] A second special feature lies in the mode of identifying legal antinomies: while, 'in a formal system, contradictions are also formally recognizable', 'in law, a purely formal, that is, literal contradiction is not sufficient to give rise to an antinomy, for the judge, in interpreting the texts, may give the same signs different meanings or another sphere of application, so as to avoid a conflict of norms'.[175] This is why one speaks, in certain cases, of 'apparent' antinomies, that is, prima facie incompatibilities that it seems possible to resolve through a reconciliatory interpretation.[176] A final special feature is found in the consequences ensuing from a legal antinomy: while the presence of a formal contradiction renders the system unusable and compels its author to reject, if not the entire system, at least the elements generating the contradiction,[177] the presence of a legal antinomy necessarily requires a solution in which the application of one norm is made to predominate to the exclusion of the other.[178]

It is with this aim that traditionally—on the levels of legislation,

171 On this, see Lenoble and Ost 1980: especially 176ff.

172 See, especially, Bobbio 1960: 80, where he reckons that among the different meanings of the term 'legal system' the most interesting is that such a system excludes 'incompatibility of norms'.

173 Perelman 1965: 393. 174 1976: 39. 175 1965: 398.

176 Foriers 1965: 37.

177 See, especially, Foriers 1967: 30; Perelman and Olbrechts-Tyteca 1970: 262; Bobbio 1960: 81.

178 Bobbio 1960: 81.

doctrine, and case law—certain general rules are developed to allow priority to be given to one or other of the norms present.[179] Based on three different criteria of solution—hierarchy, chronology, and specialization (*spécialité*)—these traditional rules are the following: *lex superior derogat inferiori* (a higher norm prevails over a lower norm), *lex posterior derogat priori* (a later norm prevails over an earlier norm) and *lex specialis derogat generali* (a particular norm prevails over a general norm).[180]

Although they cannot ensure an 'originative' kind of consistency in a legal system, such rules are capable of ensuring it a certain 'derived' or 'restored' consistency.

The limits inherent in a legal system's consistency are, however, just as evident as its special features. First, as has already been suggested, legal antinomies are common and, to a considerable extent, inevitable. Yet their existence—however problematical from a strictly formal point of view—does not pose any basic practical problem, so far as they can be resolved with the aid of the abovementioned rules of conflict. However, in certain cases that, while rarer, are no less real, such antinomies appear 'insoluble', either because the criteria selected are not applicable—which happens when the incompatible norms are contemporaneous, of the same hierarchical level, and of the same degree of specialization—or because the criteria are in conflict with each other,[181] which happens when the antinomy lies between two norms one of which is earlier and higher and the other later and lower, or one of which is earlier and specialized and the other later and general, or lastly one of which is higher and general and the other lower and specialized.[182]

In the case of conflict between criteria for resolving antinomies, the problem may be resolved theoretically by establishing a hierarchy between them. It is, however, generally accepted that, while 'the chronological criterion and the hierarchical criterion exhibit a constant and univocal relation of lower and higher, one cannot establish a constant and univocal relation where one of the two terms of the relation is the criterion of specialization'.[183] The result is that 'in the two cases of conflict between the criterion of specialization and the chronological criterion, and between the criterion of specialization and that of hierarchy, the solution is not automatic, although one should be able to find it through interpretation'.[184]

[179] Perelman 1976: 40. [180] On this, see Bobbio 1960: 94ff.; 1965: 237ff.
[181] 1960: 95. [182] 1965: 253–5. [183] 1965: 257. [184] Ibid.

The conclusion is not different when the question is of a hypothesis in which none of the above-mentioned criteria is applicable.[185]

These different hypotheses illustrate clearly the limits inherent in formal techniques for restoring consistency to a legal system,[186] limits additional to the basic fact that perceiving the very existence of a legal antinomy 'is never purely formal'.[187] This does not mean that the antinomy remains unresolved, since, in many legal systems, the judge will be bound to resolve it within the limits of the case before the court, but this at least brings out the fact that the systematicity on which such a solution rests cannot be of an exclusively formal kind.

Moreover, although the problem of the limits inherent in the formal consistency of a legal system has been introduced with reference only to norms belonging to that system, those limits would appear still more clearly in connection with the principles and values comprised in the system. It suffices here to say only that what precisely distinguishes these principles and values from norms is the fact that they do not operate in an 'all-or-nothing fashion'[188] and that admitting them to the system does not exclude the existence of contrary principles or values between which variable choices or compromises may come to appear necessary.[189]

7. *Completeness.* A last formal property of a legal system is its *completeness*. This may be defined briefly as the fact that a system contains no 'gaps' and may determine the legal status of any fact whatever by means of the set of the system's elements.

Here too, none can deny the importance that the ideal—indeed, the postulate—of completeness has acquired in law, particularly since the codification movements which dominated Continental Western Europe in the nineteenth century and culminated in the idea of 'the logically necessary plenitude of written legislation'.[190] The most developed expression of this idea can be found in two theories: that of 'empty legal space', according to which whatever is not legally regulated is legally irrelevant, and that of the 'exclusive

185 1960: 111.

186 See, especially, Malgaud 1965: 18, admitting that in these hypotheses 'one has therefore to make a decision although no logical criterion is available'. See also Silance 1965: 136, opposing 'philosophical or moral solutions' to 'practical or logical solutions' when the latter seem inadequate.

187 Perelman 1965: 404.

188 Dworkin 1978: 24.

189 1978: 27; Canaris 1969: 114–15.

190 Geny 1919: i. 193.

general norm', according to which whatever is not legally regulated is legally permitted.[191]

Without going deeply into critical discussion of these theories, the following arguments can be opposed to them. The second theory seems to confuse an absence of legal prohibition or obligation, which can be conceived as simple legal indifference or 'weak permission', with the existence of a legally protected prerogative or 'strong permission'.[192] In that sense, from a critical point of view, this theory is not logically distinct from the first.

As to the first, it can be objected that the norm according to which whatever is not legally regulated is legally indifferent, or permitted in the weak sense, is far from being applicable absolutely, as much from a logical as from a legal point of view.

From a logical point of view, although there has been support for the idea that the principle according to which 'whatever is not forbidden is permitted' is the only acceptable principle 'in a system applicable to an infinite variety of actions',[193] it is accepted that with regard to any particular type of action 'there is no logical obstacle to applying the [symmetrical] principle according to which whatever is not permitted is forbidden'.[194] Thus, at least within these limits, it appears that such a 'general law of freedom'[195] expresses not 'a logical, but a moral or political requirement'.[196] From a legal point of view, although it is clear that some branches of law, such as criminal law, correspond very broadly to such requirements by adopting the principles *nullum crimen*, *nulla poena sine lege*, it must be remembered that this is not the case in other branches such as civil law, where the acceptance of analogical modes of reasoning does not entitle one to conclude from an absence of explicit regulation the presence of legal indifference, just as acceptance of reasoning *a contrario* sometimes entitles one to conclude, reciprocally, 'from a permission associated with particular circumstances a prohibition with identical content when the stated circumstances are not present'.[197] Further, even for criminal law it has been emphasized that this subsystem is not as complete as it seems at first sight, in that it does not

[191] Foriers 1968: 14. Foriers notes that the first theory has been defended particularly by Bergbohm, Brinz, and Romano, and the second by Zitelmann, Donati, and Kelsen.

[192] See, especially, von Wright 1963: 85–7; Ross 1968: 129.

[193] Gardies 1979: 290.

[194] 1979: 291. [195] Geny 1919: i. 194. [196] Foriers 1968: 22.

[197] Gardies 1979: 291.

accept the principle *nulla absolutio sine lege*[198] and that the necessity of interpreting all criminal laws—including those that criminalize or impose a sanction—does not exclude the possibility of an extensive, particularly an 'evolutionary', interpretation, similar in many ways to an analogical interpretation.[199]

Finally: as with the problem of consistency, merely to perceive the existence of a gap in a concrete legal system is an operation that is far from relying on purely formal criteria. On one side, this perception is inseparable from an interpretative process that reveals 'the impossibility of always drawing an exact borderline between what may and may not be deduced from a particular provision'.[200] On the other, the borderline between a true gap (absence of norm) and a 'false' gap[201] (existence of a norm judged to be unsatisfactory) is extremely tenuous, in that a restrictive interpretation of a norm can lead to perceiving a gap when its extensive interpretation would have led to the opposite conclusion. Evidently, the choice between these two modes of interpretation ultimately depends on a value judgement with respect to a particular norm in force.

While these considerations reveal the limits of the formal systematicity of law, the difficulties indicated certainly do not remain unresolved, since in many countries judges are under an obligation to decide the case 'as if' the system were complete; equally certainly, that solution is not a product of completely free creation and the judge most often attempts to 'find' it in some way 'written in dots within the system'.[202] It seems however that such a discovery rests very largely not on formal but on substantive systematicity.

(*c*) *Substantive Systematicity.* The discussion thus far suggests that relations established among the elements of a legal system are not exclusively logical but also material or substantive. A wide variety of names have been proposed for this second type of systematicity, such as 'organism-system',[203] 'axiological or teleological order',[204] 'value order',[205] and 'axiological or teleological system'.[206] Although these expressions do not overlap completely,

198 Foriers 1968: 24.

199 Similarly, Gardies 1979: 291, 'Jurists know very well that analogical reasoning is not completely excluded from the domain of criminal law.'

200 1979: 296. 201 Foriers 1968: 10. 202 Ost 1978: 107.

203 Grzegorczyk 1986: 285.

204 Canaris 1969: 41. 205 Winkler 1969: 40.

206 Engisch 1957: 173ff.; Peine 1983: 107.

they have in common that they envisage 'rules as forming sets by reason of their *content*'[207] and not only of their formal relations.

This second type of systematicity will be reviewed successively in three perspectives. First, by stressing the partial interdependence between this form of systematicity and the earlier.[208] Second, by showing how it completes and extends formal systematicity when the latter reveals its limits. Finally, by grasping its specific mode of articulation and its own limits.

1. *Partial Interdependence of Formal and Substantive Systematicity.* As to partial interdependence between formal and substantive systematicity, it suffices to note that the different properties characteristic of the first are closely linked to a legal order's capacity to realize particular kinds of value, which may themselves be called 'formal'[209] and which form an integral part of the criterion of cohesion among the system's elements.

Thus, following Weber, it has been emphasized that the 'characteristics of abstraction, generality, formalism and fixing in rules which constitute stable and enduring facts'[210] have corresponded to the requirement of a 'specific value of "calculability"',[211] dominant in contemporary Western legal systems. Similarly, it has been said that 'predictability, which is the hard core of legal certainty, favours rigorous formalism in judicial solutions and brings into a system of law a requirement for consistency, non-contradiction and completeness—classic characteristics of an axiomatic system'.[212]

Other writers have correctly stressed that the at least partially deductive nature of a legal system ensures, further, the realization of formal justice, in terms of which 'entities within the same essential category should be treated in the same way',[213] as well as that of concrete justice based on the principle 'to each according to their legal entitlement'.[214]

This last value may also be called '*formal equality*'[215] or 'equality before the law',[216] conceived as the correct application of the law to

[207] Batiffol 1956: 49. See also Grzegorczyk 1986: 291, speaking of a 'system of legal contents'.

[208] See Gérard 1981: 255, 'These two requirements intertwine closely in practice.'

[209] F. Rigaux 1974: 371.

[210] Poulantzas 1965: 259.

[211] 1965: 261.

[212] Grzegorczyk 1986: 283–4.

[213] Perelman 1963*a*: 26.

[214] 1963*a*: 18.

[215] Van Quickenborne 1971: 183.

[216] Kelsen 1959: 5.

all individuals to whom it is addressed. For the same reason, it is synonymous with *absence of arbitrariness* in applying the law.[217]

Finally, these different values coincide very broadly with what Fuller has called the 'internal morality of law',[218] which he has himself made the very condition for the existence of a legal system.[219] Most of the eight criteria that he associates with such a value—which he also calls the value of 'legality'[220]—are actually inseparable from the idea of formal systematicity: the presence of general rules and their correct application recall the system's deductiveness, and the requirement that rules be public and clear refers back to the problem of axiomatization and in particular of the system's decidability, while absence of contradiction among the rules concerns the problem of the system's consistency.

A contrario, it is important to realize that other values—sometimes called 'substantive'—are either foreign to the formal systematicity of law (one may think particularly of some forms of liberty, or of social solidarity) or antinomical to them in a more or less accentuated degree (thinking particularly of some forms of concrete justice or real equality, such as equity).

To this partial interdependence between formal and substantive systematicity can now be added a certain form of complementarity between them.

2. *Complementarity of Formal and Substantive Systematicity.* It appears, then, that the limits inherent in the formal systematicity of law may constitute an essential argument in favour of the non-systematic nature of law, if one does not realize that these limits may be partially overcome through the presence of a substantive kind of systematicity.

To convince oneself of this, it suffices to look at various formal properties mentioned earlier.

On the level of decidability, first of all, one can follow Dworkin in thinking that a legal system is not composed exclusively of rules that can be identified by 'tests of pedigree', that is, specific criteria 'having to do not with their content but with their *pedigree* or the manner in which they were adopted or developed'.[221]

To use a different terminology, the validity of a legal norm can be conceived as determined not exclusively according to 'formal'

217 Van Quickenborne 1971: 182; Hart 1961: 202. 218 Fuller 1969: 4.
219 1969: 39. 220 1969: 41. 221 Dworkin 1978: 17.

criteria but also according to 'axiological' criteria that are not reducible to any precise formulation.[222]

In particular, while one can accept that the validity of legal norms said to be 'derived',[223] in the sense that their mode of elaboration is determined in advance by norms establishing the competent organs and the procedure to be followed, can be assessed according to mainly formal criteria, it is quite otherwise with legal norms said to be 'originative',[224] such as custom, general principles of law, or case law, for which no criterion of validity has been established by a pre-existing norm. In this second type of hypothesis, it is clear that recourse to axiological criteria plays a completely decisive rôle. This can be shown with respect to custom by recalling that the existence of a customary rule supposes not only the presence of a 'material' element consisting of the effective and repeated practice of a particular mode of behaviour in a given case[222] but also the presence of a 'psychological' element consisting of the 'conviction, among those concerned, that they are *under an obligation* to act as they do (*opinio necessitatis*)'.[226] Now, it is clear that this *opinio necessitatis* 'rests on value judgements implementing criteria of legitimacy'.[227] According to some, the existence of a custom would further depend on it not being 'irrational' or 'antisocial'—that is, not going against 'good sense' or 'certain higher principles which are fundamental to all forms of social organization'.[228] Such a condition obviously increases the weight of axiological criteria. The same goes, incontestably, for general principles of law. While the acceptance of a general principle of law may sometimes, be based on 'formal' criteria, in that the principle is worked out with the aid of reasoning by analogy or amplificatory induction, carried out with reference to particular rules of positive law in force,[229] it has already been noted that neither of these two modes of reasoning makes it possible to dispense with a 'value judgement on the equality of the legal value of the facts compared'[230] and with a 'teleological' kind of analysis.[231] *A fortiori*, it may be added, there are other general principles of law whose acceptance arises essentially from a particular conception 'of the equitable organization of social relations'.[232] Thus it has been

222 See, especially, Ost 1987: 105ff. 223 Virally 1960: 150, 158.
224 Ibid.
225 Carbonnier 1967: 12. 226 Ibid. 227 Gérard 1987: 62.
228 Geny 1919: i. 371. Similarly, see Lebrun 1932: 252.
229 Kalinowski 1965: 166. 230 1965: 116. 231 Klug 1966: 129.
232 Gérard 1981: 272.

thought that 'liberty, equality and the inviolable and sacred nature of property are so many concepts ... that are reflections of ideas commonly accepted and so generally held that they appear in the form of axioms or dogmas—one is tempted to say "basic truths"'.[233] Rules of case law, so far as considered to be rules of law, also seem to be very largely subject to axiological criteria. It appears that the possible binding force of such rules is not only subject to their formal acceptance by the higher courts and in particular by the Court of Cassation; it also depends, in large part, on the adhesion of lower courts, which are generally recognized to have a right not to bow to their superiors, on 'good grounds' drawn particularly from the evolution of the ideas and values that the legal system accepts.[234]

If axiological criteria can thus supplement the formal criteria for 'recognizing' legal norms, it is not hard to see that the same goes for their interpretation. We shall return to this when looking at the specific task of systematization carried out on that level by the judge.[235]

As for a legal system's completeness, while we have already had occasion to stress the important rôle played by criteria of an axiological kind in discerning gaps, this rôle can be considered equally essential on the level of their resolution, which in the last instance can only rest on the existence of 'preponderant values'.[236]

As to a legal system's consistency, finally, it can also be maintained that an absence or insufficiency of formal criteria may be offset by recourse to 'philosophical or moral solutions'[237] and that 'the criterion of criteria is the supreme principle of justice'.[238]

Recognizing the importance of axiological criteria with a view to overcoming the inherent limits of formal systematicity is quite obviously not sufficient, however, to demonstrate that these criteria themselves reveal the presence of a real systematicity, even though it be of a different order from the earlier. In this respect, it can be imagined that the values called upon derive from the free assessment and personal responsibility of the organ charged with resolving the problems created by the system's formal imperfections.

One cannot fail to be struck by the regularity with which such a solution—generally termed arbitrary—is found to be rejected in

233 Jeanneau 1954: 137.
234 On this, see van de Kerchove 1985: 233 ff.
235 See Sect. 3.2.3.
236 Perelman 1968: 551.
237 Silance 1965: 137.
238 Bobbio 1965: 258.

law, even though, on any hypothesis, a residual element of subjective assessment seems inevitable.

Although Dworkin's work on the recognition and interpretation of rules is particularly interesting, he is extremely critical of positivist theories that try to substantiate the thesis that a legal system contains more or less perfect decidability. After stressing the limits of formal criteria like 'tests of pedigree', Dworkin at once emphasizes that, with regard to acceptance of a legal principle, the solution 'could not depend on the judge's *own* preferences amongst a sea of respectable extra-legal standards, any one in principle eligible'.[239] Just the opposite: in his view, the existence of such a principle depends on 'institutional support', which is that it has already been referred to in some earlier judicial decision, has been applied in some statute, or has been cited in the preamble of a statute or in certain preparatory documents.[240] Even if the question here is not of a test as decisive as a 'rule of recognition' in Hart's sense might be, there is no doubt that the acceptance of such a principle is linked to some way of adopting it within a legal system and that the values to which it appeals should be harmonized with the 'spirit' that is dominant in that system.

The same goes for the resolution of gaps and antinomies. In the case of a gap, it is generally accepted that judges cannot simply decide according to their personal views, but must locate themselves to the fullest extent possible within 'the *spirit* of the legal order',[241] which implies that 'the solution developed to fill the gap should be *harmonized* with the law in force'.[242] In the same way, it can be supposed that, failing satisfactory formal criteria for resolving an antinomy, judges select the solution that appears to them to be not the one that most closely fits their personal preferences but 'the one that most closely fits the *general economy* of the system'.[243]

If we are to begin from these concepts of 'harmony', 'spirit', or 'general economy' of a system, we must now try to define more closely the relations inherent in the existence of substantive systematicity and the significance of its principal manifestations.

3. *Specificity of Substantive Systematicity*. The specific distinction between substantive and formal systematicity can be shown by way of a double conceptual opposition: while formal systematicity may be called 'mechanical', substantive systematicity may be called 'or-

[239] Dworkin 1978: 37 (our emphasis). [240] 1978: 40.
[241] Canaris 1968: 176.
[242] 1968: 177. [243] Huberlant 1965: 235–6.

ganic'; similarly, while formal systematicity may be characterized as 'logical', substantive systematicity appears as 'teleological'.

The first of these oppositions unquestionably belongs to the register of metaphor—which does not increase its rigour. It has crossed various currents of philosophical,[244] sociological,[245] and legal[246] thought, and obviously has an essential importance for our theme.

It is not difficult, without repeating ourselves too much, to grasp how systematicity of a formal kind can be called mechanical. First, this image suggests a basic form of similarity among its elements as well as between those elements and one of them from which the others are seen to be derived.[247] The deductive and axiomatized model undoubtedly corresponds perfectly to this idea. Secondly, the term 'mechanical' suggests that there is a rigid 'chain' among the different elements, evoked particularly by the figure of the judicial syllogism, of which it has been said that it gives the application of law 'a mechanical image that betrays its fundamental nature',[248] as well as by the idea of its possible automatization.[249] Finally, formal systematicity may also be called mechanical in the sense that it would exclude any internal or immanent purpose;[250] as would be expressed in rejecting any teleological consideration in the legal system's functioning.

It is by breaking with these lines of thought that one can understand how substantive systematicity can be 'organic'. As Durkheim has quite rightly said of the type of social solidarity that he calls 'organic', this concept evokes first not the 'replication of similar homogeneous elements' but 'a system of different organs, each one of which has a special rôle and which themselves are formed from differentiated parts'.[251] It is in this way, for example, that, when offering his conception of a legal order as 'institution', Romano has readily adopted the metaphors of 'body',[252] 'living whole', or 'organ-

244 Lalande 1962: at '*Organique*', 723, citing this 'antithesis which first appears in Kant, Herder and Jacobi, and has played a considerable rôle in the whole of German romantic philosophy'.

245 Thinking particularly of Durkheim's celebrated contrast between 'organic' and 'mechanical' solidarity (Durkheim 1984: 31 ff.).

246 See, especially, Rottleuthner 1986*a*: 218, where he shows that the oppositions organic/inorganic and organic/mechanical were established only towards the end of the eighteenth century.

247 It is particularly in this sense that Durkheim (1984: 60–1) understands the term 'mechanical solidarity'.

248 F. Rigaux 1966: 42.

249 See, especially, Reisinger 1975: 27.

250 Lalande 1962: at '*Mécanique*' 602.

251 Durkheim 1984: 132.

252 Romano 1975: 26.

ism',[253] while stressing that, as against formalist theories which reduce law exclusively to a system of norms, it is important to consider law, on the example of these different biological entities, as a 'unifying synthesis' through which 'elements distinct in themselves are found to be blended into a system'.[254] In the same way, Jhering had already developed the idea that law, like any organism, can be 'considered from both an anatomical and a physiological point of view'—that is, in terms of 'structure' as well as of 'functions'.[255] After showing that, from an anatomical point of view, a legal system is not composed only of rules but also of institutions,[256] Jhering explains that, from a physiological point of view, 'organs exist to fulfil certain functions'[257] and that 'the entire logical disposition, however complete, of the parts of a body of law is only a secondary thing, a product of the aim that it is to serve'.[258]

This functional and organic complementarity of different kinds of element also appears very clearly in Hart, in his conception of the legal system as a 'union of primary and secondary rules', when, from a functional point of view, he assimilates the different categories of secondary rules, whose formal heterogeneity he underlines, to 'remedies' for the defects affecting any régime of exclusively primary rules.[259] It also emerges when, dealing with some problems inherent in the development of these secondary rules, Hart raises, in the same metaphorical register, some questions relating to 'the pathology of a legal system'[260] or 'the embryology of legal systems'.[261]

The second feature of 'organic' systematicity appears in a form of fluidity of the relations that can be established among a system's elements. It is in this sense, it seems, that one can characterize substantive systematicity of law in terms of 'equilibrium', 'harmony' or 'cohesion', rather than in terms of logical consistency; in terms of a 'spirit of consistency' (*Folgerichtigkeit*), rather than in terms of rigorous deduction.

The idea of equilibrium is raised particularly by Batiffol, when he characterizes the mutual conditioning of legal solutions not 'as a kind of solidarity determining the rules' content in a necessary and, as it were, mechanical way' but as 'an organic kind of bond' which 'manifests itself, if one does not take it into account, in a multiplica-

[253] 1975: 8. [254] 1975: 31. [255] Jhering 1969: 27.
[256] 1969: 37.
[257] 1969: 48. [258] 1969: 49. [259] Hart 1961: 91.
[260] 1961: 114.
[261] 1961: 116.

tion of difficulties ... like any organism defending itself against an unassimilable foreign element'.[262] Pursuing this comparison on the level of the investigation of legal institutions, Batiffol also refers to the idea of a 'network'. In his view, '"institutions" hang together—more or less: to alter one of them makes trouble for its neighbours, which consequently must also be reformed'.[263]

The idea of a legal system's harmony, found particularly in the existence of 'general principles of law', is also set out by Huberlant: 'In a doubtless imperfect yet very real way, there is ... among the rules of a system of law not only a consistency that excludes contradiction but also a harmony which flows from the general spirit animating the system and is manifest in the concordance of the solutions chosen'.[264]

The 'spirit of consistency', finally, is perfectly expressed in the thought of Canaris, according to whom 'both legislator and judge are obligated, once they have encountered values, to adopt them afresh in a "consistent" way, to follow all of their particular consequences through to the end and to depart from them only in a reasonable way, that is, for objective reasons—in other words, to proceed in a spirit of consistency'.[265]

We now turn to the last feature of organic systematicity, its 'teleological' character.

Unquestionably, to take into account 'aims', 'ends', or 'objectives' reflects a tradition of legal thought at least as deep as that which stresses the logical form of law. In particular, methods of teleological interpretation—although believed to occupy a smaller place in those periods in which an exegetical model has predominated—have always existed alongside interpretative methods that have been termed logical. It has even been said that 'the aim of the law appears as the true *measure* of interpretation',[266] even when it has to be joined with other criteria.

On the level of legal systematicity, the honours probably go particularly to writers like Jhering, then to the *Interressenjurisprudenz* and *Wertungsjurisprudenz* tendencies, for having rehabilitated the importance of this dimension, which had gradually been obscured by formalist theories of law and by *Begriffsjurisprudenz* in particular.

The basic idea here is that law can be presented, at least in

262 Batiffol 1956: 50. 263 1956: 51. 264 Huberlant 1965: 212.
265 Canaris 1969: 16. 266 Pescatore 1978: 342.

part, as a 'teleological system',[267] that is, as a set of rules considered as so many means for realizing ends, which can themselves be expressed in terms of interests, values, or social stakes. The specific linkage supposed by this type of systematicity is thus no longer to be found in a deductive kind of logical relation but in a practical relation of means to end.[268] This type of linkage is unquestionably manifested most clearly in the concept of a legal institution.[269] Although a legal institution appears as 'a set of rules necessarily ordered according to a "spirit" that is the institution's animating and federative principle', one can conceive that 'among the rules thus linked together there reigns a *hierarchy* whose key is furnished by the institution's purpose and by the degree of proximity of means to end, the most distant means being subordinated to the closest means and so on'.[270]

There is, however, no doubt that the general principles of law, as well as the branches of law, constitute other forms of linkage of different kinds of rule whose basis is also essentially teleological. It has thus rightly been said that the basic principles are 'very general rules characterizing the aims actually pursued by a particular legal order or the essential values inspiring those aims',[271] in the same way as 'the unity . . . of the branches of law appears to be of a functional' (rather than a logical) 'type, in the sense that this mode of organization gravitates around the *purposes* served by the rules concerned'.[272]

Here too, however, it is important to avoid any form of idealization. Just as the formal systematicity of law cannot be conceived as totally completed, it is impossible to think of its substantive systematicity in a fully realized form. Especially, one can conceive the existence of what Engisch has called 'teleological contradictions' (the adoption of norms not suited to attaining the desired ends),[273] as well as cases of 'disharmony' or 'axiological inconsistency' (that situations that are 'equal' with regard to the desired ends are treated 'unequally')[274]. In either case, however, one can grasp the importance of the phenomenon of substantive systematicity in the form of

[267] Canaris 1969: 41; Peine 1983: 123; Weinberger 1970: 291; Diederichsen 1966: 700.

[268] Poulantzas 1965: 320.

[269] See, especially, Lachmayer 1975: 107; Poulantzas 1965: 312ff.

[270] Dabin 1969: 101 (cf. 1950: 286).

[271] Renauld 1958: 178.

[272] 1958: 173 (our emphasis).

[273] Engisch 1956: 161.

[274] 1956: 162; Canaris 1969: 115–16.

a 'permanent requirement' running through the elaboration of law, as well as in that of a true 'postulate' usually guiding its application.

3.1.3. *Linear and Circular Systematicity*

If any single description seems traditionally to have dominated legal thought, it must be the idea that law is basically a hierarchized system. One of the apparently most obvious consequences flowing from this is that the action of applying a legal norm is subordinate to that of creating it, and that, between application and creation, there can exist only a purely linear and hierarchical relation, the lower being always grounded and determined by the higher.

Although an important part of legal theory does support this description, some tendencies seem concerned to reverse its terms (American legal realism), to emphasize its limits or, finally, radically to question whether it is well founded. In this last case, the paradigm of circularity is substituted for that of linearity. To the attentive observer of legal realities, however, it appears that neither of these two paradigms is capable of describing adequately the entanglement of jurisdictions and norms that is evident today. Another form of systematicity comes onto the scene and to deal with it requires new instruments. These may be found in contemporary systems theory, which proposes, following writers like Hofstadter and Morin, the concepts of 'tangled hierarchy' and 'strange loop'.[275]

(*a*) *Linear Systematicity*. The traditional hierarchical conception of a legal system, according to which a higher norm is the basis of the validity of a lower norm, undoubtedly finds its best illustration in Kelsen and particularly in his pyramidal presentation of a system. Since this model has already been queried abundantly in our earlier arguments, we will not return to it here.[276]

Seeing the very great creative and normative power that courts and tribunals actually exert, many American writers, adhering to the tendencies of 'sociological jurisprudence' and 'American legal

[275] On the whole question, see Ost and van de Kerchove 1987: 183–253.

[276] For a critical discussion of the Kelsenian 'pyramid', see, especially, Golding 1971: 69ff.; Troper 1981: 518ff.; Amselek 1978: 5ff. [The 'pyramid' image is more prominent in the French version of *Pure Theory of Law* than in the English version or the German original; e.g.: the heading of sect. 35 is 'Der Stufenbau der Rechtsordnung', 'The Hierarchical Structure of the Legal Order', and 'La pyramide de l'ordre juridique'. The image should not be taken strictly: Kelsen's conception of hierarchy does not imply the even-sidedness of a pyramid. Tr.]

realism', appear to have radically contested the well-foundedness of the Kelsenian model. At least, they have inverted its terms, this time locating the ultimate site of validation no longer in some higher rule (a Constitution or a *Grundnorm*), but in the most individualized lower rule: the judge's decision. Often invoked as origin of this movement of ideas is the judge Holmes's declaration: 'The prophecies of what the courts will do in fact, and nothing more pretentious, are what I mean by the law'.[277] The change of perspective thus effected has been termed a 'Copernican revolution': while traditional legal thought places general rules in the centre of a system and thinks it can deduce specific decisions from them mechanically, the realist movement, instead, places judicial decisions in the heart of the system.[278] This new point of view has often been described as that of the 'bad man', the gangster who is preoccupied solely with avoiding the disagreeable consequences of his acts. His question is no longer, 'What is my duty?' but rather, 'What are the chances that my behaviour will be punished by a court?'[279] One then understands that the rule is no longer a justification for the decision, in that it no longer binds the decision-maker *a priori*; rather, the rule represents a prediction of the future decision. The decision no longer derives from the rule, rather the rule flows from the decision. It is also no longer important to speak of the rule's validity; rather, one has to admit that a rule is verified *a posteriori* if it states that the prediction that it formulates is actually fulfilled.[280]

This conception evidently shatters the traditional hierarchical picture; but, on looking closer, its terms are permuted rather than repudiated. To continue with the 'pyramid' metaphor: while the classical normativist perspective (especially Kelsen's) envisages a pyramid standing on its base and culminating in a single higher rule, the realist perspective proposes an inverted pyramid, in which the multiple distant sources of law flow into the singular decision of the judge. Although the movement of validity is therefore clearly inverted, nevertheless it is not abolished. The realist movement—not very surprisingly in a régime of judge-made law—tends to consider the judge's authority as supreme in relation to the legislator's, even that of the makers of a constitution. Nor does any of this question the hierarchical nature of a legal system or the linearity of its logic.

[277] Holmes 1897: 461.
[278] Frank 1932: 578.
[279] Holmes 1897: 459.
[280] Llewellyn 1941: 22–3.

(*b*) *Circular Systematicity.* Other tendencies have also raised these questions. Some writers, although without presenting alternative views, are content to state their perplexity in the face of the many kinds of phenomenon that seem to thwart the linear logics of authorization and validation. Thus Virally, asking himself the real significance of the hierarchical principle, notes: 'One cannot assert *a priori* that a norm can never alter that from which it draws its validity'.[281] The same embarrassment is found in Amselek, who, after confronting French public law with the *Stufenbautheorie* (construction of law by degrees), concludes: 'Reality—in this case, the legal regulation of normative competences—is much more complex, more tangled than the Kelsenian schema allows it to appear: the different public authorities draw the principle of their normative competence from the most varied categories of legal norms, which, from this standpoint, are in no way linked together on a continuous scale'.[282]

These observations finally lead some writers—we refer here principally to the teaching of the German sociologist of law Luhmann—to abandon the hierarchical model totally in favour of that of circularity. Thus Krawietz, referring to Luhmann, argues that, if one wants to escape from any dogmatic *a priori* and observe the reality of contemporary legal phenomena, one is forced to conclude that there are systems that have neither centre nor summit and within which the traffic is not only one-way, in that the multiple structures composing it maintain relations of interaction, the 'lower' elements helping to determine the 'higher'.[283] Luhmann himself presents legal systems as concatenations of elements determining each other reciprocally through self-referring processes that do not conform to any '"grounding" principle' or 'metanorm'. In this way, the relations—even of validation—maintained by the various legal norms are circular or recursive, foreign to the idea of hierarchy and to mechanisms of causality and deduction.[284]

(*c*) *Tangled Hierarchies.* We therefore find ourselves before two totally opposed conceptions of legal systematicity: a hyper-centralized, hierarchical, and linear model; and a hyper-decentralized, circular, and recursive model. Although they are not devoid of application, these radical conceptions seem to us to account adequately

281. Virally 1960: 174.
282 Amselek 1978: 13–14.
283 Krawietz 1984*a*: 269.
284 Luhmann 1988: 21–2.

only for the most extreme phenomena of any legal order. Nineteenth-century public law, within the framework of the *Rechtsstaat* (or *État de droit*), probably corresponded fairly well to the hierarchical model; likewise, in the absence of supranational authorities endowed with really effective powers, contemporary public international law can well be conceived as an 'an-archical' domain in which there is hardly any distinction between authorities and subjects, so that the relations within that domain correspond to a 'horizontal' or 'transversal' rather than 'vertical' logic.[285] So far as the principles of sovereignty and equality of States prevail in the international sphere, the competence of any authority and validity of any rule claiming to bind in that sphere will necessarily be subordinate to the States' formal consent, which quite obviously leads to questioning the very existence of a true 'system' of international law.[286]

Both the disciplinarian (*caporaliste*) model and the anarchical model therefore seem poorly suited to describing the most contemporary legal phenomena, those lying between the two extremities of the spectre we have just raised. To deal with those phenomena requires theory and concepts that give hierarchy its due, since hierarchy is unquestionably present in jurists' representations and therefore in the institutions and norms that they adopt, while also fitting in the innumerable situations that more or less explicitly thwart its efficacy. Contemporary systems theory appears to possess precisely those concepts that make it possible to articulate this new approach, which takes the name of 'paradigm of complexity'. While the first generation of systems theories was limited to envisaging 'complicated' systems, one speaks nowadays of 'complex' systems. The idea of complexity lies both in these systems' relative unpredictability (some of the information about their functioning escapes the observer, so that that functioning can suggest apparent disorder) and in the structures of retroaction that develop in them. While complicated structures are perfectly predictable, inasmuch as the ordering of their elements is purely deductive or linear, complex systems are more unpredictable, to the extent of the multiplication in them of recursive relations. The essential change therefore consists of taking 'looping' processes into account—a change that has also coincided

[285] Combacau 1986: 90.

[286] Similarly, see Verhoeven 1978: 69: 'One must not delude oneself: today there is hardly any international legal order; there are only disparate rules, powerless to define a mode of ordering outside the minds of those who arbitrarily discover a system there.'

with the birth of cybernetics. The question is then to oppose relations 'in cascade, open chain, sequence, series, tree form'—relations spreading like a tree—to relations 'that loop or close, or are reciprocal or conflictual, or recycling'—relations of retroaction: a passage from 'tree to trellis'.[287]

Hofstadter tries to conceive these relations of retroaction systematically with the help of the concepts of 'tangled hierarchy' and 'strange loop', defined as 'an interaction between levels in which the top level reaches back down towards the bottom level and influences it, while at the same time being itself determined by the bottom level'.[288] 'Tangled hierarchy' must none the less be distinguished from both simple 'feedback' and 'heterarchy'. While feedback supposes a simple relation of non-paradoxical control, in that it does not involve any violation of levels, heterarchy aims at a program without a 'monitor', composed solely of 'recursive transition networks' that are 'all tangled up'.[289] In the first case, no hierarchy is set up; in the second, hierarchy is totally absent. The interest of the 'strange loop' model, on the other hand, is that it makes it possible to conceive the phenomena of distortion of presumed hierarchies. Is this not just the kind of model we need? For we are claiming that the operation of legal sources corresponds to a systematicity of a 'tangled hierarchy' type: the presence of a gradation, a relation of superiority, a position of command, is, in law, beyond doubt, even though it is usually interfered with. In this lies the strangeness of the loops observed: they are strange because they disappoint a natural expectation—that, precisely, of a respected hierarchy, of a superiority in act.

Such an expectation develops as much among the ruled as among the rulers. Each of these, at its own level, interiorizes the pyramidal model, locates itself in the place provided for it, adopts the conventional discourse—the 'rôle', as sociologists say—and tries to situate, indeed to maintain, all the others in the exact echelon of power that is to be recognized as theirs. None the less, the hierarchy does not fail to affirm itself and to punish the waywardness of those, whether public or private agents, who could be tempted to step out of line. Thus, many controls of legality are imposed on the actions of subordinate powers, while criminal provisions aim to prevent encroachments of power between constituted authorities.

287 Le Moigne 1977: 89–91. 288 Hofstadter 1980: 709.
289 1980: 134, 691–2.

While it is therefore beyond question that there is hierarchy in law, such hierarchy seems largely to be tangled. This can be seen, in general terms, as much in processes of validation as in those of interpretation. What is the interpretation of a norm, if not the gift of meaning that is imposed on it by the organs applying it? What is the validation of a norm, if not the recognition, by the organs applying it, that its authors' claim to draw its legal effects from it is well founded? For the idea of *a priori* meaning and bindingness imposed by a higher organ is now substituted the idea of collaboration between organs that create and apply law—indeed, in some cases, of a pre-eminence of a lower organ whose decision as to the real significance of a legal text is not subject to appeal. Although case law and administration thus continue to subscribe to the postulates of the legislator's 'sovereignty' and 'rationality', this apparent discipline does not prevent those authorities from taking an active and sometimes unforeseen part in the process of legal creation, thus revealing the real systematicity of law in the form of a chain of strange loops. Three examples of this, among many others, may be offered.

In public law, the question of control over the constitutionality of statutes gives rise almost necessarily to 'tangled hierarchies'. Two things come together: either positive law excludes all judicial control over the conformity of statutes to constitutional provisions and the legislative power appears sovereign in that statutes that have been signed into law are incorporated in the legal order, whatever criticisms of their constitutionality may arise; or a supreme court exercises control over the constitutionality of statutes and thus places itself, at least in fact, in a position of pre-eminence with regard to the constituted powers. In both hypotheses, respect for the Constitution is entrusted to an organ of the legal order whose actions are removed from any control. Thus, one acute observer has written, with reference to the Constitutional Court of the Federal Republic of Germany: 'possessing a monopoly over interpretation of the Basic Law, it states what the Constitution requires and appears as the holder of a sort of constitution-making power prevailing over the three powers'.[290]

More basically again, this 'strange loop' reminds us that, when the legislative body exercises supreme power (constitution-making power), it acts only as representative of the true source of power, the sovereign nation. Of course, Parliament usually takes the place of

[290] Fromont 1984: 1215.

the nation from the moment that the latter delegates its powers to Parliament. As Carré de Malberg has observed: 'The idea of sovereignty of the general will has been exploited in order to ground the sovereign power of Parliament itself.'[291] The difficulties generally encountered by the proponents of popular referenda—which, in the end, do no more than re-establish the true hierarchy of powers—bear sufficient witness to the resistance potential represented by this 'strange loop'.

A second illustration may be taken from the domain of administrative law. Although, in this area, the principle of legality, understood as the subordination of regulation to statute (the public service—that is, the executive power—can do only what it has been strictly authorized to do), traditionally prevails, today one is forced to recognize that the State's growing interventionism leads to serious alterations of the principle—so that one can speak, with Loschak, of at least partial 'mystification' in relation to the executive's alleged submission to statute.[292] To be sure, the principle is always referred to, by way of legitimation, but it can no longer hide the now obvious fact that administrative law, largely instrumentalized, serves more to authorize than to constrain the executive's actions, while one expects from the executive ever-increasing effectiveness. For statute often has only an indicative value and takes form only through the executive's intervention. Upstream, laws are drafted by the officials who will be charged with their application. As a result, their content is, to that extent, largely determined by the constraints operating on the specific level of execution. Moreover, downstream of the legislative process, the executive's mastery over the norms that are supposed to regulate its actions is still more evident. It is well established in this respect that a statute is applied only if, and so far as, the executive really wants to do so. One can conclude, with Loschak, that under these conditions administrative regulation is to be conceived as a 'provisional and relative self-limitation of and by the executive',[293] which comes back once again to observing the installation of a strange loop.

Our third example is taken from criminal law, the area in which the paradoxical aspect of the phenomenon we are looking at appears the most clearly. Would one not expect in criminal law, as in tax law,

291 Carré de Malberg 1984: 215.

292 Loschak 1981: 387–92.

293 1981: 392.

a reinforced respect for the principle of legality? Certainly the Public Prosecutor, the organ for applying criminal statutes, is required to conform to that principle in the task of prosecuting crime. Prosecutory practice, however, reveals a curious slippage from the principle of legality in prosecution to that of discretion to prosecute. As a customary kind of rule, justified by the requirements of the general interest, the principle of discretion to prosecute authorizes an 'organ of the law' to apply the law selectively. There is a double strange loop: here is a customary rule *contra legem* which confers upon an organ of application a true discretionary power, in the sense that, evaluating the discretion to prosecute freely, it ensures that the criminal laws will be applied permissively.[294]

Other examples could also be mentioned, particularly in the area of the relations established between different legal systems. It is obviously not possible to reduce legal systematicity either to Kelsen's strictly hierarchical model or to Luhmann's acephalous model.

3.2. The Different Forms of Systematization

3.2.1. *Systematization and the Legislator: Codification*

(*a*) *Definition and Historical Background*. Of all the forms in which law is systematized, the most effective and the most laden with consequences is certainly that of the legislator, codifying legal solutions. The code is probably the most tangible example of systematicity in law. As Sève writes, 'The idea of system has long been identified less with an abstract totality—a legal system as conceived in contemporary legal theory—than with the system—a special case, to be sure, but much more tangible, if one may put it that way—that is a code'.[295]

The fruit of a very long historical evolution, which began with the imperial codes of Theodosius and Justinian, really got going with the codes of Frederick II of Prussia, and triumphed in the nineteenth century with the Napoleonic codes, the idea of codification proves to be singularly complex and demanding.

To codify means to gather together in a single text (whether *codex* or collection is not very important) the greatest possible number of legal provisions—in contrast with an earlier situation, judged *ex*

294 On this point see, especially, van de Kerchove 1986: 77 ff.
295 Sève 1986: 81.

hypothesi to be open to criticism, in which the sources of law are dispersed. In this way the most diverse rules are brought together and put in order, as much according to their source as to their object; logic provides these rules with systematic ordering, while the Prince's stamp endows them with binding force. Passed through the crucible of the code, the law as a whole takes the form of legislative law, while the several attributes of perfection seem to accrue to it naturally—as if the cult of statutory law, in that age when jurists were nomophiles, increased tenfold when the law was written down in a code, a veritable incarnation of political Reason. No less than eight attributes, according to Vanderlinden's excellent study of them, combine to achieve that perfection:[296]

1. Above all, a code is consistent in the sense that it achieves a concentration of legal material, a quality that appreciates by contrast with the dispersion and fragmentariness of legal sources that reigned prior to codification.
2. A code benefits from wide publicity in that its authors seek to bring it effectively to the knowledge of its addressees, so that 'ignorance of the law will be no excuse'.
3. A code is handy. Although it cannot always be reduced to the size of a single short volume, it will contain only the essentials. Excluded from it will be laws that have fallen into desuetude, repetitive provisions, *obiter dicta*, and other formulae that are not strictly normative.
4. Logical structuration: a reasoned arrangement of the codified materials will make it easier to consult the code and will help to make the law accessible to everybody.
5. This is reinforced by a code's clarity: written in clear and simple language, it is meant to avoid doubt, ambiguity, fictions, latinisms, and archaisms, all of which so often characterize jurists' style.
6. Absence of contradiction between the solutions instituted by it. In this connection too, a code makes a *tabula rasa* of the past by reducing the diversity of often contradictory rules, customs, usages, and case law to the unity of its own logic.
7. Not content with formulating existing sources into a clear and harmonious system, the idea of a code also entails the codified law's conformity with the law applied. That is to say: once

[296] Vanderlinden 1967: 163ff.

adopted, a code can claim exclusivity among the various sources of law. No question of a subsidiary body of law surviving on the margins of the code; rather, the solutions deduced from the code's text are exclusively binding.

8. Last but not least, completeness: whatever the field envisaged by the codifier (whether a branch or a source of law, or even the law as a whole), the codifier's work is marked by a concern for exhaustiveness. To express this idea, Bentham forged a neologism: a code would be a 'Pannomion', a collection of all the laws, a 'complete body of legislation', or nothing.[297]

Of so perfect a work, the codifiers expected several effects: unification and simplification of the law, no doubt, but also its diffusion among the whole citizenry, and very often also a reform in depth of the codified material itself.

(*b*) *Quantitative and Qualitative Codifications*. Such a conception of a code probably marks the high point of the evolution of codification, which might be said to have shifted gradually from a quantitative to a qualitative ideal.[298] Quantitative codification consists, at one extreme, in simply writing the law down and bringing it together in a single document (such as the Twelve Tables or the commandments of Yahweh given to Moses). In this case, the nature of the law codified is hardly affected. The exercise is confined to compiling solutions, which remain juxtaposed, so that the code only reflects the casuistic process which reigned when those solutions were created. The ambiguities, antinomies, and gaps that inevitably emerge when these diverse rules are brought together still could not be overcome, for lack of a systemic vision of the law. Sometimes, even, the sacred origin of these codifications accentuates still further the rigidity and punctiliousness of rules brought together in such a mechanical fashion. In the hypothetically intermediate cases—which are surely the most numerous—there is some rationalization of the data: for example, the French Civil Code, which continued on from the doctrinal work of Dumoulin, Loysel, Domat, and Pothier with the aim of gradually systematizing the customary law and case law, without however claiming to produce a truly scientific work. Arnaud has shown clearly how the history of the Civil Code was one 'of constantly balancing two contrary intellectual movements, one

297 Bentham 1829*a*: iii. 91–5; see also 1829*c*: i. 366–70.
298 Similarly, Varga 1977.

empirical and the other rationalist, before witnessing the final victory of modern axiomatic rationalism'.[299]

At the other extreme, qualitative codification emerges as a systematization of legal material in axiomatic form. In this hypothesis, there is a real transubstantiation of law, the solutions being no longer juxtaposed, but hierarchized on the basis of rational and universal principles and each deduced from another according to rules of logical inference. In this case, the code is endowed with its own rules of transformation, application, and interpretation, so that, with the aid of those rules, the remaining legislative imperfections can be overcome. The rationality that emerges from this form of codification expresses in exemplary fashion an essential property of systems, that the whole appears with a value greater than that of the sum of its elements; systematization can even bring out emergent properties not to be found in each element, taken in isolation.

Pushed to that point, the requirement of rationalization verges on utopia. What is envisaged is a code of laws that would be perfectly simple, pulled together in the unity of a single volume and expressed in a language accessible to natural intelligence. It would probably be extremely simple to criticize in familiar ways each element of this ideal of systematization. Let us, however, agree that the rationalist utopia is an integral part of the very idea of a code and that, without it, we very likely would not have any of the codes that, historically, have attempted, with varying degrees of success, to realize that ideal.

Yet it must also be observed that the successful codifications do not depend entirely on a process of formal rationalization; they also suppose a radical simplification of the legal material and concomitantly a levelling of the social system itself. In making a *tabula rasa* of the past, inspired by a unitary conception of society, the codifier rewrites the law by assembling it under a few essential categories. Writers have often stressed this labour of simplification and unification, effected by the Napoleonic codes—work made possible by the Revolution, which had done away with the differences obstructing the nation's unity and the possibility of putting the law in order: differences of religion, suppressed by a secular law; differences of

299 Arnaud 1969: 216. See the judgement on Domat by Portalis, principal drafter of the Civil Code: 'The judicious Domat and some other contemporaries began to doubt that legislation is a true science. We call something a science that is a pursuit of truths or rules linked to each other, deduced from first principles and gathered together in a body of doctrine and system concerned with some of the principal branches of our knowledge' (1844: 298).

birth, suppressed by an equalitarian law; and local differences, suppressed by a national law.[300]

To generalize this point: one can observe a remarkable coincidence between the high tide of codification and a consolidation of political power. Whether one thinks of Justinian, Frederick II of Prussia, Napoleon, the Soviet Revolutionary codes, or the codes imported by some developing countries, in every case successful codification has gone together with either a completed revolutionary process or the triumph of a form of enlightened despotism. On any hypothesis, one can see a seizure by the State of the whole process of legal production. For a decentralized and many-formed kind of law is substituted a single formulation emanating from a sovereign whose henceforth all-powerful will is imposed in a quasi-hierarchical fashion on the other agents of legal production.

(*c*) *Codification Today.* Are the conditions, intellectual as well as political and social, favourable to codification still present now, at the end of the twentieth century? This is doubtful, in that, as has been seen, codification seems to involve a general context of simplification and unification: 'Codification', the sociologist Bourdieu explains, 'makes things simple, clear and communicable'.[301] Yet have we not resolutely entered the age of complexity? Are not the four paradigms on which the enterprise of codification rested in the period of its triumph (legal monism, political monism, deductive and linear rationality, and Promethean temporality) now profoundly altered?

Anyone can surely see that legal monism (the supremacy, indeed exclusivity, of written law) is giving way on all sides under the pressure of a reduced number of sources of law. Or that political monism must now compromise under the pressure of concurrent forces on the supra-national, infra-national, and indeed corporative and extra-territorial levels. Evidently, the model of strictly linear and deductive rationality has found itself opposed with increasing frequency by a dialectical logic—plural, reversible, and recursive—which corresponds to the entanglement of competences (above). Finally, there is an erosion of Promethean temporality (a time orientated towards a future governed by reason and law) following a multiplication of precarious and provisional legal forms characteristic of what we shall call a hazardous temporality (below: Sect. 4.5).

300 Similarly, Cambacérès, in Fenet 1827: i. 3.

301 Bourdieu 1986: 42.

One has therefore to speak today not of codification but of 'de-codification', in the framework of ever more diversified and conjunctural legislative policy (that of the Welfare State). There multiply today, on the margins of the classical codes, blocs of ever more specialized legislation. 'Codes', it has been said, 'are no longer at the heart of a legal system, which has burst open with the increase in the number of special laws, veritable microsystems with their own principles and methods of interpretation'.[302]

And while in France one can see a certain renewal of codification, the term 'code' is understood there in a different sense from the one we have been analysing. Far from representing a body of general rules applicable to the population as a whole, these new codes sometimes express sectional interests (like the Rural Code or the Craft Industry Code), sometimes the power and autonomy of particular administrative departments (such as the Customs Code or the Tax Code), so that this renewal of codification arises sometimes from corporatism and sometimes from bureaucracy. Reinforcing the compartmentalization of law, this kind of codification breaks up rather than unifies.[303]

If the contemporary legislator is still unable to attain this kind of systematization of law, can doctrine and case law succeed instead?

3.2.2. *Systematization and the Jurist: Doctrine*

(*a*) *The Jurist's Rôle.* Even if they are capable of carrying out many other functions and, in particular, to become 'decision-makers'—as political representatives, civil servants, or judges—it has rightly been emphasized that the 'only essential function' of *jurists* is 'the function of knowing' the law,[304] the other rôles not always being reserved 'solely for those called jurists'.[305]

It must, however, be made clear again that this assertion is true only if one has in mind the very specific form of legal knowledge called 'doctrine' in French-speaking countries,[306] or 'legal dogmatics', especially in the Germanic and Slavic countries,[307] and which expresses exactly the kind of knowledge that jurists have of

302 Viandier 1986: 79.
303 Fourré 1986: 728, 735.
304 François 1978: 197.
305 1978: 190.
306 See, especially, Ziembiński 1986: 9, recalling that, particularly in English and Polish, this term is little used.
307 Kalinowski 1969: 1. On the term's origins, see, especially, Perrin 1987: 49ff.

law as 'specialists' in that discipline. It may also be added that, according to a long tradition, this form of knowledge of legal phenomena is called 'science of law' and is sometimes even understood to monopolize that name.[308]

We shall confine ourselves here to emphasizing, as to the level of systematization, the specific rôle that the 'science of law' thus understood is able to play, the way that that rôle is linked with the functions peculiar to the legislator and the judge, and finally how other and more recent conceptions of the science of law open up new perspectives.

That doctrine or legal dogmatics fulfils a function of systematizing law seems to be unanimously accepted. Some writers even seem to attribute to it that function and no other. Carbonnier, for example, holds: 'All sciences systematize; but law, in one aspect, seems to be nothing but that . . . In this kind of science (which in other countries' doctrine is readily called "dogmatics"), systematic exposition of rules constitutes legal ordering, where the rules are logically co-ordinated with the unity of the system'.[309] Likewise Pescatore writes: 'It is doctrine's job to systematize these scattered elements and unite them in consistent and harmonious wholes. This labour of synthesis and systematic generalization forms the domain and the special value of doctrine.'[310]

Other writers, on the other hand, recognize that doctrine performs this function, while accepting that it also fulfils others. In Kalinowski's view, legal dogmatics is 'the science that makes explicit *and* systematizes the content of the legal norms constituting a legal system in force at a particular moment in a given territory or for a particular population'.[311] Likewise Van Hoecke thinks that 'legal dogmatics operates in two different ways . . . On the one hand, legal dogmatics *systematizes* the law. On the other, legal dogmatics *concretizes* the law, in that, in the interpretation and application of law, it develops more concrete rules on the basis of legal norms formulated in a fairly general fashion.'[312] This double function of interpretation and systematization is pointed out by many other

[308] See *Pour une Critique du Droit* (1978: 94), 'Doctrine monopolises legal knowledge. It turns all science of law into an abstract commentary on statute.'

[309] Carbonnier 1967: i. 24–5.

[310] Pescatore 1978: 118. See also Rials 1986: 74.

[311] Kalinowski 1969: 1.

[312] Van Hoecke 1986: 218.

writers,[313] some of whom, however, stress their necessary interdependence.[314]

(*b*) *The Methods of Doctrinal Systematization*. This interdependence raises, moreover, the question of the privileged methods by which doctrine is able to contribute to the systematization of law. It appears that *interpretation*—as much in the provisions of statutes and regulations as in judicial decisions—forms one of these methods.

While doctrinal interpretation enjoys, in principle, less authority than that of legislative or judicial interpretation, in reality it is traditionally 'more systematic and more generalizing'[315] than they. This systematic character is probably due largely to the fact that one finds at the core of legal dogmatics, as a veritable paradigm, the postulate of the rational legislator,[316] which is one of the most obvious bases for systematic interpretation of law and leads the doctrinal writer to reformulate the legal norms as clearly, consistently, and completely as possible. However, as will be seen later, one must not forget the essential place that this postulate also occupies in judicial interpretation, even though the systematization that it produces can operate, *ex hypothesi*, only more fragmentarily.

It also seems clear that the systematic arrangement of law, with regard to its 'material' and the content of its rules, arises in a privileged way from the intervention of doctrine and requires further specific methods.

Among these methods is firstly that of *definition*,[317] some writers also readily describing a jurist as 'a professional definer'.[318] This method of delimiting and determining the contents of concepts borne by legal norms is probably relevant not only to doctrinal work

313 See, especially, Alchourrón 1986: 171; Bulygin 1986: 193. Bulygin adds, however, a third function of 'the modification or transformation of legal systems' (ibid.).

314 See, especially, Aarnio 1986: 162; Van Hoecke 1986: 218.

315 Pescatore 1978: 328; Orianne 1982: 154.

316 On this, see Ziembiński 1969: 224; Lenoble and Ost 1980: 161 ff.; Ost and van de Kerchove 1987: 100 ff.

317 On definitions of law, see, especially, Belvedère, Jori, and Lantella 1979; Scarpelli 1958: 127 ff.; Ross 1958: 139 ff.; Eisenmann 1966: 25 ff.; Dabin 1935: 111 ff. Similarly, Portalis could say: 'everything that is definition, teaching or doctrine falls within the sphere of science ... Though there are definitions of which the legislator has to make himself arbiter, they are those belonging to the changeable and purely positive part of the law; but it is otherwise with the definitions that are concerned with morality and with things that exist independently of arbitrary acts of human will' (Fenet 1827: vi, 42).

318 Dabin 1935: 111.

but also to intervention by legislator and judge. It is often accepted, however, on the one hand, that 'the normal method of legislation is to posit terms without defining them',[319] starting from the principle *omnis definitio in iure civile periculosa*[320] and, on the other, that definitions in case law are of a more 'marginal'[321] nature, the judge being content most of the time to 'categorize'[322] the concrete dispute situation—that is, to decide whether or not it belongs to the extension of a concept, without going so far as to define the concept comprehensively. Each time this happens, the doctrinal writer cannot be content to 'reproduce' a pre-existing definition, but will 'construct' it on the basis of the ordinary methods of statutory interpretation, or by 'eliciting' from a set of categorizations used in case law the concept on which they rest.[323]

It further appears that, in some cases, doctrinal writers are called upon to 'create, themselves, concepts with legal content that will help them to know and systematically analyse law'[324]—the kind of concept that Eisenmann has called 'concepts of typology'.[325] While it seems obvious that in this case the method of definition performs a function of systematization, the same goes for the earlier cases, in that this method helps both to clarify the legal norms containing such concepts and to connect the concepts together in terms of non-redundancy, consistency, and completeness.

To the method of definition may be added that of classification, that is, of 'grouping concepts under common predicates',[326] which is a method *par excellence* of 'arranging legal material systematically'.[327] While, on this level, the legislator's rôle is far from negligible,[328] it is clear that doctrine also occupies a quite central place, in that the aim of this method is not only 'didactic' but also an aim of 'rationalizing and simplifying the legal system'.[329] Eisenmann has even gone so far as to say that 'establishing classifications . . . is the special mission, hence the responsible task, of theoreticians alone (that is, of people devoted to the systematic knowledge of law).'[330] 'To jurists themselves, and to them alone, falls and belongs the task

319 Pescatore 1978: 214. 320 Ibid. 321 1978: 215.

322 Eisenmann 1966: 28.

323 1966: 26–8. In the last case, Eisenmann speaks of 'induced concepts'.

324 1966: 29.

325 Ibid. 326 Dabin 1935: 163. 327 Renauld 1958: 170.

328 See, especially, Ray 1926: 229, 'The classifications to be met with in the Civil Code are often . . . fragmentary and exterior. They appear almost like aids to exposition rather than as the true armature of the system of laws.'

329 Van Hoecke 1986: 220. 330 Eisenmann 1966: 29.

of imposing intelligible order . . . on this mass of materials, of constructing a system of classes or categories of types each with its own characteristic, its constitutive definition of a concept.'[331]

As to the systematic organization of rules, with regard to their content, one can again refer to the essential rôle incontestably played by doctrine on those different levels of organization that are *institutions*, *branches of law*, and *general principles of law*.

According to Dabin, 'what distinguishes a legal institution from a legal rule as such is the systematic note—of a kind of systematization that is not logical but primarily and essentially organic'.[332] An institution thus appears as 'a set of rules necessarily arranged in terms of a "spirit" constituting the institution's animating and federative principle'.[333] Now, while, in modern codes, frequently 'all the rules relating to one and the same legal institution are grouped together'[334] and 'the Civil Code appears as the ideal framework for expressing institutions',[335] this is certainly not necessarily so and in many cases 'a host of scattered rules ... recover their unity or "complementarity", at the same time as their precise significance, when they are read in the light of whatever idea is common to them and in terms of which they are ordered'.[336] Such regrouping generally emerges from doctrinal work, the more because 'positive laws do not usually contain statements of the ends that they serve' and because the task of identifying those ends tends to be abandoned to the interpreter's intervention.[337]

The same seems to go for the different 'branches of law'. While codification appears here too as the method by which 'an entire branch of law, or an important part of a branch, is given systemic form by the legislator',[338] it is clear that 'the question of distributing the material of law among its different branches is infinitely complex'[339] and it is not surprising that the drafters of the Napoleonic

331 1966: 35. 332 Dabin 1969: 100 (cf. 1950: 285).

333 1969: 101 (cf. 1950: 285–6).

334 du Pasquier 1967: 145. 335 Ray 1926: 230.

336 Dabin 1969: 103 (cp. 1950: 285–5).

337 Batiffol 1956: 54. Batiffol also explains that 'doctrine should concern itself with the reasons why the rules have come into existence' and that 'positive law needs doctrine in order to organise itself' (1981: 182). See also Renauld 1958: 177, 'Normally the decision, on this point, is the interpreter's task. In fact it is rare for the legislator to proceed formally to classifying the rules that he or she develops.'

338 Pescatore 1978: 226.

339 Ray 1926: 202. Ray recalls, especially, that 'one finds in the Civil Code some provisions of criminal law and of procedure'.

codes may have suffered from 'a degree of empiricism and unevenness in distributing material among the different codes' and, 'instead of forging a system, just about abandoned themselves to their instinct and tradition'.[340]

It therefore seems that, generally speaking, 'to perceive a set of legal rules as linked together supposes doctrinal reconstruction'[340] and that this task, already necessary in the branches of law that have been codified, is necessary *a fortiori* for areas in which 'codification is lacking'.[342]

As for general principles of law, while it is generally recognized that they 'make the law a consistent system in the sense that they make it possible to ensure systematic unity of the law amid the disorder of the positive rules',[343] they too reveal the importance of doctrinal work. Some principles, of course, are to be found in statute itself and one cannot neglect their decisive institution by a judge when they are unwritten.[344] Nevertheless, writers are often concerned to stress the essential contribution of doctrine to their formulation, believing that most of the time the rules concerned are 'discovered by legal doctrine', are 'doctrinal rules',[345] and that 'recourse to these principles and to the use made of them . . . shows . . . the nature of *law made by jurists*, and not only of systems of legislative norms, which belong to the types of law in the Romano-Germanic family'.[346]

Finally, although this method can be understood in partially different senses, it seems undeniable that doctrine participates in systematizing of law through the elaboration of *constructions* or *theories*.[347]

In a broad sense, it may be thought that legal construction means the 'in one way or another constant activity of the jurisconsult',[348] consisting of a 'perpetual reshaping' of the legal edifice, whose materials, at every moment, are to be assembled in new ways[349] and manifest 'a general tendency of doctrine' to set in operation 'the resources of legal dialectics in order to elaborate a system that is more complete and more consistent than a strictly statutory system'.[350]

In a more specific sense, however, one can intend by this expression

340 Ibid. 341 F. Rigaux 1974: 113. 342 Pescatore 1978: 228.
343 1978: 120.
344 On this point see, especially, Jeanneau 1954; Gérard 1981.
345 Roubier 1951: 12.
346 David 1971: 150.
347 On this see, especially, Dabin 1935: 186 ff.; Atias 1987.
348 Ray 1926: 253. 349 Ibid. 350 Pescatore 1978: 222.

the 'formal explanation' of legal rules 'by attaching them to an ideal principle able to unify them in a harmonious system'.[351]

Here too, while some have spoken of 'statutory or case-law theories',[352] indubitably the specific work of systematization comes more from doctrine or dogmatics,[353] and moreover at the point where the same terms are often used indifferently to refer both to that discipline and to the intellectual method that the discipline is required to apply. It is in this sense that one speaks, especially, of 'doctrinal systematizations',[354] 'doctrinal systems',[355] or 'dogmatics'[356] to indicate precisely constructions of this type.

(*c*) *Relationships Between Doctrine and Other Processes of Systematization.* The review of these methods should be enough to highlight the essential rôle that doctrine plays in the systematization of law, constituting, beyond the activities of legislation and case law, a true 'scholarly order', fruit of 'the co-ordinating action of the community of jurists'.[357]

It goes without saying, however, that these various activities can be separated only on an abstract plane and that, concretely, they are in constant interaction,[358] and indeed at a certain point they can become confused with each other.

It clearly appears, first of all, that doctrine is *par excellence* a site of *mediation*: mediation between legislation and case law, in that it is a 'site of privileged encounter' between them,[359] since doctrinal commentary refers not only to statutory provisions but also to their application in case law;[360] and mediation for each of these two formal sources, in that doctrinal work frequently finds itself simultaneously upstream and downstream of each of them.

First, everybody knows that 'a legislative project, however little it may be meant to be comprehensive, cannot be accomplished without having been prepared by an effort of doctrinal insight'.[361] Con-

351 Dabin 1935: 186.
352 See, especially, Atias 1987: 28.
353 See, especially, de la Marnierre 1976: 125, 'Legal construction ... can be carried out only by doctrine.'
354 See Atias 1987: 35.
355 See Pescatore 1978: 222.
356 See du Pasquier 1967: 170.
357 Atias 1987: 115.
358 See, especially, Bergel 1985: 70.
359 Leurquin-De Visscher and Simonart 1980: 187.
360 It is usually only from a theoretical point of view that it is possible to distinguish between a 'doctrine of legislation' and a 'doctrine of case law' (ibid.).
361 Pescatore 1978: 118. On this point, Arnaud 1969 may usefully be consulted. As to the various ways in which the influence of doctrine may bear upon the legislator, see, especially, Polak 1984: 7–17; Desmet 1984: 19–43.

versely, however, as already mentioned, even projects of codification have left to doctrinal writers the task of putting the finishing touches to systematization.[362]

The same goes for the interaction between doctrine and case law. On one side, 'doctrine prepares case law'[363] and receives from it an application without which 'doctrinal elaborations are useless';[364] on the other, doctrine 'comments on' case law[365] and sees to it, as much by the information that it provides about case law[366] as by critically examining it[367] in a systematic form,[368] that case law 'is an effective source of law'[369] and integrates harmoniously into the legal edifice as a whole.

These phenomena of interaction are not, however, the only ones to emphasize: in some cases it can be observed that these different activities eventually become truly confused with each other.

Sometimes, in fact, as was the case in Rome through the mechanism of the *ius respondendi*, a doctrinal writer might turn him- or herself into a kind of 'legislator'.[370] It also happens, as is sometimes now deplored, that writers make themselves, if not veritable 'judges', at least either 'consultants'—so that it has been said that doctrine 'descends into judicial debate'[371]—or 'case-noters',[372] meaning that 'doctrine is shut up inside commentary on case law'.[373] The Belgian jurist Laurent has already condemned that attitude by saying of such writers that 'they are not architects, but builders'

362 See Ray 1926: 214, 'The Code ... calls not just for "commentaries" but for "treatises"'.

363 Bellet 1980: 5.

364 Scalfi and Romagnoli 1980: 16.

365 Bellet 1980: 5.

366 See Malaurie 1980: 89, 'Case law that is not published or that is published only in confidence lacks any normative value ... One must even go a step further: a divergence of case law, a wavering of case law, and even a reversal of case law, in which doctrine is not interested, in practical terms do not exist'. See also Verougstraete 1984: 83, 'Doctrine itself, in a sense, creates case law by publishing it. Without publication, a judicial decision is of use only to the parties: as long as it is not appropriated by doctrine, it does not actually become a source of law.'

367 Scalfi and Romagnoli 1980: 16, 'The case-law rule cannot resist the criticisms of doctrine.'

368 1980: 18, 'It is doctrine that eventually has the task of formulating the rule, linking the different judgements, setting in relief the limits and exceptions to the rule stated'; Esmein 1902: 15, 'The courts ... provide and fashion the materials, but are in no way asked to construct the edifice. That is for the theoreticians, the studious men.'

369 Malaurie 1980: 89.

370 See Ray 1926: 73, where he indicates that, with 'the organization of the *ius publice respondendi*', 'the interpreter is found promoted to the rank of legislator'.

371 Bredin 1981: 116.

372 See 'Un thème de recherche' (1981: 57).

373 Bredin 1981: 117.

labourers' and in holding that their work 'is not a task of science' but 'bookselling'.[374]

In either case, it seems evident that the function of systematization specific to doctrine undergoes a considerable impoverishment because of its excessive dependence on the individual case or its reduction to a simple task of classification. Moreover, it has to be grasped that this last function of doctrine can be gradually supplanted by 'a judicial computer system that would provide to order, and better than doctrine can, the whole body of decided cases'.[375] As for the hope of actually seeing doctrine rediscover its traditional rôle through judicial computerization, while one can easily see in databases 'a tool for validating and monitoring' the 'grand syntheses' of doctrine and an instrument for 'discovering the regularities and distortions of case law',[376] it has rightly been emphasized that 'a case-law information glut threatens to alter the nature of enquiry into case law, obscuring its effort at prediction and wiping out its critical spirit'.[377]

The converse confusion, however, is also conceivable and presents fairly comparable difficulties.

Legislators also run a risk, of transforming themselves into 'doctrinal writers' or 'theoreticians'. While the drafters of the Civil Code denied having produced that kind of confusion, it has nevertheless been remarked that 'the legislator's work finds itself, by force of circumstance, coming close to that of the jurisconsult'[378] and that 'the Civil Code was less a code, a collection of prescriptions, than "Institutes", that is, a systematic exposition of the law'.[379]

The same goes for judges, who sometimes turn themselves into doctrinal writers. Sometimes it is 'the judiciary who publish in the form of a note on the judgement the submissions or findings preceding their decision'.[380] In other, more extreme cases,

> the very same person is by turns the drafter of a piece of legislation at the Chancellery—hence a legislator; commentator on the statute in a theoretical analysis—hence a doctrinal writer; and drafter of ministerial replies—so that this person is first the executive power, then a judge, applying all together the text itself, the commentaries and replies, and finally a commentator on his or her own decisions. The same person becomes simulta-

[374] Laurent 1881: i. 115.
[375] Bredin 1981: 118–19.
[376] Bourcier 1986: 93.
[377] Malaurie 1980: 82.
[378] Ray 1926: 72–3.
[379] 1926: 75.
[380] Malaurie 1980: 85.

aneously legislator, doctrinal writer, administrator and producer of case law.[381]

In such hypotheses, it seems obvious that this kind of 'cabinet of mirrors'[382] can end only in systematic approval of the decisions taken rather than in their genuine systematization.

(*d*) *Doctrinal Systematization and Creation of Law.* These different forms of interaction—indeed, of confusion—between doctrine, legislation, and case law require a few further comments.

In the first place comes the problem of knowing how far the activity of systematization specific to doctrine is of a 'creative' nature and effects an at least partial transformation of the legal order to which it applies.

We have already seen that the development of any scientific theory presupposes a requirement of systematicity and it is clear that satisfying such a requirement amounts to 'reconstructing', in the broad sense of the word, the object studied and results in altering, if not the object itself, at least the way it is described.

According to some writers, the function of systematization specific to legal dogmatics is limited precisely to presenting the contents of the norms studied in a 'new perspective', but without making any alteration to the normative conclusions following from them.[383]

Although one can accept that, within certain limits, this is indeed the specific task of a scientific theory of law,[384] it is clear that a particular feature of doctrine or legal dogmatics is that it does not limit itself to a theoretical activity of knowing its object but also includes a practical activity of transforming that object.[385] And, though it therefore seems possible to introduce a 'conceptual distinction' between these activities of systematizing and transforming law,[386] it is not sufficient to note that that distinction is not always respected in practice;[387] one has to add that it does not explain the mode of functioning specific to that discipline, which characteristically is, precisely, a 'semi-scholarly discourse',[388] thoroughly mixing together theoretical construction and practical aim, descrip-

381 Ibid. 382 Ibid.
383 See, especially, Alchourrón 1986: 171; Bulygin 1986: 199.
384 On this see, especially, Ost and van de Kerchove 1987: 52ff.
385 Bulygin 1986: 193.
386 1986: 207. 387 Ibid. 388 Cf. Bourdieu 1988: 17.

tive intention and normative perspective,[389] knowledge and action.[390]

Similarly, Aarnio has proposed to speak of 'theory *in* law', to describe this specific activity of systematization, as opposed to 'theory *of* law'.[391] Likewise, Dabin has emphasized that legal 'theories' or 'constructions' aim less 'at a value of theoretical truth ... than at a value of practical utility with regard to the effective operation of regulation'.[392]

While it might now be concluded that the activity of systematization peculiar to doctrine is truly 'creative', in the sense that it helps to transform the norms that are its object, one has also to accept the idea that this creation is not completely 'free', inasmuch as it normally supposes a commitment to the ends inherent in the legal order studied and is closer to the pursuit of the requirement of systematicity located in the very heart of legal phenomena than to the imposition of a new mode of ordering that would be completely foreign to it. In spite of the objective alterations that it involves, doctrinal systematization thus makes it possible to grasp what Aarnio has called a 'weak identity' between the state in which a legal system finds itself before the intervention of such an activity and the succeeding state.[393] This identity tends to recall the 'game' to which the interpreter, and particularly the judge, is dedicated at their own level of intervention.[394]

A second question concerns the different directions that doctrinal systematization may follow.

Up to now, we have placed exclusive stress on the rôle that doctrine can fulfil at the level of what may be called an 'internal systematization of law',[395] in the sense that the stress has been placed exclusively on the formal perfection and substantive structuration of a legal system, conceived as to its internal organization.

Parallel to a certain shift of stress observable in contemporary legal thinking, from studying the structure of law to studying its functions,[396] it has also been emphasized that legal dogmatics is able to perform a task of 'external systematization',[397] conceived as the

389 See, especially, Pescatore 1978: 50, defining legal science as a 'normative science, that is, a science providing us with precepts for action'.

390 F. Rigaux 1974: 113.

391 Aarnio 1986: 165 (our emphases).

392 Dabin 1935: 200.

393 Aarnio 1986: 170.

394 See below, Sect. 3.2.3.

395 Van Hoecke 1986: 224; Luhmann 1974: 29–30.

396 See, especially, Bobbio 1977.

397 Van Hoecke 1986: 224.

task 'of maximal integration of the legal system into the particular society, which is constantly in evolution, as well as into the system of values and norms dominant in that society'.[398]

With this question is immediately connected another, concerning more specifically the methods employed by doctrine in its activity of systematization.

(*e*) *Doctrinal Systematization and Interdisciplinarity*. While internal systematization of law is achieved essentially 'by paths of a logical kind' (in a broad sense)[399] and thus—to all appearances—makes doctrine 'monodisciplinary', external systematization cannot do without the empirical and explanatory methods of the different human sciences, thus making doctrine ever more explicitly 'interdisciplinary'.[400]

So far as this form of systematization involves a concern to adapt law to social changes, it is not surprising to find that it is at the moment when 'the evolution of social life exhibits a divergence between mores and institutions' that 'the labours of doctrine make greater use of sociological' or 'economic' research.[401]

This methodological change gives rise, however, to a final question about the practical interests underlying the adoption of an interdisciplinary perspective.

To employ Habermas's terminology, it appears that interdisciplinarity, in the form in which it is generally practised by doctrine, proceeds essentially from a 'technical' interest[402] and aims at the best possible adequation of the legal means employed to a set of social objectives taken as 'given', that is, as most often in keeping with the dominant social rationality. As Commaille has put it, '"legislative sociology" as conceived by contemporary legal sociology represents a will to rationalize legislative production in order to improve the adequation between social and legal norms'.[403]

It is, however, essential to grasp that interdisciplinarity can also proceed from an interest that Habermas calls 'emancipatory'[404]

398 Ibid. 399 1986: 225.

400 1986: 227–8, 'Concerning the systematization of law on the external level ... other methods are required besides those of logic. These are the methods of sociology, as well as those of psychology, history, economics, and so on.'

401 Dalloz, no. 13. Likewise Arnaud (1975: 195) observes that, since the 1960s and 1970s, 'doctrine has applied the methods of the social sciences daily in order to understand better the society to which the legal system is applied'.

402 Habermas 1972: 308. 403 Commaille 1982: 16.

404 Habermas 1972: 308.

and can contribute to a scientific theory of law that furthers critique of the dominant social rationality as well as possible search for alternative ends.

While this second perspective does not exclude any form of systematization, either at the level of developed theory or at that of the practical effects that it proposes, systematization of this kind clearly cannot be confused with the first.

3.2.3. *Systematization and the Judge: Case Law*

(*a*) *Systematization or Casuistry?* Surely it is paradoxical, even somewhat blind, to try to associate the judiciary with systematization of law? Certainly judges, as legal practitioners, close to everyday conflict, tend towards 'problem-oriented thinking' rather than 'system-thinking';[405] they try to resolve the problems of the moment, the issues put before them, rather than to develop learned doctrinal syntheses or majestic normative systems. Put in the front line on the legal battlefield, the judge is necessarily faced by the antagonistic interests of the parties and their legal advisers, who argue to the best of their ability in the direction most favourable to them, thereby inflicting sometimes considerable distortions on legal systematicity. The judge is then surely drawn more to casuistry than to systematization and one is struck by the contrast between the consistency and timelessness of the great works of doctrine, and the fragmentation and precariousness of law reports and legal databases.[406]

One might conclude, for instance, with Haesaert, that 'judges do not follow fixed rules' and that their logic 'has nothing but the name in common with the logic of treatises'; that the source of a decision is found 'to a large extent in the judge's feelings about the case'.[407] This idea is, of course, clearly excessive, as if a lack of strictly deductive logic amounts to a lack of rationality as such. With more sophistication, Perelman, all of whose work is dedicated to promoting a non-formal rationality, of the order of dialectic or rhetoric, observes that judges take care to adapt the interpretation of rules to the desired social result. Trying to avoid manifestly 'unreasonable' or iniquitous solutions, judges introduce into the legal system conditions relating to appropriateness, justice, and the general interest—so that

[405] Wróblewski 1986: 16. [406] Similarly, Bourdieu 1987: 824.
[407] Haesaert 1948: 318, 358.

the system is constantly made more flexible and adapted, and seems closer to a teleological rather than a structural perspective.[408]

Flexible, yes; yet none the less a system. In this respect it can be observed that, at least in our own legal traditions, the judge is a legal professional, different from the popular juries or elected judges that France had during the revolutionary period. Now, the specifically legal competence of a judge necessarily involves, because of the technical mastery that it supposes, a 'disqualification of the non-specialists' sense of fairness, and the revocation of their naïve understanding of the facts'.[409] A discrepancy thus arises between vulgar vision and learned description of the dispute; to this discrepancy, the various techniques for putting a dispute 'in due form'—translating the facts into legal language, choosing the particular 'law-ways', and judicial rituals—contribute decisively. The judge then appears as the incarnation of a vast institution that mediates conflict, subsumes the triviality of rival interests under a transcendent form, and transforms the claims thus far articulated on a factual level into a regulated exchange of legal arguments. As Bourdieu excellently shows, recourse to a judge signifies entry into the legal 'field'—one can say 'system'—which necessarily involves tacitly accepting the rules and conventions, both explicit and implicit, determining that field's boundaries and regularizing its functioning. Among those rules and conventions, the 'fundamental law of the legal field' takes the form of a constitutive tautology: one has to accept that, within the legal field, conflicts can be regulated only legally. This initial commitment entails that, once involved in the game that one has agreed to play, one will also accept the set of visions and divisions constitutive of that field. Judges too, despite the position of mastery that they occupy within that field, are 'immersed in the game' and obliged to assume the 'rôle' allocated to them. This rôle, a set of 'habitus' communicated by the system of training and guaranteed by *esprit de corps*, involves the adoption of what Bourdieu goes on to call an 'overall attitude',[408] a veritable world-view, or specific intellectual space, which is nothing other

[408] Perelman 1984: 91, 73. Similarly, Krawietz (1981: 328–55; also 1984: 50 ff.) notes that, in the Federal Republic of Germany, case law derive[d] predominantly from the *Interessen- und Wertungsjurisprudenz* (jurisprudence of interests and values) model, whose conception of a legal system is more functional than structural and its modes of reasoning more teleological than analytical.

[409] Bourdieu 1987: 828.

[410] 1987: 829.

than the judge's description of the overall legal system and the place that a judge is called on to occupy within it.

Clearly the systematization to which the judge contributes is complex, and this has sent commentators like Haesaert on a false trail. It seems to be as much dynamic (creative) as static (tautological), as much formal (deductive) as substantive (dialectical), and as much linear (disciplined) as recursive (rebellious). The system that emerges from the judge's everyday intervention seems, therefore, to contain as many elements of determinacy, guarantees of legal certainty (or, some would say, immobility), as of indeterminacy, guarantees of adaptation (or, others would say, uncertainty). It is as if, in order to be operational, legal logic has to put up with such elasticity, due particularly to the presence of many 'confused notions' (the public domain (*ordre public*), good morals (*bonnes mœurs*), fault, urgency, normality).[411] As if the syllogistic and binary logic of truth and falsity had to compromise with 'dialogic' or 'polyphonic' logic, which takes into account simultaneously values that might not harmonize and may even be contrary. One passes, then, into a form of reasoning that introduces indeterminacy and variability into the process of elaborating norms.[412]

One concept seems to be of central importance in describing the legal systems that emerge from such a process of rationalization: the concept of 'fuzziness', in the sense in which modern mathematics already refers to 'fuzzy subsets'. Carbonnier, in his time, had risked the expression 'flexible law'[413] in order to cast doubt on the superb rigour that legal constructions are so proud of. Today, it seems necessary to go a step further and recognize the 'fuzziness of law'—now drawing this expression from Delmas-Marty, who understands it as 'ability to conceive and order multiplicity, but without reducing it to unity or abandoning it to fragmentation'.[414] Wróblewski in particular uses the concept of 'fuzziness' to characterize a legal system as a whole.[415] In his view, legal systems are marked by 'fuzziness' or 'vagueness' when a complete and absolutely rigorous formal determination of rules' membership of those systems (the problematic of validity) turns out to be impossible, their higher rules or rules of recognition being affected by fuzziness themselves.[416]

411 Perelman and Vander Elst 1984.
412 Similarly, Timsit 1986: 113–20.
413 Carbonnier 1971.
414 Delmas-Marty 1986: 12.
415 Wróblewski 1983b: 313 ff.
416 1985: 96.

And, in the same way, the complete and absolutely rigorous formal determination of the meaning given to those rules (the problematic of interpretation) turns out to be equally impossible, each norm displaying, beyond a core of clear meaning, a 'penumbra of doubt' leaving open the question of knowing just what realities it applies to.

(*b*) *The Game Model.* How can one conceive together both the determinacy and the indeterminacy of a system, its rigour and its fuzziness, its systematicity and its casuistry? We would like to propose the metaphor of the game (*jeu*), which often comes from the pens of legal theorists without ever being properly thought through or exploited systematically. We would define a game as a social activity combining, in varying proportions, an element of convention or regularity and an element of invention or creativity. The English word 'game' bears witness to the first meaning, 'play' to the second. That is: while every game, even the most unrestrained such as the inversion of tradition during Carnival, supposes a minimum of rules, nevertheless the rules do not exhaust the game's potentialities. A 'game space' opens up to the players, who then exhibit within it their 'sense of the game' or skill in utilizing the game's 'openings' (its margins of uncertainty) to score 'hits' that can enable them to win the match. But this game space, in its turn, is not to be understood as pure indeterminacy: on the contrary, the sense of the game supposes an adjustment of the player's behaviour to the objective possibilities of the field or system. Implicit rules—probably the more effective for remaining largely implicit—guide the experienced players, imbue their habitus, and determine the game's 'stakes' and 'aims'.

This model seems to us to provide the necessary conceptual instruments for describing the way that a judge intervenes in the collective task of systematizing law. The subtle dialectic that it involves, between closure and openness, discipline and audacity, and rigour and flexibility, seems particularly suited to theorizing judicial decision-making, which, while rejecting the limitations of formalism on the planes of decidability, consistency, and closure, also helps in a way to restore a form of systematicity—albeit affected by fuzziness—to those different levels.[417] We shall try to show

[417] For an application to the question of decidability, see van de Kerchove 1985: 207–42.

this in relation to the judge's two main tasks: the interpretation and validation of legal rules—that is, determination of their meaning and of their authority.

(*c*) *Interpreting a Legal Rule.* First is the problematic of interpretation. The recurrent oscillation among theorists of interpretation, between a concern for fidelity to the legislator's will (the 'Exegetical School') and a concern for adaptation to the social needs of the moment (the '*Freies Recht* School') attests, in its way, to the dialectical tension characterizing judicial statutory interpretation. This activity seems simultaneously both to follow rules *and* to involve at least a mimimum of latitude and inventiveness. Some of those rules are known: the judge can reach a decision only according to general rules, must decide the case even though the law is inadequate or obscure, must give reasons for the decision, and must take the letter of the law into consideration yet not stick to it where it appears to contradict the legislator's intention. Beyond those rules that constitute the framework of the very act of interpretation, legal tradition proposes to judges countless arguments and maxims which offer them a keyboard to use to the best advantage in order to produce the 'hits' authorized by the particular features of the case before them.

In no case, however, is this endowment with meaning reduced to a mechanical application of rules; the uncertainty affecting both the statutory formula (characterized by its polysemicity and 'open texture') and the legislator's intention (sometimes lacking, occasionally contradictory, and often obscure) cannot actually be removed simply by recourse to pre-established maxims. It is necessary to employ meta-rules or preference directives guiding the interpreter's choice among various methods of interpretation. The recourse to these meta-rules, too, is in no way automatic or programmed, so that the interpreter has a real choice.

The writers who accept this irreducible indeterminacy—contrary to classical dogmatics, which entertains the illusion of a legal certainty that unicity and clarity of a statute's meaning could confer—usually conclude that, beyond that, interpretation is a matter of political and ethical choice. One such is Kelsen, for whom 'the law to be applied constitutes only a frame within which several applications are possible'.[418] However, this is far from saying that, in the reality of legal practice, all interpretations theoretically com-

[418] Kelsen 1967: 351.

patible with the frame formed by the applicable higher norm possess the same value, having regard to what is 'in play' during the process of interpretation. The fact is that, in the course of the game, the players are not free to adopt just any kind of behaviour, from the moment when they acknowledge the letter of the game. Indeed, to understand a regulation or a right literally or observe it 'to the letter' can be quite an effective way of no longer 'playing the game'—as can happen, for example, in a work-to-rule or the misuse of a right.

It is therefore important, once the explicit rules have been discerned and the margin of manœuvre structuring the game of interpretation has been measured, to pick out the game's implicit rules, as well as its aims and stakes. If these implicit rules are not brought to light, it will never be possible to understand how a legal system rejects some interpretations as unassimilable noise, while others are retained as generating information capable of reorganizing the earlier equilibrium. Our thesis here is that the judge should try to choose, among the range of possible meanings of the norm to be interpreted, the meaning that will naturally support 'the legislator's rationality'.[419] In other words, judicial strategy aims to guarantee and reinforce the legal order's consistency, understood as both logical congruence and ideological harmony.

Whatever the interpretative context of reference—be it language, system, or society—there is a prevailing concern to support the legislator's rationality, and this necessarily leads to reinforcing the systematicity of legal ordering on those three levels. The terms of the statute to be interpreted can be represented as located at the centre of a set of three concentric circles of ever-increasing area. The first circle is formed by the provision's lingustic context: natural and legal language, which are partly separate. Contrary to what doctrine and case law often maintain, once inserted in a legal text the terms of natural language hardly ever retain their 'ordinary' meaning. There is an attraction effect making these terms acquire a new and technical meaning resulting from their place and function in the institution or branch of law from which they come. Portalis already noted that 'one mistakes the meanings of laws when one takes their wording in the acceptation that it has in everyday language'.[420] Accordingly, without giving too much away to the rationalist illusions of a pure legal language as dreamed of by Leibniz, Wolff, or Bentham, one

419 On this, see Ost and van de Kerchove 1987: 355–419.
420 Portalis, in Fenet 1827: xiii. 47.

should nevertheless record the continuous semantic operation of legal language in distributing and redistributing the meaning of each term with regard to the economy of the system as a whole. To invoke the rationality of a legislator who is supposed always to use legal language correctly amounts to guaranteeing this continuous work of semantic integration with an argument of authority.

The second circle of reference is formed by the whole set of legal provisions to be found in the same legal order as the provision to be interpreted. The judge will draw from them innumerable resources for getting around the statute's obscurities, gaps, and inconsistencies: thus, recourse to general principles will allow the judge to fill a gap, and use of a 'collision rule' (priority of a higher over a lower rule, of a recent over an old rule, and of a special over a general rule) will resolve an antinomy. The dominant idea on this level is that, while the letter of the law may be accepted in default, the system's spirit cannot take its place, the legislator being supposed to demonstrate praxeological rationality: it avoids antinomies, gaps, and redundancies, and adapts the means used to the ends employed. All the sources of logical reasoning (argumentation *a contrario*, *a pari*, *a posteriori*, *a rubrica*, and from absurdity), and the whole gamut of legal sources, will be mobilized to mend the net of legal systematicity in the case where a new claim, expressing an unanticipated configuration of interests, comes to threaten its solidity.

Lastly, the third circle in which the rule to be applied and interpreted is found is constituted by the social context, the widest possible context, in which one can perceive the set of values and descriptions operating in the social field. The judge, however legalistic and formalistic, cannot ignore the fact that the statute has been enacted in order to attain a particular social objective and that the interpretation that he or she, as judge, will give it will have—on the level of the particular case—a practical effect of sustaining or modifying the aspirations that gave rise to the claim before the court. One might believe that, at least at this level, the greatest possible openness would prevail; surely, in a pluralist society the gamut of values obtaining throughout the society is very extensive. Study of case law, however, shows a very important labour of systematization on this level too, connected once again with the idea of the legislator's rationality, which this time is considered to demonstrate axiological rationality, in the sense that it would guarantee the rule of justice and conform to a consistent hierarchy of values. The reference to values, be they formal or substantive, again reinforces, in this spirit, the legal order's consistency, understood here as 'ideological harmony'. On a formal plane, the judge is concerned to promote the value of justice, which requires equal treatment of similar cases. This requirement, whose strength and recurrence are familiar, of course exerts very powerful pressure to conform to precedent or the generality of statutory rules. As a result, it is only with great difficulty that the achievement of equity in the specific case clears a path for itself in judicial argumentation; although judges are not prohibited from innovating, they must always at least propose a solution that can be generalized: one mode of systematization can be rejected only in favour of another, considered more congruent with the economy of the whole. In the train of conformity to this rule of justice understood as equality of treatment also comes a vital series of other values, each thought to express legal certainty: stability, order, social peace, predictability, and so on. And while in the end one has regard to substantive values (the 'external' morality of law, as against its 'internal' morality, to take Fuller's categories—above), on this plane too one has to notice the significance of an axiological 'hierarchy', representing what German doctrine calls the 'spirit of the legal order' (*Geist der Rechtsordnung*),[421] requiring the judge to elicit an order that is just and apposite, and conforms to the nature of the case and the idea of law.[422]

Dworkin has recently provided a very stimulating formulation of this postulate of the legislator's rationality, imposing itself on the interpreting judge. For Dworkin, judges may be said to be in a situation comparable to that of a group of writers compelled to write a chain novel. Each, with the exception of the first, has to add a chapter of their own to the plot, on the understanding that each writer will of course maintain a certain continuity of style and content. The rule—which, very happily, Dworkin calls the 'rule of the game'—is to respect the 'principle of unity' which leaves each novelist not only to assimilate the production of their predecessors but also to anticipate that of their successors, so as to make the story move on in a direction that is both compatible with its earlier stages and capable of ending in a credible conclusion. Moreover, each writer will long to impress on the story and its style their personal stamp—which, on the plane of law, appears as the need to interpret a statute not only in conformity with the set of sources in force but

[421] Larenz 1969: 450. [422] Canaris 1961: 165, 172.

also in the light of ethical and political principles that the judge thinks he or she ought to apply.[423]

The metaphor of the 'novel written by chain' shows clearly that, while statutory interpretation is very largely a matter of the law's own interpretation of itself, a self-production of meaning, this probably belongs less to achievements intrinsic to that legal order itself (clarity of its text, consistency and completeness of its construction, and appropriateness of its explicit rules of interpretation) than to the strategic skills of its actors, who know how to take advantage of its many sources of uncertainty in order to reproduce a game that their very intervention reinforces. To state this yet another way: the legal production of meaning results less from a unilateral intentional consciousness—that of the legislator, who binds the judge, or that of the judge interpreting a statute as he or she pleases—than of a collective, uninterrupted, and multidirectional process of circulation of meaning: 'meaning *of* the game', 'spirit *of* the system', not as a desire for any old hypostatized legal order but as 'practical faith' shared by the players.

(*d*) *Validating a Legal Rule*. We are led to analogous conclusions when examining the question of the validity of legal norms. Here too, theory seems constantly to vacillate between a dogmatic attitude, fixing criteria of validity that are *a priori*, exclusive, and non-graduated, and a sceptical attitude, limited to an *a posteriori* statement of the rules that are in fact obeyed by officials and/or throughout society. But the real processes of validation seem to lie at some distance from either of these poles, so it makes sense to try to describe those processes in terms of the game model.

In our legal systems, deeply impregnated with legal-positivist philosophy, the validity of rules is assessed by reference to formal criteria—of competence, procedure, and sometimes basis—that are fixed by the legal order itself, generally by its higher norms on the constitutional level, or even, for such a writer as Kelsen, on a supra-constitutional level. Validity is then understood in an exclusively formal way, as a norm's membership of a given legal order. It is then a matter of a 'test of pedigree', as Dworkin puts it, set up with reference to some 'master rule' considered to crown the legal edifice.[424] The validation process is at once unilateral (taking into account only the rule's formal validity: that it has been enacted

[423] Dworkin 1986: ch. 7.   [424] 1978: 17.

in conformity with intra-systemic criteria), absolute (leading to unambiguous results: a rule will be declared absolutely valid or totally void), and hierarchized (validity is always assessed in terms of basis, which necessarily supposes an ascent from a lower to a higher norm). Now, it seems clear that, to describe legal practice, the judgement of validity has to be portrayed as plural (based on criteria that are formal but also empirical and axiological), relative (able to portray different degrees of intensity and therefore highly variable effects), and circular (not only produced from above or below, but resulting from continuous interaction of the whole group of legal actors).

Thus, if one wishes, following Wróblewski, to associate conceptions of validity and descriptions of a legal system, one would need to refer to a much enlarged form of systematicity to describe the operation of validation in which judges actually engage. It would be a question, in this case, not only of the system formed by the rules officially enacted by the competent authorities but also of the set of formal derivations arising from them and the interpretative conclusions that can be drawn from them; there may also be added here a set of ethical and political principles and standards prevailing in a society and inflecting the legal rules' significance—such as the frequent references to 'democracy' appearing in the European Convention for the Protection of Human Rights and Fundamental Freedoms. If one also wants to describe the decisions by which a judge manages to conclude that a legislative norm has been repealed by desuetude or that the norm is inapplicable in terms of a theory of necessity or some equivalent theory, the system of reference is further enlarged by now fitting those decisions themselves into it.[425]

Such an enlarged conception of a legal system is highlighted by the anglophonic debate on 'hard cases'. It appears that, on these difficult issues, judges readily apply solutions that are not necessarily derived from rules officially belonging to the system, rules given authority by the formal test of 'pedigree': what Perelman has called 'rules in uniform'.[426] In these hypotheses, judges, alerted precisely by some gap or iniquity in the official system, readily accord binding force to 'guerilla rules'—today, following Dworkin, called 'principles', operating on the margin of statute law and sometimes even against it. What lesson is to be drawn from these paradigmatic cases, if at least one wants to accept that what is at work here in an exemplary

[425] On all this, see Wróblewski 1986: 5–19.

[426] Perelman 1971: 316.

fashion also operates, though no doubt to a less extreme degree, in simple cases?

It should be remembered that a judgement of validity incorporates, more or less explicitly, according to whether they are or are not contrary to formal criteria, empirical considerations (whether the norm whose application is envisaged is effective or on the way to desuetude, and, even if the norm is still in force, whether it is appropriate to apply it *hic et nunc*) and axiological considerations (whether the norm whose application is envisaged is legitimate, and whether it conforms to the dominant ethical and political principles).[427] In answering these questions, judges are guided by principles that Raz calls 'discretionary rules', rules that orientate judges' choices without determining them absolutely.[428] In this way, legal systems would culminate not in a single rule of recognition but in a variety of rules, some imposing on judges imperative criteria of validity (rules of recognition) and others guiding their search for the reasonable solution in delicate cases (discretionary rules).[429] Hart, for his part, is far from endowing the rule of recognition with absolute rigidity; the rule of recognition, let us not forget, exists 'as a matter of fact' in so far as it is 'accepted' as a rule of recognition, 'established by reference to actual practice: to the way in which courts identify what is to count as law'.[430] The rule of recognition can therefore vary through time and remains dependent on an interpretation[431] that is reducible neither to 'blind, arbitrary choice' nor to 'mechanical' deduction.[432]

But, while the validation process is plural (and, by the same token, graduated), it is also circular. Contrary to the Kelsenian image (not without religious connotations) of a pyramid where the top validates or authorizes the bottom, and against the American realists' model in which the bottom validates the top (only the norm actually applied can be considered valid), the interactional nature of the judgement of validity should be stressed. Hart had already introduced this idea by decentring the validation process: validation is no longer secured exclusively through authorization by a higher organ but also depends on the recognition accorded to that organ by officials situated on a less elevated level of the hierarchy. Kelsen takes that

427 Similarly, Ost and van de Kerchove 1987: 257–314.
428 Raz 1979: 96–7.
429 1972: 852–3.
430 Hart 1961: 105–7.
431 1961: 144.
432 1961: 200.

reality into account only in the extreme case of a successful revolution. But, as was seen earlier, it is permissible to generalize that hypothesis and maintain that, if the higher norm's claim to be necessary is to be fully accepted—that is, if it is to produce its legal effects, be declared valid—it must form the object of a recognition by the lower organ of application.

The multiplicity of criteria governing the judgement of validity, like the plurality of the organs that combine in recognizing the binding force of legal rules, sufficiently attests to the latitude that the validation process allows, within the framework outlined by the formal criteria of validity fixed by the legal orders in force and sometimes even beyond those orders. One must not, however, conclude—no more here than in the case of statutory interpretation—that the whole approach is indeterminate and all its results are equivalent. Here too it is important to pick out the implicit rules of the game which, on a heuristic plane that is the more effective for being barely conscious, guide the organs charged with assessing the restrictive scope of legal norms. In our view, just as the operation of interpretation was polarized by the vision of a 'rational legislator', recognition of validity is polarized by the image of the 'sovereign legislator'—by which is envisaged the necessarily valid (and therefore binding) character that must attach to rules whose origins can be traced to the sovereign's omnipotence. As if their origin in the state naturally conferred on them—an almost irrefutable presumption of legal dogmatics—a certificate of legitimacy and an assurance of effectiveness.

The judge, it can be seen, is associated decisively with the process of systematizing law. The undeniable discretionary power at the judge's disposal—larger, indeed, than the authorizing texts recognize—does not, however, degenerate into an arbitrary exercise of the judge's competences. The social efficacy of a decision derives precisely from the judge's skill in rationalizing his or her grounds for the decision—that is, in the last analysis, in proposing their connection with an order transcending the interests in conflict, an order imposing itself almost naturally, simply by virtue of its logic.

(*e*) *A System of Case Law*. Thus are gradually formed not only a body of case law (a set of legal rules that it is possible to deduce from the multiplicity of individual decisions) but even what Serverin calls a 'system of case law', that is, a vast apparatus of case-law production, selection, memorization, and transmission. This involves, among other things, mechanisms, both official and unofficial, for publishing decisions, doctrinal practices commenting on and synthesizing them, and systems of teaching that ensure the spread of knowledge of them. There thus occurs a passage from 'litigation' (the sum of individual decisions, to be found in judicial statistics) to 'case law' (a rational system of decisions of 'legal interest'). In that way, 'case law no longer appears as an instrument for discovering social movements through disputes, but as an instrument for producing and integrating rules within an autonomous legal universe'.[433]

At a time when, as has been seen, the legislator is less and less capable, in a pluralistic society and in a State divided between the 'legalistic' model of the nineteenth century and the 'welfare' model of the twentieth, of maintaining the legal order's consistency and stability, some have turned to the judges in order to invest them with a mission of restoring the system's integrity and the values of order and certainty that it is supposed to guarantee.[434] Are the judges in a position to respond to these hopes? The answer to this question cannot be definitive, since, although in many cases before them judges still behave as 'referee-judges' adhering to the legalistic model, in other areas (for example, protection of juveniles or supervision of firms in difficulty) there appear 'trainer-judges' who mean to associate themselves actively with the interventionist State's plans by now acting in the fashion of social engineers rather than as technicians of law.[435] Here again, the systematization of law does not appear as definitively given. For law cannot be conceived independently of the social context, in which it operates. This will be the subject of the following chapter, which will study the relationships binding a legal system to its environment.

[433] Serverin 1985: 390. On this concept of a 'system of case law', see 1985: 15ff., 48ff., 81ff., 325, 339, 343. To give one indication, among others, of this will to systematize: Serverin mentions that publication of the judgements of the French Cour de Cassation in the *Bulletin des arrêts* (an official publication) is accompanied by the inclusion of each judgement in a *series*, by way of a list of judgements referred to that go in the same or the reverse direction. This practice is obvious evidence of a search for internal consistency of a normative whole, like the systematic elimination of given facts in favour of a single 'legal solution' that fits into ramifying conceptual structures (for the judgements of lower courts not published in their entirety) (on this, see Serverin 1986: 113).

[434] See e.g. Belaid 1974: 317, 333.

[435] On this point, see Ost 1983.

4
A Legal System and Its Environment

After tracing in Chapter 1 the main outlines of the general problematic of systems, we examined in Chapter 2 the constitutive elements of legal systems and in Chapter 3 the variety of relations that structure them. We have now to explore the peripheries of systems, investigating their environment. New and important questions arise, whose solutions will particularly help to clarify some of the problems dealt with earlier. Are legal systems closed or open? Are they self- or hetero-regulated? Do they maintain relations with other normative systems and, particularly, other legal systems? Each of these questions is widely debated. We shall therefore begin by summarizing, in a first section, a radical idea proposed by Luhmann: the conception of a legal system as autopoietic, that is, as a system that is not only self-organized but even self-produced. We shall propose to substitute for this extreme view the conception of law as a game—a model already employed in the preceding chapter. As a game of order and disorder, determinism and indeterminism, a legal system appears to be endowed with a 'relative autonomy' in relation to society. This relative autonomy is undoubtedly the necessary condition for a legal order's exercise of the functions peculiar to it. Those functions will be reviewed in a second section. However, since law never acts in a 'social void', the effectiveness of its interventions will depend on its mode of articulation to society. In a third section we shall study the interchanges between legal system and social order and there we shall bring out the concept of 'infra-law (*infra-droit*)'. This theme will be continued in a fourth section with a discussion of legal change in its various relations to social change. Then, in fifth and sixth sections, we shall try to unravel the complex tangle of relations woven between legal systems and other normative systems, as well as between the various legal orders.

4.1. LEGAL SYSTEM AND AUTOPOIESIS

If it did not possess an at least 'relative' autonomy, law obviously would not take the form of a system; it would lack that minimal differentiation with regard to its environment which alone makes it possible to identify a specific whole. Is it possible to push this idea a bit further and, rejecting the concept of 'relative autonomy', describe law as a self-referential, indeed even 'autopoietic', system: not only self-organized but even self-produced?[1] This is the view now held by an important tendency in sociology of law, led by Luhmann, and itself inspired by recent work done in biology, cybernetics, and information theory.

We must now describe and discuss this new theory, called autopoiesis, which confronts us with a choice whether the autonomy of a legal system is complete *or* relative.

4.1.1. *The Paradigm of Autopoiesis*

Luhmann and his disciples take the paradigm of autopoiesis from work on the organization of living forms by two contemporary biologists, Maturana and Varela. Their approach to living forms is deliberately mechanistic: living systems, such as the cell or the brain, are to be understood as machines, which are to be explained by their internal organization.[2] But whereas, in an allopoietic machine such as a car, the product of its operation is different from itself, the product of the operation of an autopoietic machine is nothing other than itself. A cell can then define itself by its self-generation, on the model of an artificial machine able to construct itself. An autopoietic system can therefore be understood as a machine organized in the form of a network of processes of component-production, in which the components, through their constant interaction and transformation, endlessly regenerate the network of processes of component-production and thereby provide the machine with a particular spatial unity.[3] An autopoietic machine is thus a network of tangled or 'looped' processes, which ensures a continual regeneration of its constitutive elements and thus defines its unity in space. This initial conception has several consequences.

1 Similarly, Luhmann 1989.
2 Maturana and Varela 1980: 75–6; Varela 1979: 4.
3 Maturana and Varela 1980: 89; Varela 1979: 17.

First, an autopoietic system may be said to be autonomous. Autonomy should be understood here as capacity to subordinate any kind of change to the maintenance of its self-organization. It will be observed, secondly, that such a system is individualized: to the extent that it maintains its identity constant through a process of continual adjustment, this identity is somehow self-produced and owes nothing to the intervention of an external observer. An autopoietic machine defines its own borders by determining what is and what is not itself. Lastly, it can be said that such a system has neither 'inputs' nor 'outputs'. No doubt it can be aware of exogenous impacts, events independent of its internal logic, 'disturbances'; but these, far from acting as information that could contribute to programming the system, generate internal compensatory actions so that the homeostatic equilibrium characterizing the system is maintained as invariable.[4]

This last feature is probably the most significant, requiring a radical change of paradigm. While classical scientific thinking, in order to conceive a system's relations to its environment, sticks to a paradigm of 'coupling by inputs' (changes of a system are determined from the outside, as in the Darwinian theory of evolution), what is proposed here is a paradigm of 'coupling by closure': a system's development is determined by its internal consistency. The environment alone generates 'disturbances' which the system absorbs and digests thanks to its self-organization. In that respect, a system's closure may be termed 'operational'. And if therefore the autopoietic system is neither autarchic nor isolated, neither is it programmed from the outside: entering into a relation of 'structural coupling' with other autopoietic systems, it maintains its identity by compensating for the impacts that it receives. If by any chance this continual adjustment is caught on the hop, one will see the system disintegrate.[5] The theory is thus very radical: either the system's autopoiesis (self-organization and self-production) is maintained or the system disintegrates.

Luhmann, a sociologist of law whose earliest works largely followed the structural-functionalist ideas of Parsons, later resolutely adopted the autopoietic paradigm in order to conceptualize a legal system. Stripping the autopoietic thesis of those of its connotations that are too directly biological, Luhmann begins from the idea

[4] On all this, see Maturana and Varela 1980: 80–1.
[5] Varela 1979: 32–3, 50ff.

that the minimal constitutive element of a legal system, a sort of legal atom, is found in acts of communication.[6] More precisely, Luhmann's disciple Teubner takes the legal act to be the basic element of systematicity in law.[7] A legal system can be called autopoietic so far as the self-reference characterizing it affects not only its structures, its mode of organization, but also its basic elements themselves. Law, as with any other operational and well-differentiated social subsystem, presupposes and reproduces itself: its unity, as well as its mode of organization, its constitutive elements and its borders, result, through 'reduction of complexity', from specifically systemic achievements: they proceed neither from nature nor from any condition deriving from the environment. Consequently, there is no law other than positive law (in the form of legislation, case law, or contract).[8]

An autopoietic system is thus, above all, a closed system. In law, this closure is normative. Only legal norms are able to decide the pertinence or relevance of any element to a legal system. After centuries of debate, it is now admitted that neither nature, nor morality, nor religion possesses this power to create law. Only a legal system, through its autopoietic functioning, has the capacity to confer on the elements that it determines the quality of being law. There thus reproduces itself an endless and non-intentional process of reproduction of legal elements by themselves.[9]

But the progress that the autopoietic paradigm claims to represent consists of superseding the classic opposition between openness and closedness formerly important in systems theory. An autopoietic system, defined as functionally (normatively, as concerns law) closed, is also a system open to the environment, which is a source of information for it. Normative closure thus goes hand in hand with cognitive openness. A legal system can be programmed in such a way that it deliberately makes itself dependent on the evolution of external circumstances; modification of the program itself, under pressure from the environment, is also possible[10] inasmuch as, after this search for optimal adaptation, the system does not lose control of its transformations.

Combining in this way closure and openness, a legal system cannot lay claim to complete self-determination. Thus no legal sys-

[6] Luhmann 1988: 16–17. [7] Teubner 1988: 221.
[8] Luhmann 1988: 18.
[9] 1988: 20. [10] Ibid.

tem can aim to determine in advance the content of every judicial decision. It is sufficient that the act of deciding legally should refer normatively to the necessity of perpetuating the legal system's self-production—for the rest, it is able to integrate all external information necessary to its larger functionality. In this order of ideas, it can be seen, most legal norms are conceived as programs dedicated to the normative handling of external information[11] (if a particular fact is recognized, then a particular normative conclusion will be applied).

It will now be understood that, to ensure its autopoietic development, it is enough for a legal system to possess a binary logic—the logic of permission and prohibition, and of legal and non-legal. Because they manipulate this code of identities and differences, legal systems are well able to open themselves to the outside without losing their identity, the reality thus produced—and, we would say, imposed—being actually 'nothing but the correlate of a self-referential mode of operation which reproduces itself according to this code'.[12] Luhmann maintains explicitly that such a conception is akin to 'the juristic descriptions to be found in legal dogmatics':[13] it describes a form of autopoiesis of law by itself (here, by legal actors seeking to know it), which contributes directly to its reproduction. The interaction of a self-referential system's operations actually occurs only on the basis of such self-observation, which selects, amid the infinity of possible internal relations, those that are most capable of reinforcing the system's consistency and performance.

4.1.2. *Critical Discussion of this Paradigm. Relative Self-Organization*

What is one to think of these ideas which transpose to law the radicality of the views proposed by Maturana and Varela in the field of biology?[14] Following Treves in particular, one might stress the implicit political conservatism inherent in this conception of a hyper-autonomous and hyperfunctional legal system, as if it could operate independently of the intervention of social actors and sheltered from their conflicts of interest. It is clear that the consensualist and functionalist paradigms operate here the more effectively because they disguise themselves completely beneath a scientific vocabulary borrowed from bio-cybernetics.[15]

[11] 1988: 24. [12] 1988: 16. [13] 1989: 59. [14] See Ost 1988.
[15] Treves 1987: 313 ff.

One could also attempt an internal critique of Luhmann's views. First, as to the limit of modes of formalism: just as Gödel's theorem has demonstrated that no mathematical system can completely loop itself—an essential incompleteness which necessarily supposes a more embracing meta-language—the cybernetician Ashby, one of the first theorists of self-organization, has managed to prove that absolute autonomy is a logical impossibility.[16]

Taken literally, reflexive expressions like 'self-programming program', or 'self-organizing organization' reveal themselves as contradictory. One could of course push autonomy rather far and conceive systems with a capacity to alter not only the information that they handle but also their own rules of functioning. But the ability to alter their principles of organization can only be partial: for the rules of change determining those alterations are themselves determined, so that the self-control possessed by the program is only partial. No doubt the program is not immutable, its rules of change being able to alter themselves in their turn, but to take these things into account supposes a form of 'jump', qualitative leap, to a more complex and comprehensive level of organization. In other words, only changes affecting the organization itself—and not only the different states of the system, which are merely the phases of a continuous program—have to be products of the system's outside.

The theory of self-organization thus faces an essential question: how can self-organized systems claim to alter themselves without losing their identity whenever they correspond completely neither to internal programming, as Ashby has shown, nor to external programming, which would remove the pertinence of the very idea of self-organization?[17]

With that question, it seems, the self-organizational model embarks on a new and decisive path. This is the path of 'relative self-organization', explored by Atlan, who admits that 'a change in the mode of organization can occur as an effect not of a meta-law governing alteration in a constant and predictable way but of chance disturbances'.[18] For the paradigm of 'organizational closure' (Varela) is substituted that of 'organization by chance' or 'order through noise'. As Atlan says, debating with Maturana, 'changes in the mode of organization can come only from the outside. Therefore

16 Ashby 1962; referred to, Dupuy 1982: 226.
17 Similarly, Dumouchel and Dupuy 1983: 97.
18 Atlan 1983: 122.

there cannot be self-organization in the strict sense.'[19] But what has to be well understood is that, on one side, the environment does not act as a central regulator and, on the other, the message that the system receives does not necessarily have a destructive effect on it. We therefore have to manage to conceive a form of non-deliberate co-operation of chance external to the system's mode of organization or, conversely, a form of autonomy in dependence.

How can chance help to create complexity (the system's more sophisticated mode of organization ensuring it improved adaptive results) instead of being only a disorganizing factor? This question is by no means gratuitous, since it envisages the process illustrated by the phenomena of the evolution of species, and to answer it one will probably have to rely again on the structure of living systems. These, Atlan explains, are found somewhere 'between the rigidity of metal and the decomposition of smoke'—hence the title of his work *Entre le cristal et la fumée* (*Between Crystal and Smoke*).[20] Living organizations equilibrate two types of property: on one side, repetition, regularity, and redundancy; on the other, variety, improbability, and complexity.[21] In this way living automata achieve a form of compromise between determinism and indeterminism, as if a certain quantity of indeterminacy were necessary to a system, beyond a certain degree of complexity, to allow it to adapt to a certain noise level—a result that Atlan very significantly relates to a theorem in von Neumann's game theory.[22]

In these ways, then, sufficiently indeterminate systems have an ability to transform noise, external chance disturbances, into an organizing factor able to generate increased complexity. In other words, rather than speaking of a 'self-programming program', one must analyse the logical nature of systems 'in which that which acts as a program endlessly modifies itself, in a way not established in advance, in response to chance environmental factors'.[23]

To summarize: the revelation by writers such as Ashby of the logical limits of the self-organization model, on one side, and on the other the development, with Atlan, of a theory of 'relative self-organization' supposing systems whose functioning combines regulation and indeterminism, definitely facilitates the attempt to apply the self-referential paradigm to social organizations. But the question this time is of a 'relative' self-reference ('relative autonomy', if

[19] 1974: 181. [20] 1979. [21] Ibid. [22] 1979: 41.
[23] 1979: 56.

you prefer), for which we resort, once again, to the model of the game. It will be remembered that we defined a game as a type of social activity that combines regularity and creativity, convention (game) and invention (play), determinism and indeterminism. Thus understood, the concept of 'game' shows itself to be a very fruitful instrument for the analysis of social and legal systems.[24] It has been used particularly by Crozier and Friedberg in their book *L'acteur et le système*.[25] They write: 'The game, essential instrument of organized action, reconciles freedom and constraint.' The players remain free, but, if they want to win, they must 'adopt a rational strategy in accordance with the nature of the game and conform to the game's rules'.[26] This instrument of analysis has the advantage, Crozier and Friedberg believe, of making it possible to supersede both the strategic perspective, which is confined to the actor's subjective point of view, and the systemic perspective, which is limited to the system's determinism.[27] In a game, 'the rules condition the actors' strategy, but in return are also conditioned by it'.[28]

A whole series of characteristics of a game emerges. Thus, the closeness of play activity in relation to the world of ordinary activities, the game being an end unto itself. Also repetition, or incessant reprise of the game's motif (as in a refrain), the to-ings and fro-ings of movement determined by the game's rules. Finally, the distinction, as an effect of the same rules, between an inside and an outside, between the field of the game and the domain of the 'out of play'. However, to insist on the game's objectivity or neutrality must not make us forget the player. The interest of the concept of game lies precisely in superseding the categories of subject and object, even if we find ourselves having to use those descriptions in order to express ourselves. A game is neither the effect of anonymous programming nor the product of a sovereign will. As a space of creativity, it measures the effect of the subject's intentionality, which is largely unpredictable, on the rigidity of a convention; as a regulated field, it expresses the will's re-orientation in response to a largely uncontrollable collective structure.

Does the concept of game take us away from self-organization? Yes, probably, if one conceives self-organization as autopoiesis or

[24] For a substitution of the game model for the self-referential model, see Febbrajo 1984: 30ff.
[25] Crozier and Friedberg 1977. [26] 1977: 97. [27] 1977: 103.
[28] 1977: 212.

the machine-like accomplishment of a program that can be disturbed only by exogenous 'impacts'; but not if it is conceived as 'relative self-organization' where the program's execution, which remains partially indeterminate, modifies itself in response to external information which, although appearing to an external observer as noise and disorder, emerges for the organization itself as meaning and more complex order. As living forms evolve between 'crystal and smoke', a social and legal game develops between order and disorder—or, to put it differently, a legal system is animated by a game that, because it involves the intervention of players who are not exclusively their own product but also participate in other social games, necessarily modifies itself in response to its environment. It is as if, at the level of society as a whole, the game of law would appear only as a particular scenario or a single incident in an overall strategy. In the following sections we shall explore the various components of this social environment and the relations that it forms with a legal system.

4.2. LEGAL SYSTEM AND SOCIAL ORDER. THE FUNCTIONS OF LAW

4.2.1. *Dialectic of Law and Society*

A legal system is obviously a subset of a social system: while every legal norm is a social norm, the converse is not true.[29] There are countless relations between legal order and social order, so that, as has been seen, law cannot lay claim to absolute self-generation but rather seeks, in return, to discipline society. As Chevallier writes, law, 'aiming to act on society, is also the product of society's determinations'[30] —a phenomenon that Kelsen, though he did not deny it, never tried to study. In a sense, law means to impose order in the heart of what can appear as social disorder: 'order' in the double sense of command or instilled discipline and of the ordering or putting in logical form of scattered elements. From this point of view, law can carry out that function of order, certainty, and stability only on condition that it attains, itself, a high degree of abstraction and generality and presents itself as a logical and consistent whole.[31] Legal professionals occupy themselves with this, when, as occasion arises, they resort to the resources of mytho-logic. Conversely, how-

[29] Chevallier 1983: 30. [30] 1983: 20. [31] Ibid.

ever, society can itself appear as largely ordered and ordering,[32] whether in response to subsystems distinct from law, such for example as the economic or political systems, or because of the significance of the vast structures underlying the whole of a given social formation. The first of these hypotheses may be illustrated by Weber's analyses, taken up by writers like Poulantzas and Gérard.[33] According to Weber, the logical formalization of law is the result of an inherent requirement of a capitalist economic system, for which the predictability of behaviour is an essential basis for calculating economic profit. Concerning the vast 'macro-social' structures, one may especially mention the views of Castoriadis, who shows that every society is 'instituted' by a sort of symbolic and founding power-bid which has the effect of affirming particular inaugural descriptions, imposing a code of canonical statements, and publicizing authorized models of behaviour—in short, of producing a consistent set of authorized meanings which are endowed with both authority and self-evident truth and, as such, form a kind of matrix for the range of discourses and disciplines that will be vital to that society.[34]

Reviewing these ideas witnesses to the inanity of any theory of a legal system that would insist radically on its closedness or openness, its self- or hetero-regulation. A dialectical conception of the relations between legal system and social order is obviously required. As Chevallier shrewdly remarks, juridicity does not operate like a Midas transforming into law every reality that it touches: in that case, indeed, society itself would lose all consistency and movement. What appears as external disorder from the standpoint of law is only partially ordered by way of legal classification (coding) and handling: facts continue to 'hum' in the heart of the legal machinery, ensuring it the element of disorder that it needs to survive and progress. In other words: 'The legal dynamic does not result from processes purely internal to a legal order, but rather from the dialectical tension between law and fact.'[35] Conversely, law is not limited to

32 On this double movement, see Castoriadis (1984: 194), in whose view it is urgent 'to render intelligible the relationship—at once complementary and antagonistic—that exists between these two aspects; to explain, that is to say, how the social system generates the particular and historically specific technique-logic that holds sway in the social domain in question, how it overdetermines that, and how, and to what extent, this particular technique-logic acquires autonomy and may eventually run counter to the overall goal of the system'.

33 Poulantzas 1965; Gérard 1981.

34 Castoriadis 1987: 359.

35 Chevallier 1983: 21.

reproducing mechanically the determinations imposed on it by any social infrastructure: it transcribes them into its own order, imbuing them with something of its logic and majesty and makes them, thus transformed, act reciprocally upon society. Here too the ideas of complexity and circular causality must be substituted for dogmatic reductions, whether they proceed from some jurists' internal point of view or from the radical external point of view of some theoreticians in the social sciences.

4.2.2. *The Functions of Law*

A better way of dealing with the complexity of the relations established between legal system and social system would also permit a more precise grasp of the range of the functions performed by law. Those who study this question usually concern themselves with denouncing the way in which the conception of the rôle taken by law is often reduced solely to the register of the prescriptive—as if law confined itself to regulating behaviour on penalty of sanction, or could be reduced to a 'rule of behaviour' (Dabin) or a 'coercive order' (Kelsen). Strongly rejecting this reductive description, writers like Summers and Howard devote several hundred pages of their *Law: Its Nature, Functions, and Limits*[36] to presenting the rôle of law as instrument of individuals' self-realization and development. With this aim, law promotes public health and the quality of the environment, protects private life and secures the family, maintains order in the group and guarantees civil rights, reduces inequalities of opportunity, ensures the certainty of settlements and the redressing of grievances, and recognizes and orders private property. To attain these various objectives, law uses various techniques indifferently and sometimes concurrently: sometimes it provides for the award of damages, sometimes it applies repressive penalties or equivalent measures, sometimes it provides a framework for activities through administrative regulation, sometimes it sets up public services, and sometimes, finally, it recognizes and guarantees the efficacy of private transactions.[37]

While there is an element of idealism in thus reducing the whole set of functions assumed by law to the single design of promoting individual development, at least this way of looking at it has the merit of wrong-footing the usually offered classical conception of it, which

[36] Summers and Howard 1975. [37] 1975: 16–17.

is unilaterally prescriptive. And, while one would like to get free both of this disciplinarian perspective and of the opposed individualistic conception—an opposition that, in the end, reflects fairly well two of the principal senses of the term 'law' (*droit*): objective state law and subjective individual right—it is possible to discern, following Orianne, the very varied functions that legal systems are called on to perform in our highly complex modern societies.[38] Of course, because of the variety of rôles that law plays in society, the effectiveness of its interventions is highly variable, its action never taking effect in a void: sometimes social pressures, indeed antagonistic mechanisms, hinder its operation or even stop it in its tracks; sometimes, instead, favourable conjunctures and convergent movements accelerate its motion. It can be observed, moreover, that the effectiveness expected from law can belong as much to the order of instrumentality as to that of the symbolic; thus a law can be passed either to alter a given state of affairs and achieve a particular purpose directly (instrumentality) or with a view to realizing an 'other' (symbolic, unexpressed) purpose, the end declared not being really desired.

The primary functions of a legal system aim to achieve social structuration and integration. In this order of ideas, one can perceive the action of law upon the choice and diffusion of a common language: on one side the officialization of a dialect through its authorized recognition and, on the other, the diffusion of a specifically legal language whose nominatory functions are seen to be paralleled by genuinely normative functions of institution, in the sense that here it is really true that 'saying is doing'—to designate is to create a legal reality. In this direction, law plays a preponderant rôle in identifying persons and things: registration of births, marriages, and deaths; land registration; registration numbering; many techniques, that is, of labelling and classifying individuals and goods. But, here too, to identify is to bring to legal life—as appears particularly clearly in the case of legal persons, which are fictional entities with only a 'legal' existence. The legal system also ensures the recording and distribution of this information, thus allowing social life 'to be carried on with the continuity of a common memory whose data are permanently accessible to all'.[39] But law is not confined to naming, classifying, and recording; more basically, it ratifies common means of measurement (standards, technical norms) and

[38] Orianne 1982: 259–302. [39] Ibid.

distributes social rôles; while it is true that, in any society, individuals' actions conform to models or rôles, it is clear that, in large part, the allocation and imposition of these models and rôles is the business of law. The stratifications effected by legal language result in a great variety of statuses to which are attached rights and duties, burdens and privileges (this ambivalence shows clearly the reductiveness of an approach to law exclusively in terms of constraint). The actors in the social game are thus designated and the rôle of each—their 'status'—defined. Each finds themselves allocated a social function, in suitably planned situations; derived from this is a set of consequences, positive and negative, legal and non-legal. Finally, the legal system's participation in setting up the framework of societal life culminates in affirming a bundle of options and basic values which are considered to enjoy some degree of consensus and thereby ensure the cementing of collective life. Constitutional declarations of rights endow these values with a solemn mode of expression, while criminal prohibitions ensure that they are backed up with a more effective sanction. The legal transcription of these choices made by society not only provides precise information on their content but also has the advantage of allowing them to be debated: whether in judicial controversy on the level of particular applications or in parliamentary debate on the level of their creation or possible alteration.

Apart from the structuring of social life, a legal system contributes to its regulation. On this score, and in a general way, law, as Orianne again maintains,[40] ensures the 'planning of actions' for the long term, thus guaranteeing certainty—to be exact, 'legal' certainty—and the economic, social, and political predictability following from it. By moulding behaviour according to model programs that are obeyed, law contributes effectively to the development of social life, in the sense of an increasing complexification, everyone becoming more and more deeply involved in the process of division of labour and exchange to the extent of the increase in promise-keeping and sanctioning by pre-established rules. This effect is produced not only by statute, 'which provides only for the future' (Civil Code, Article 2), but also by private contract, the instrument *par excellence* of transaction and exchange.

Finally, there emerge the most classical functions of law: regulation of behaviour and conflict management. But one can see that it is

[40] 1982: 284.

only in the extreme that law *imposes* a particular behaviour and by authority inflicts a *sanction* on the lawbreaker.[41] Usually, recourse to the judicial apparatus is left to the initiative of the parties, while a rule generally appears as a model offered to individuals, arranging for them new and broader possibilities of action associated, of course, with a set of constraints and limits. Sometimes, even, as with excludable statutory implied terms, law confines itself to proposing to the interested parties various models of behaviour, to which they are free to prefer arrangements invented to suit themselves.

Lastly, this range of functions performed by a legal system can be carried out with different degrees of intensity and linked together in a variety of ways: sometimes the repressive function and the authoritative direction of behaviour are primary; sometimes, on the contrary, as in the framework of the nineteenth-century liberal *État de droit*, law confines itself to providing a framework for the free play of the market. In the course of the twentieth century, the emergence of what is conventionally called the Welfare State has brought with it a powerful intensification of regulation, the law attempting to regulate some modes of behaviour in detail, such as those of economic entrepreneurs, judged essential to the social progress of which the State now believes itself to have a duty to take charge. The result is a fundamental alteration of the meaning of legal intervention: while, in the *État de droit*, the legal system limits itself to distributing rôles and arbitrating a mode of game-playing left to the actors' initiative and imagination, in the Welfare State law means to take the lead both as general guide and in the details of its execution. Besides its traditional missions, it now takes on a rôle that Bobbio has called 'promotional',[42] witnessed by the vogue for prospective norms (plans, laws coming into force in stages, contracts of conditional State aid to industry) and the multiplication of 'positive' sanctions (various incentives and benefits aimed at rewarding conformity to the law rather than penalties aimed at sanctioning deviance from it).

Can law keep all its promises? To answer the questions of effectiveness (is the law applied?) and efficacy (does the law applied obtain the desired result?), it is important to see plainly how the legal system is linked to the social system. In this respect, sociologists of

[41] On the different styles of social control that a legal system can establish, see especially van de Kerchove 1987: 332 ff, 353 ff.

[42] Bobbio 1977: 13–22 (ch. i: 'La funzione promozionale del diritto').

law have shed a clearer light on the 'immediate periphery' (*proche périphérie*) of law: a set of 'para-legal' or 'infra-legal' phenomena, practices, discourses, and claims that sometimes facilitate and sometimes retard its progress. Its nature will be discussed in the following section.

4.3. LEGAL SYSTEM AND SOCIAL ORDER. 'INFRA-LAW'

One could try to explore methodically the immediate environment of legal systems, that uncertain beach recording the ebb and flow of law—'that fringe', Carbonnier writes, 'running in chiaroscuro the whole length of the positive legal system'.[43] This zone of exchange between law and 'near-law', Carbonnier calls 'vulgar law', a sort of lower law produced in non-technical circles and combining with autonomous usages elements borrowed from the legal order of the State.[44] Arnaud attempts to formalize these rough expressions. He finds here a phenomenon of 'simultaneous polysystemicity'.[45] The positive law 'is only one legal system among others—the one that, among all those possible, has been posited and imposed by an author invested with the power to state the law'.[46] This is to distinguish between the system of imposed norms and, operating under it and indeed against it, the multiple systems of 'spontaneous law' formed from the conjunction of 'imagined legal entities' and 'law-like experiences' that are not officially recognized but none the less have a claim to juridicity—multiple systems that Arnaud places in the category of 'infra-law',[47] which would be to law what infra-red is to the colour spectrum—a marginal case, yet not a heterogeneous element[48]—a set of phenomena that only the limitations of habit keep us from seeing as 'legal'. While imposed norms have been subject to a process of 'institutionalization',[49] 'potential norms' do not of course enjoy such official recognition but nevertheless detach themselves 'from the indeterminate mass of social phenomena'[50] in that their authors see law in them and that the expectations they express materialize in rôles effectively performed in social life.[51] How far, however, can one speak of 'legal *systems*' among this infra-law? There is system,

[43] Carbonnier 1972: 159. [44] Ibid. [45] Arnaud 1981: 25.
[46] 1981: 20. [47] 1981: 26. [48] 1981: 325. [49] 1981: 323.
[50] 1981: 324. [51] 1981: 344–5.

according to Arnaud, even if these systems 'are not as evidently systematic as imposed law' because—and inasmuch as—each of them is 'ordered in terms of a form of legal reason'.[52] For Arnaud, legal reason—that is, 'the motor by which a system organizes itself consistently and in a way appropriate to attaining certain ends'—is 'the necessary and sufficient condition for the existence of a legal system'.[53]

One can also ask what is the content of these phenomena or systems of 'infra-law'. Do we find here a form of bastardization of official law, leading to a kind of vulgar law combining autonomous usages with positive norms—for example, the summary jurisdiction exercised in police stations—as Carbonnier maintains,[54] or do we only find 'practices that their actors perceive and intend as law yet which, nevertheless, are not law', as Arnaud is inclined to believe[55]—for example, 'the communitarian utopia of the 1970s'?[56] The question seems to have little importance, inasmuch as both hypotheses are 'non-legal' from the standpoint of positive law and, moreover, considered dynamically, infra-legal phenomena always in some way rival the law in force and often end up intertwining with it, so that the distinction between the 'para-legal' and the 'pseudo-legal' loses its pertinence.

This dynamic approach is the main point of interest in the investigations of Carbonnier and Arnaud. Infra-law is truly a site of confrontation between spontaneous and imposed law and, by that token, reveals a field in which each is constantly being transformed into the other. 'Sometimes', Carbonnier writes, 'vulgar law will corrupt learned law, or even wound it with a kind of languor, close to desuetude; sometimes learned law will go onto the counter-offensive, trying with greater or lesser success to strike vulgar law down with penalties and with declarations of nullity; sometimes a compromise will be reached, learned law considering it more politic to incorporate a dose of vulgar law'.[57]

One of sociology of law's major contributions to theory of legal systems is to have thus relativized the frontiers of the legal, while, in the same movement, providing it with the conceptual instruments necessary to a dialectical theory of change of these systems.

[52] 1981: 26. [53] 1981: 27. [54] Carbonnier 1972: 159.
[55] Arnaud 1981: 344.
[56] 1981: 338–40. [57] Carbonnier 1972: 159–61.

4.4. LEGAL SYSTEM AND CHANGE

4.4.1. *Change and Homeostasis*

None will deny that legal systems experience changes—sometimes endogenous, sometimes exogenous, sometimes continuous and imperceptible, and sometimes abrupt and deliberate. But change itself can be evaluated only in relation to stability. No system would be viable and operational if it could not manage to maintain its equilibrium, at least within certain limits. It also seems inappropriate to adopt, at least within a realist perspective, the idea proposed by some legal theorists who think that legal systems can only be 'momentary'.[58] Believing that the addition of any norm whatever to a system or the repeal of any one of them has the effect of creating a new legal system, these writers readily define a legal system as the set of norms in force at a given moment in time. As if, in some way, these systems necessarily appeared with the fixity of a photograph, as opposed to an image in a movie.[59] Although this thesis can make sense within the axiomatic perspective that these writers share, it corresponds neither to current terminology nor to the requirements of a theory of change in law. This conception of law as spasmodic succession of different systems seems to have the effect of making the problem of change completely void. Would it not be better to show the adjustment mechanisms and rules of change that legal systems use to ensure their gradual adaptation?[60] This is just what distinguishes a system from a simple collection of elements, that it has at least partial control over its own transformations. Thus the problematic of change presupposes that of homeostasis. Wróblewski defines this property thus: a system is homeostatic if it reacts to internal and/or external stimuli so as to maintain its equilibrium and existence within certain limits which determine the system's degree of tolerance.[61] Examples of artificial

[58] To our knowledge, the first writer to formulate this idea was Raz (1970: 34 ff.); it was later adopted by Alchourrón and Bulygin (1971: 77, 89–90) and, more recently, by Gardies (1987: 176).

[59] See, especially, Bulygin 1982: 66.

[60] Nevertheless, these writers often find themselves having to introduce another concept, in opposition to that of a momentary system, to account for the element that remains constant throughout its transformations: in 1971, Alchourrón and Bulygin speak of 'law' ('French law', conceived as 'the sequence of all momentary legal systems that have been in force in France'—1971: 89), while in 1982 Bulygin came to oppose (momentary) 'legal system' to 'legal order' (a set of momentary systems succeeding each other within a given time span—1982: 66–7).

[61] Wróblewski 1983*a*: 302; see also Wróblewski 1981: 1 ff.

homeostatic systems are an automatic pilot or a thermostat. A human society can also have properties of this order; thus Wiener, founder of cybernetics, remarked that, while a small society possesses a high degree of homeostasis, in a complex society, on the other hand, anti-homeostatic factors multiply.[62] A legal system, as with any system, also tends to reinforce its conditions of equilibrium and thus helps to guarantee social homeostasis, whether with reference to the relations existing between human societies and the ecological environment, to relations of coexistence between peoples, or to the essential socio-political relations obtaining in each social formation.

Homeostasis does not, however, mean rigidity or immobility; rather, the system constantly adapts to new conditions through a self-regulating process—that is, according to the system's own rules of change (for example, a constitutional reform carried out according to the procedures provided by the Constitution itself). In such phenomena it is easy to discern legal 'changes'. These, however, are changes in a weak sense: more important is the invention of a new combination, or a new 'hit', within the framework of still unchanged rules of the game. On the other hand, when it is the rules of the game themselves that are altered, it must be admitted that another game is progressively instituted. One will speak in this case of change in a strong sense. Arnaud defines it in these terms: 'Legal change is specifically linked to change of the form of legal reason in the system of imposed law . . . One will then speak correctly of legal change only when it is possible to observe . . . a transformation of the deep structure of a system of imposed law, such as when one equilibrium is succeeded by a new equilibrium, based on a different or at least renewed form of reason.'[63] For Arnaud, the occurrence of such a situation requires the conjunction of two conditions: a gulf must have opened up between the official legal system and its unofficial rivals in the category of infra-law; and the latter must lay an effective claim to substitute themselves for the imposed model. Sociologists of law have the task of measuring the thresholds of legal change by the yardsticks of these two criteria; needless to stress, however, this search for the (in)effectiveness of law obviously cannot be subject to rigorous calculation. Following Friedman and Arnaud in particular, the important thing is to emphasize that society's pressures on law are rarely direct; they operate only through the filter of what Fried-

62 Cited in Wróblewski 1981: 5. 63 Arnaud 1981: 369.

man calls 'legal culture' (ideas, attitudes, beliefs, expectations and opinions about law)[64] and Arnaud calls the 'infra-legal'; for instance, litigated claims, which can sometimes entail important breaks with precedent, proceed from a series of prognostications that form part of this set of social descriptions of law's rôle and potentialities.

4.4.2. *Legal Change and Social Change*

This leads to the observation that legal and social change do not necessarily go together; precisely so far as there is no direct causal relation between social order and legal system, their evolutionary rhythms are at least partially autonomous. Even if one does not accept the Marxist thesis that transformations of law are determined by changes in the relations of production,[65] it may be interesting to attempt a typology of the relations existing between the two forms of change. Among the abundant literature on this point in sociology of law, we shall look at two attempts of this kind, the first taken from Friedman and the second from Wróblewski. Combining the criterion of the origin of change with that of its point of impact, Friedman distinguishes four varieties:[66]

Change originating from society and affecting only law, without a consequent social effect. This hypothesis would suppose the action upon law of two antagonistic social forces whose practically equivalent effects cancel each other out.

Change originating from society, and both affecting the legal system and having a social impact. This hypothetical case envisages the truly significant legal changes that, according to the legal traditions present, can be made sometimes by the legislator and sometimes by the higher courts (for instance, the rôle of the Supreme Court of the United States in the policy of racial integration). As a type of break, such changes occur in a fairly revolutionary way; as factors in a process of social construction, they take the form of planning.

Change originating within the legal system and affecting only the legal system. These are cases of 'giving the building a facelift' or limited changes that form the greater part of jurists' activity (the problematic of 'reform' constantly on the stocks . . .), but hardly ever concern important social stakes.

Change originating within the legal system and having a social

64 Friedman 1975: 15–16; 1977: 7.

65 Carbonnier 1972: 169.

66 Friedman 1975: 269 ff.

impact. The rather special hypothesis of a purely formal internal alteration that unexpectedly produces social effects of some importance.

To be complete, this classification should include a fifth hypothetical case: that of a purely social change that does not affect the legal order. In view of the legal order's considerable autonomy and the resistance that it sometimes offers to social movements, this hypothesis should not be treated as simply academic.

Wróblewski too distinguishes four paradigmatic situations:[67]

Legal change accompanied by social change. This situation can result from a direct influence of law on the social environment or the converse relation. In the first case, one would say that the law is effective: the effect predicted by the legislator is achieved in social reality. But lateral and sometimes perverse effects, whether predicted or not, can also be produced. In the second hypothesis, pressures exerted by particular interest groups lead the decision-maker (judge or legislator) to stamp a change on the system. Today, in the framework of the Welfare State, this instrumental conception of law is extensively developed. There are, however, a number of limits to the legislator's freedom of action in planning and transformation: perverse effects may multiply if the legislator is not in full control of the facts that he or she is called upon to regulate, the economic efficiency (social cost) of legal change may turn out to be disproportionate to the objectives pursued or the axiological value of the ends that legal means have been mobilized to serve might no longer be given priority.

Legal change not followed by social change. This possibility can have three explanations: sometimes one will find 'legalistic', purely formal alterations, hardly affecting real life; sometimes a piece of legislation may attempt a real social change but remain ineffective; and sometimes the legal arm has been used successfully to prevent a social change that there had been reason to fear.

Social change not followed by legal change. For example, a failure of the previous possibility: a piece of legislation designed to control a particular social evolution remains largely ineffective.

Absence of both legal and social change: a hypothesis possible in periods, probably very short, of generalized stability.

Finally, Wróblewski mentions a fifth situation, which is perhaps the closest to social realities because it is the most complex: here one

[67] Wróblewski 1983*a*: 300ff.

records a 'relative change' of law, presupposing a dissociation—which is indeed very common—between the written law and the law applied. The hypothesis here is of an unaltered written law that nevertheless puts up with a law 'in action' renewed in unison with a significant social change. For example, the case of judicial or doctrinal interpretation of a law whose letter remains unaltered, which is done in order to respond to unforeseen needs produced by social life. One can, therefore, accept that written law might not respond to social conjunctures immediately and that case law, mobile and specific by nature, is occasionally used as an experimental laboratory for new solutions. There is thus an equilibration of the functions expected overall of a legal system: while the code guarantees some degree of legal certainty, the judge ensures the indispensable adaptation of the normative order. However, the converse is also found. For legislators sometimes enact 'symbolic' legislation, which neither the executive nor the courts ever apply. In this fashion, in the framework of a pluralistic society, one can hope to satisfy the antagonistic interests of conflicting social groups: while some obtain the symbolic satisfaction that a law meeting their wishes has been enacted, the others are content with a legal practice that remains unchanged.[68]

Any rigorous study of change in law should trace this path of internal diversification of the elements of a legal system. In that spirit, we shall offer in the final chapter of this book a differentiated presentation of the various temporalities of law, which we shall then relate to the diachronic transformations of legal systems. For the moment, we must continue to investigate the environment of legal systems by now enquiring into their relations with other normative systems.

4.5. LEGAL SYSTEM AND NON-LEGAL NORMATIVE SYSTEMS

4.5.1. *Rules of Experience*

That law is a technique for directing human behaviour is a truism. Unless it is to embody all available knowledge and evaluations, law cannot attain this objective on its own resources. The application of law to fact obviously requires the mediation of rules borrowed from other registers: moral assessments, rules of logic, rules of grammar, psychological judgements; rules of economics, accounting, and medicine; and many others. Italian and German doctrine calls 'rules of experience' those non-legal norms whose operation is nevertheless

[68] For an application of this phenomenon in criminal law, see Ost and van de Kerchove 1987: 344 ff.

indispensable for guiding the application of a legal rule.[69] For example, to determine the capital due to the beneficiaries of a fatal accident victim, 'judges fix the probable length of human life with the aid of a mortality table and calculate the capital sum due by means of a capitalization table'.[70] The lawmaker's adherence to these rules of experience is an important aspect of the rationality that the judiciary, interpreting the laws, ascribe to the legislator. These rules of experience are therefore regularly applied, especially by the judiciary. Yet this does not necessarily make them legal. The rules of syntax, the rules of logic, or even mortality tables exist independently of law and are vital to every rational speaker and to everyone who tries to determine, to the highest degree of probability, the probable length of a person's life.

Nevertheless, it is possible for these rules of experience, as in the cases of certain moral principles, to undergo a substantive reception by the legal system. The rule of experience is then transformed into a legal rule. Sometimes it is the very legislator who incorporates the rule of experience into the system of statutes (many statutory presumptions are the result of such a procedure); sometimes the transformation results from a process formed by custom; and sometimes the reception is the work of case law, conferring on the rule of experience the authority attaching to its own decisions—hence, for F. Rigaux, a rule of experience applied by a court turns into a normative fact clothed with the authority of a judicial precedent.[71]

One may then ask how far such a transformation leaves intact the substance of the rule incorporated: is there a reception pure and simple, or does the rule get altered by the fact of its integration into a legal system? The two hypotheses come together: while mortality tables remain unchanged, on the other hand the lexical meaning of certain statutory terms is sometimes simply their ordinary meaning and sometimes largely determined by their legal contexts of utterance and application. Likewise, although judges must apply the ordinary rules of interpretation, they cannot ignore certain specifically legal rules of interpretation; for example, the precept that criminal and tax laws are to be interpreted restrictively—a principle constituting, one might say, a creative application of the general principle that exceptions and derogations are to be interpreted restrictively.

69 F. Rigaux 1966: 112–22, 222–6.
70 1966: 115.
71 1966: 119–22, 224–5.

Here, then, is a new aspect of legal systems' permeability: their practical operation, their relation to social life, suppose the mediation of rules borrowed from other normative systems. In some cases, these rules are simply applied by the decision-maker-jurist; in others, they are incorporated into the legal system and transformed into legal rules. This very general capacity of law to make norms coming from other normative codes its own constitutes the frequently studied phenomenon of 'internormativity', which, though it represents a specific feature of law, also expresses its great openness towards its environment.[72] Nevertheless, a legal order that did not apply generally recognized rules of experience would not *ipso facto* lose its validity, understood in the formal sense. In the short or fairly short term, however, its lack of correspondence with reality would threaten its effectiveness and eventually its formal validity.

4.5.2. *Legal System and Morality (or Moralities)*

This problematic finds paradigmatic application in the relations existing between a legal system and the morality, or rather moralities, prevailing in a society. Originally, as will be seen in the following chapter, this question was hardly ever put: law and morality—just as, later, with religion and mores—were largely woven together. But, as evolution proceeded, law and the other normative systems became dissociated, so that the problem of their compatibility had to be posed. Attempting to resolve it in a descriptive perspective and using, to do so, a description that has become classic, it can be said that while, earlier, law and ethics formed two concentric circles, today their relationship is that of secant circles, whose area of intersection is greater or larger according to the period and part of the world envisaged.[73] One finds the greatest variety of situations. Sometimes legal regulation intersects with accepted morality: for instance, civil rights, which are the translation into positive law of the moral requirements implied by human rights—a translation that is also incomplete since, while the so-called 'first-generation' human rights (freedom of conscience, personal security, and so on) have been integrated into legal orders, on the other hand the 'second-generation' rights (economic and social rights) have not necessarily received constitutional recognition, while the

[72] On internormativity, see Carbonnier 1979: 258; see also Romano 1975: 32–3.
[73] Similarly, du Pasquier 1967: 317; Virally 1960: 27.

juridicity of the 'third generation' of rights (rights to peace, to development, and so on) continues to be vigorously contested. Sometimes positive law confines itself to an overall *renvoi* to common morality without otherwise trying to specify and modify that morality's prescriptions: as, for example, with standards like the reference to '*bonnes mœurs*'. Sometimes, too, law develops with a degree of indifference to ethics, for instance by permitting what ethics condemn. Sometimes, lastly, they are in outright opposition—in so far, of course, as one can distinguish 'a' dominant moral option, which in our own pluralist societies is not always easy. It must be stressed here that the ethical bases of political community are now difficult to examine otherwise than in terms of 'fragile convergences'[74] at a time when one can observe an increasing heterogeneity of collective morality. It appears that collective morality is gradually fragmenting into a plurality of segmentary moralities distributed according to divisions in terms of age, social class, status, religion, and cultural orientation. Moreover, this diversified social morality seems itself sometimes to enter into conflict with strictly individual moral convictions or with the critical claims of moralities with claims to universality.

It can be observed, moreover, that the relations between law and morality are not only one-way, since, while traditionally law is thought to derive from ethics, the converse relation can equally be found, as Bentham already noted: 'In many cases, morality derives its existence from the law.'[75] Here too, it is important to conceive the relations between systems in terms of interaction and not of linear causality. In this order of ideas one finds—always on a simply observational level—that the greater the convergence the more intense the collaboration between law and morality, and the more assured the development of both systems.

Seen more closely, however, the question becomes more complicated, since it is not of course posed solely on an observational level; from the outset, the relations between law and morality raise normative questions, to which legal thinking has provided completely contradictory prescriptive answers. Schematically, one can recall here the opposition, as old as the debate between Antigone and Creon, between iusnaturalism and legal positivism. The battle is joined over the question of knowing whether there is a *necessary* link

[74] The expression is borrowed from Ricœoeur (1985: 10).

[75] Bentham 1829*b*: 39.

between law and morality. This question, in its turn, raises two others: 'Does law necessarily have a moral content?' and 'Is there a moral obligation to obey the law?'

To these questions, iusnaturalist thinking, at least in its most radical formulation, replies that unjust law is in no way law and that, accordingly, a legal order can claim to be unconditionally obeyed since, by nature, it intersects with the prescriptions of morality. This is, in particular, the teaching of Saint Augustine, for whom States without justice are only 'robber-gangs on a large scale'.[76] Conversely, legal positivism maintains, at least in its most extreme formulation, of which Kelsen is an important representative, that 'Legal norms may have any kind of content'[77] and that the obedience to which law may lay claim is sustained by an obligation internal to the legal system—in Kelsen the *Grundnorm*, which commands that the Constitution be obeyed.

Often, it is true, standpoints in the controversy are stated with more qualification. One example is the recent debate between Hart and Fuller.[78] Opposing Bentham and Austin, who attempted a radical separation between law and morality, Fuller maintains that there are two counts on which ethics forms the basis of law's bindingness. On one side, it provides the criteria that make it possible to evaluate rulers' legitimacy and to make the Constitution stand not only for law but for just law ('external' morality); on the other, it establishes a number of formal principles which legal regulation must necessarily respect—generality, publicity, and non-retroactivity of norms, and so on—on pain of no longer being law and of releasing the subjects of law from their duty of obedience ('internal' morality, see above).[79] Although he insists on the interaction between these two forms of morality, Fuller mainly stresses the second, no doubt aware that agreement can more easily be reached, in our pluralist societies, on this 'procedural version of natural law',[80] which in fact answers to the requirements of the modern *État de droit*, than on material values arising from external or substantive morality. None the less, in this renewed form, he reaffirms a commitment to the classic iusnaturalist thesis: a legal order, such as Nazi law, that does not adhere to these minimal rules

76 *City of God*, book 4, ch. 4. 77 Kelsen 1946: 113.

78 This debate has six stages: Hart 1958; Fuller 1958; Hart 1961; Fuller 1964; Hart 1965; Fuller 1969: ch. 5, 'A Reply to Critics'.

79 Fuller 1958: 645. 80 Fuller 1969: 96.

of the game constituting internal morality cannot claim the name of law.

Hart, on the other hand, places himself in the lineage of positivism, albeit by way of some important concessions. For him, the distinction between law as it is and law as it ought to be, or that between law and morality, must be maintained. There is no *necessary* connection between law and morality, even if observation leads us to note the existence of 'many different types of relation' between them.[81] Thus the criteria of *legal* validity of legal rules used in a system need not necessarily include a reference to morality or justice.[82] From this (strictly legal) point of view, Nazi law is definitely law, even though we have high *moral* reasons not to conform to its commands. In fact, Hart explains, there is every advantage in retaining a broad concept of law (to include unjust laws) rather than a narrow concept. On the scientific plane, study of a phenomenon should include investigation of its deviations and abuses; while, on the ethical plane, it is equally preferable to maintain the dissociation between law valid from the formal point of view and legitimate law. To entertain confusion between these two levels exposes one either to the danger of anarchism, in that everybody would arrogate to themselves the right to decide, on the basis of their own moral conceptions, what is law and what is not, or, conversely, to the danger of social conformism by weakening citizens' vigilance with regard to a power with respect to which one has become systematically habituated to thinking that the norms it pronounces constitute just law.[83] On the contrary, Hart believes,

> This sense, that there is something outside the official system, by reference to which in the last resort the individual must solve his problems of obedience, is surely more likely to be kept alive among those who are accustomed to think that rules of law may be iniquitous, than among those who think that nothing iniquitous can anywhere have the status of law.[84]

While therefore there are good reasons *de principe* to keep the two spheres of morality and juridicity separate, on the other hand realism leads one to record, on the *observational plane*, countless forms of relation between them. Thus no positivist would deny the influence of 'accepted social morality' and of 'broader moral ideas' on legislation and case law. And a Constitution like that of the United States explicitly includes, among the ultimate criteria of legal validity, prin-

[81] Hart 1961: 181. [82] Ibid. [83] 1961: 204–7. [84] 1961: 206.

ciples of justice and a reference to positive moral values. Again, since judges' interpretation of statute is neither purely mechanical nor purely at hazard, it appears that 'Very often their choice is guided by an assumption that the purpose of the rules which they are interpreting is a reasonable one, so that the rules are not intended to work injustice or offend settled moral principles.'[85] Or, again, it is perfectly correct to maintain that a legal system that rests on a conviction, widely shared by the citizens, of its moral value provides a greater guarantee of stability than a system based on exploitation and brute force. Yet here too one cannot speak of a *necessary* connection between law and morality, since allegiance to the system can rest on very many reasons other than a feeling of moral obligation and history also offers many examples of legal systems imposed by force on large sections of the population.[86]

On two points, however, Hart is prepared to make important concessions to the opposite thesis. The interest of this here is that the connection thus admitted between law and morality is established not at the level of isolated norms but at that of the legal system as a whole. Just as each legal norm is not necessarily to be either sanctioned or obeyed, but rather there is little sense in speaking of a legal system as a whole that would lack sanctions and effectiveness, if the question of the relationship between law and morality is to receive a satisfactory and complete answer it must be conceived on the plane of the overall legal system.[87] On this level one can establish a double and necessary, although tenuous, connection. On one side, it is correct that respect for the principle of legality and for the rules of due process ('natural justice', 'fair trial', and so on) guarantee a minimal form of justice. Hart thus comes considerably closer to Fuller, although not without remarking that this 'natural justice' is 'unfortunately compatible with very great iniquity'.[88]

Elsewhere, Hart also remarks that, whenever a legal system means to ensure the survival of the group from which it emanates, it has necessarily to include certain rules made indispensable by the shape of the world around us and the characteristics of our human nature. These rules, relating especially to the prohibition of violence, the institution of property, and the keeping of promises, constitute the 'minimum content of natural law' (see below, Sect. 5.4). As history still shows, however, such rules need not be established for the benefit of everyone; it is enough for these elementary protections to

[85] 1961: 200. [86] 1961: 198–9. [87] 1958: 621. [88] 1961: 202.

benefit the dominant groups or classes—so, to iusnaturalists, Hart's concession may seem pretty thin. For the rest, Hart is very careful to insist that the deduction of the 'minimum content of natural law' rests exclusively on empirical considerations, following a method traceable to Hobbes and Hume: that the formulation of the rules that any social organization needs to include in order to be viable flows simply from 'the modest aim of survival', linked to a few elementary truisms about human nature.[89]

This does not prevent the form of argumentation used by Hart from being evidently capable of leading to still more significant results and thereby reinforcing the connection between law and morality. The type of argumentation in this case is transcendental: beginning from a fact of experience, selected as an *a priori* given, one attempts to discover that fact's conditions of possibility by a reflexive effort of thought.[90] Hart began from the 'modest aim of survival' and derived from it the 'minimum content of natural law'. Other writers, however, would readily defend a broader conception of nature and of the meaning of human life and then derive from it a richer normative content.

Thus, for Cotta, every human being is characterized by coexistence or sociality (*Dasein* is a *Mit-dasein*, existence is coexistence): mutual recognition is the fundamental condition for individual existence.[91] Through its requirement of universality, natural law shows itself to be the expression of this essential and basic factum; its prescriptions are rationally justified by the fact that they guarantee the greatest extent of human coexistence, that of a universal audience. On the other hand, although positive law subscribes to that aim, it guarantees only partial coexistences and only in particular parts of the world. This does not prevent the justification of its prescriptions from having necessarily to refer to their functionality in relation to the requirement of coexistence and, in this logic, the movement towards universalization from being irresistible. In the end, only a difference of degree separates positive law from natural law.[92]

The same argumentative strategy is used by Apel, who is known to

[89] 1961: 187.

[90] It can be seen that this way of reasoning makes it possible to escape the 'naturalistic fallacy' objection made by Hume against iusnaturalists (the logical error of deducing a normative conclusion from a factual premiss). The question is not to deduce a norm from a fact but to investigate the conditions of possibility of a fact.

[91] Cotta 1982: 17.

[92] 1983: 273–90.

have decisively influenced the thought of Habermas. Starting from the *a priori* factum of the existence of 'communicative communities' (people speak, and exchange ideas and arguments), Apel believes that to engage in such a 'language game' is necessarily to accept that game's implicit rules, whose nature is basically ethical. To argue is necessarily to presuppose the recognition of all speaking beings as discussion partners with equal rights; it is to commit oneself to recognizing all the possible claims by members of the communicative community that can be justified by reasonable arguments; and this is to force oneself to ground one's own claims upon others only on arguments of the same kind.[93] Apel brings out in this way what he calls the 'basic principles of a communicative ethic'.

It has to be recognized that, since modernity, the establishing of this 'public space' of free discussion has begun to receive institutional realization with the gradual emergence of an outline of human rights and the construction of democratic régimes. Human rights and democracy are bearers of a requirement of universality and unconditionality which expresses the ethical nature of their inspiration. What in fact are human rights, if not the recognition that everybody has, in Lefort's happy expression, 'a right to have rights'[94]—that is, the initiation of a historical process that is not subject to the control of the power through which unprecedented forms of social life are ventured as fast as the demand for recognition of the dignity of human life is deepened and the circle of the beneficiaries of those rights is enlarged? As for democracy, it is probably less the government of the city by the majority than the régime that, tolerating at its core a representation of social division, accepts the (peaceful) expression of dissensus and, in so doing, respects the minority's rights. It then appears as the régime 'in which participation in decision-making is guaranteed to an ever greater number of citizens'.[95]

It can now be accepted that, from this discussion, the connection between a legal and an ethical system emerges reinforced: on the theoretical plane, it has been shown that the rational justification of positive-legal solutions necessarily subscribes to a universalizing aim concerning coexistence or communication, while, on the practical plane, one can observe institutional realizations inspired by that logic. One has nevertheless not to conclude in favour of confusing law and morality. In this regard, the position of Hart, who wishes to maintain a distinction of principle between the two spheres, seems

93 Apel 1987: 94, 124–6.

94 Lefort 1984: 37.

95 Ricœur 1985: 10.

perfectly justified. This is because, on one side, an ethical requirement, by its very indeterminacy, necessarily transcends its positive realizations; to reduce ethics to law would be to expose oneself to the risk—realized in totalitarian régimes—of a complete legitimation of law that would not fail to sterilize, before long, the ethical inventiveness from which it originated.[96] And also because there would be some naïvety in tracing the sole source from which law is inspired to the fact of communication; history and the present day offer a quite sufficient spectacle of violence for one to accept that, although law and State give form to coexistence, they can just as well bring about situations of force and exploitation.

Law thus intersects as much with the field of relations of force and conflicts of interest as with that of universalist ethical aspirations and unconditional demands. Turning again to the figure of secant circles, one can say that the sphere of legality in the strict sense partially intersects with the spheres of politics and ethics. While it is true, as Ricœur writes, that 'the *État de droit* is the carrying out of ethical intention in the sphere of politics',[97] it is probably no less correct to maintain that State and law (which do not necessarily take the form of an *État de droit*) can give form and consistency, in the ethical sphere, to dominant interests and prevailing forces. Legal life is marked by constant oscillation and fragile compromises between political pressures and ethical inspiration. At its limit, this movement can tip over into two extreme and equally pathological hypothetical cases: either the legal system is reduced to giving form to the volitions of raw and totally illegitimate power, such as that wielded by foreign occupying troops, or, on the contrary, law, totally deprived of effectiveness, acquires its authority and continued existence only from the ethical aspirations of the community from which it emanates. It can happen that these two models—marking a splitting of law between force and good—may coexist in a particular historical situation: to the occupier's coercive but illegitimate order correspond the legitimate but clandestine demands of the oppressed populations. In both cases, legal forms and rituals may be mobilized: decrees can be issued and trials set up, but the absence of one essential component of law (legitimacy in the one case, force in the other) quickly shows the now odious, now derisory nature of what thus parades itself as a parody of law and justice. A return to normality can be achieved after recentring the previously dissociated poles:

[96] On this point, see Ladrière 1984: 95.

[97] Ricœur 1985: 9.

either, in time, the régime initially based on force and usurpation will end by legitimating itself or, conversely, the demands of the exploited classes or peoples will end by taking control.

Does this recentring mean complete overlap? Such, probably, is the utopia contained in embryo in all totalitarian thought fascinated by the mirage of a society in which no distance any longer separates the ethical, the legal, and the political. In our view, such a society would be thoroughly non-human and ahistorical—Paradise or Hell, as you will—as would also be the equally utopian society of anarchical inspiration, in which there would be no convergence among the moral, legal, and political orders. In short, in either of these societies law would no longer have any place: in the one case, the complete overlap of ethics by politics would mean the disappearance of State and law, as in the dream of a communist society totally lacking in alienation, while, in the other hypothesis, anarchy would obviously be accompanied by the most complete anomy. It therefore seems that, for the same reasons, the autonomy and specificity of a legal system in relation to other normative systems—such as ethical, political, or religious systems—should be preserved, even though we possess good reasons to think that they are only partial and precarious.

4.6. RELATIONS BETWEEN DIFFERENT LEGAL SYSTEMS

Does a legal system's environment consist exclusively of 'non-law', or perhaps 'infra-law'—that is, of a space (structured or not, normative or not) that is not strictly legal—or does the environment also include other legal systems separate from the first, but with which it is capable of entering into certain specific relations?

As can be seen, two questions arise in succession, the second supposing logically that the first can be resolved in positive terms: is it possible to conceive the existence of a plurality of legal systems separate from one another? and what relations can exist between them? The first question poses the problem of a legal system's *identity* and of the criteria necessary to distinguish one legal system from another.[98]

[98] Several writers clearly distinguish the problem of a legal system's identity from the problem of relations between legal systems. See particularly, Raz 1979: 78 ff.; François 1978: 163 ff.; Lenoble 1984: 51.

The second question concerns the degree of a legal system's *openness* or *closure* in relation to others.[99]

4.6.1. *The Identity of a Legal System*

(*a*) *Monism or Pluralism?* In the history of legal thought, the first of these questions has received two opposite answers, corresponding respectively to what may be called a 'monist' or a 'pluralist' conception of law.

A *monist* conception of law is understood as the idea that law exists only in the form of a single and universal system.[100] As Carbonnier has plainly demonstrated, this conception is generally expressed in the form of a dilemma:

> *Either* the phenomena depicted as forming another body of law are taken into consideration by the overall legal system ... and unity is restored through that overall system, which takes over the whole; *or* the phenomena of an alleged other body of law remain outside, not integrated into the system, in a primitive state, and cannot be truly classified as law but at the very most as *sub-law*.[101]

This, as has already been mentioned, is the position of Kelsen, for whom 'No one can serve two masters'[102] and 'a monistic construction is inevitable'.[103] It is also, particularly, the conception of Dabin, for whom 'the legal order of political society ... seen as supreme, is the only *true* law'[104] and 'law, conceived as obligatory rules, exists only from the moment when the State, through its designated organs, shall have put it in the form of a State law, whether explicitly or implicitly ... directly or indirectly'.[105]

By a pluralist conception of law we shall understand neither the fact that 'the same persons are subjected to several legal orders independent of each other'[106] nor the fact that there exist, 'within a particular society, different legal mechanisms applying to identical situations',[107] nor 'the fact that several equivalent legal norms involving the use of coercion coexist on one and the same territory'.[108]

99 See, especially, Virally (1960: 200–1), distinguishing a legal system's tendency to form 'structurally, a *closed* system' and its tendency to '*open* itself to other systems'.

100 Bobbio 1960: 186.

101 Carbonnier 1972: 213.

102 Kelsen 1967: 329.

103 1967: 333.

104 Dabin 1969: 24 (cf. 1950: 239).

105 1969: 34 (cf. 1950: 244).

106 F. Rigaux 1977*b*: 439; 1977*a*: 113.

107 Vanderlinden 1972: 19.

108 Ingber 1972: 83.

We shall understand by it the simple fact that several legal systems coexist at the same moment.[109] As distinct from the last two definitions, such a conception of legal pluralism supposes a plurality of systems and not just a plurality of legal *mechanisms* or *norms*. As distinct from each of the three definitions quoted, this conception does not require any supplementary condition, neither in terms of the identity of subjects of those systems (in many cases those subjects will be different) nor in terms of difference of those systems' contents (their contents can be at least partially identical), nor in terms of relations between those systems (in particular, such a relation is not necessarily one of equivalence or independence).

Accordingly, such a pluralist conception of law accepts first of all the coexistence of a plurality of legal systems of the same kind and, in particular, a plurality of state legal systems (unitary, federal, and federated), contrary to some writers' opinion that each state legal system would by nature be 'exclusive' and 'unique',[110] and would consider 'as legal only its own norms', regarding 'all others as irrelevant'.[111] Following Bobbio, one can speak, within such limits, of a 'state or national pluralism'.[112]

A pluralist conception of law is, however, also able to accept the coexistence of a plurality of legal systems that are different in kind, such as suprastate legal systems (the international legal order, or supranational legal orders like the legal order of the European Communities), infrastate legal systems (corporative legal orders), or transnational or deterritorialized legal systems (the legal order peculiar to a transnational group of commercial companies, or an ecclesiastical order).

This is what Bobbio calls 'institutional pluralism',[113] meaning the coexistence of legal systems of different kinds, corresponding to the diversity of 'institutions' or organized social groups.[114]

While we accept the idea that such a pluralist conception of law—which does not, in itself, prejudge any specific relation of independence between one legal system and others—gives a better account of legal reality than a monist conception,[115] to be convinced of the

[109] Similarly, in particular, Romano 1975: 77. [110] 1975: 106 n. 1.
[111] 1975: 107n. [112] Bobbio 1960: 188. [113] Ibid.
[114] This distinction largely intersects with that mentioned by Carbonnier, between a 'statist' and a 'spontaneist' orientation of legal pluralism (1972: 217). On the historical development of theories of legal pluralism, see, especially, Belley 1986: 11ff.
[115] On this, see Ost and van de Kerchove 1988.

pluralist conception it is not sufficient to maintain that 'the multiplicity of legal orders is a fact so obvious that no-one would dream of denying it'.[116] It is also necessary to agree on the criteria required for determining the *identity* of one legal system in relation to another and being able to establish that, in different types of hypothesis, such criteria find themselves effectively united.

(*b*) *Criteria of Identity*. How is one, first of all, to determine the identity of a legal system, or, if one prefers, what makes it separate from another?

One can easily accept, it seems, the idea that this identity is linked directly to a principle of unity binding different elements together so as to make them into a system. As has been seen, however, this principle of unity can itself take different forms: static or dynamic, formal or substantive, and hierarchical or circular. And it may be added, owing to the relative autonomy of law from society, that this unity is also largely determined by the existence of a social group of which the legal system forms a subset. However, in that none of these principles of unity seems able by itself to account for a legal system's specificity, it seems logical also to accept a plurality of criteria able to determine a concrete legal system's identity. Among these may be mentioned three distinct forms of autonomy, which may be termed 'social', 'organic', and 'organizational'. Contrary to most writers, who seem inclined to privilege one or other of these criteria exclusively, it seems to us preferable to accept that the identity of a legal system may have degrees, according to the extent to which the different criteria are united. In other words, one can accept that a legal system's autonomy in relation to other legal systems is as relative as its autonomy in relation to the social system and to other non-legal normative systems.

Such a hypothesis, it seems, can shed a lot of useful light on many classic legal debates.

As to the criterion of social autonomy, first, one may look at private agreements. Traditionally, as is familiar, most writers have refused to see in private agreements the existence of true legal norms. While one argument often called upon in support of this conception is that such acts' significance is individual and not general,[117] the

116 Virally 1960: 199.

117 Dabin 1969: 92, 'A legal rule has always been defined as involving generality' (cf. 1950: 281).

most decisive argument[118] seems to lie in the idea that 'the agreement of the parties . . . is never anything but a *private* law, which for that reason escapes the category of law defined as a social rule emanating from a group and created for the group'.[119] Consequently, it seems more correct to maintain that private agreements do not form a legal system separate from that of the state, albeit that they emanate from individuals, for the simple reason that individuals do not act as members of a group separate from society as a whole. This is also what such a writer as Romano seems to have accepted in the end. After maintaining that 'a legal act, which only creates relations, is not sufficient to give birth to objective law',[120] he came to recognize that legal acts 'give birth not only to relations but also to norms that regulate those relations and that are legal, in that the autonomy on which they are based derives from the State and that the State sanctions them'.[121] Even if one can speak in this case of an autonomous mode of production of legal norms—corresponding to the principle of autonomy of the will—this kind of production is not carried out within the framework of a legal system pertaining to individuals themselves, in the absence of what may be called a certain form of *social autonomy*, which would suppose the existence of a specific 'social body'.[122] On the other hand, in the case of what are called 'corporative rules'—that is, rules issued by a private group for the benefit of its members—one surely does find such a social entity, and these rules may therefore form a legal system separate from the state legal order, a system that could be termed 'corporative law'.[123]

Although some consider this first form of autonomy sufficient to determine a legal system's identity,[124] obviously one can conceive of other forms of autonomy whose presence could only reinforce that identity and moreover is considered by other writers to be equally necessary.

In this regard, we shall mention only the classic problem of a distinction to be drawn between a devolved administrative unit, a

118 Dabin himself maintains (1969: 96): 'Perhaps the argument often called upon in favour of the generality of a legal rule—that law, whose vocation is to govern the generality of the members of the group, itself includes generality—misses the point. For the terms *social* (or societal) and *general* are not necessarily in a relation of equivalence.' (cf. 1950: 283).

119 1969: 98 (cf. 1950: 284).

120 Romano 1975: 51. See also F. Rigaux 1974: 151.

121 Romano 1975: 51 n. 2.

122 1975: 25.

123 Dabin 1969: 44 (cf. 1950: 244).

124 See, especially, Romano 1975: 29–31; Lenoble 1984: 50.

decentralized territorial community, a federated State, and a unitary State. While one can accept that each of these entities presupposes the existence of a social organization endowed with a certain autonomy, it none the less appears that the differences between them also relate at least partially to other forms of autonomy.

As distinct from other entities, firstly, devolved administration possesses no *organic autonomy*,[125] which means that its agents, even though they are 'local managers' seconded to specific territorial communities, 'command in the name of the State'.[126] In consequence, the devolved agents act by delegation[127] and find themselves hierarchically subordinated to the State's central authorities.[128] Thus 'government remains *unitary* and only its exercise is geared down by the presence of an agent at the point where decisions have to be made'.[129]

A decentralized territorial community, on the other hand, is characterized by the existence of special organs that 'give rulings in the name of the secondary community from which they originate',[130] possess 'special prerogatives' and are able to oppose their 'sphere of autonomy' to the central government,[131] the latter possessing with regard to them only a power of tutelage and supervision.[132] *A fortiori* it can be accepted that this organic autonomy exists in the case of a federated State and a unitary State.

From the standpoint of such a criterion of autonomy, one could be tempted to accept as specific legal systems only the decentralized community, the federated State and the unitary State, excluding the devolved administrative unit. This would particularly seem to be the position taken by François,[133] who is prepared to call a 'legal order' only 'the set of legal norms resting directly or by delegation on a single non-delegated authority'[134] and considers two legal orders to be separate 'as long as there are several authorities, of which none is simply an organ of another'.[135] One cannot, however, avoid recalling that this criterion of autonomy not only is not the sole one conceivable but also is itself essentially relative. It is not in fact

125 Buttgenbach 1966. 126 Burdeau 1967: 363.
127 Buttgenbach 1966: 111.
128 1966: 107. 129 Burdeau 1967: 369. 130 1967: 363.
131 Buttgenbach 1966: 108.
132 1966: 107.
133 The ambiguity of his position is rightly stressed, however, by Lenoble (1984: 48).
134 François 1978: 155. 135 1978: 164.

difficult to grasp that, owing to the diversity of legal organs (constituent, legislative, regulatory, administrative and judicial organs, and organs of execution) with which a community may provide itself, one can perfectly well conceive that an entity may possess certain organs to the exclusion of others. In this way a territorial community may well possess a form of administration ensuring 'the operation of prerogatives similar to the functions of governing, regulating, compelling and even judging'.[136] However, these prerogatives are usually limited both in their content (only certain matters are envisaged) and in their nature (certain functions are excluded).

One may now take the view not only that decentralization 'may have degrees' but also that 'all cases are cases of relative decentralization'.[137]

This relativity, however, does not affect decentralization alone, for it can also be extended to entities other than decentralized communities. In fact, while in principle federated States probably enjoy very broad organic autonomy, in the sense that they have 'their own legislation, system of courts and public service ... to ensure the efficacy of their internal legal order',[138] it is no less certain that the powers devolved to their own organs are limited. The result is that federalism, like decentralization, 'expresses a way of sharing powers between the general community and particular communities'[139] and that, from the standpoint of the extent of their autonomy, 'the difference between a federal State and a decentralized unitary State is only a *difference of degree*'.[140] This remark may also be extended to other legal systems such as the international order. Although it can be observed that an international treaty containing directly applicable norms sometimes sets up 'organs peculiar' to the interstate legal order thus formed, as is the case with those 'supranational' orders which are the European Communities and the legal order created by the European Convention on Human Rights,[141] it has to be admitted that this situation is exceptional and that 'these organs are normally those of the States themselves, which are alone competent to administer and judge the particular situations subjected to their rules'.[142] The organic autonomy of the international legal order is thus also very limited—without it being necessary to

136 Delpérée 1980: 434. 137 Burdeau 1967: 370. 138 1967: 471.
139 Delpérée 1980: 436.
140 Rousseau 1974: 165. *Contra*, Carré de Malberg 1920: 170.
141 F. Rigaux 1984: 179. 142 1984: 177.

conclude that, for that reason, it does not form a specific legal system.

In addition, the relativity of a legal system's organic autonomy sometimes also arises from the existence of a 'functional duplication', in terms of which the same agents are organs of several different legal systems. In this case, it must be accepted that such a legal system, while possessing its own organs, has no organs that are exclusive to it. For example, it has been said in France that, 'because of the double interest involved, mayors exercise their governmental function as much in the capacity of an organ of the commune as in that of an agent, in the commune, of the State'.[143] Likewise, in Belgium it is thought that 'the organs of provincial and communal administration frequently intervene in matters of general interest, where they act not as decentralized authorities charged with the management of regional and local interests but as devolved organs of central government'.[144]

Though one can perceive in these various phenomena that the criterion of organic autonomy has some inherent limitations, one can also mention a last form of autonomy, capable of determining, or at least reinforcing, a legal system's identity: what is sometimes called *constitutional autonomy*,[145] which could also be called organizational, in the sense of a legal system's 'faculty of self-organization'.[146]

Traditionally, it can be observed, it is this last form of autonomy that has often been called upon to distinguish a federated State from a decentralized community. Thus Carré de Malberg, following Jellinek in particular, thought that a State that is a member of a federal State would be characterized by its 'autonomy', while a decentralized community would be defined by a simple faculty of 'self-administration' (*Selbstverwaltung*).[147] It can be seen, however, that Carré de Malberg does not state the concept of autonomy in its organic sense but in a constitutional or organizational sense, since he explains that 'for a territorial community to be a State, it is necessary and sufficient for it to possess and exercise by virtue of its *own Constitution*, that is, its *own power to organize itself*, all the functions of state power'.[148] Likewise, Burdeau has held that 'The most

143 Carré de Malberg 1920: 180.
144 Buttgenbach 1966: 114.
145 Rousseau 1974: 167.
146 Ibid.; Burdeau 1967: 407.
147 Carré de Malberg 1920: 171.
148 Ibid.

important illustration of this difference is taken from the power of *self-organization*. States that are members of a federal State *give themselves their own constitution*; contrarily, a decentralized community owes its mode of organization to the laws of the State on which it depends'.[149]

The interest of such a concept here is obvious. On one side it overlaps remarkably with the terminology and hypotheses developed by recent theories of autopoiesis. On the other, it equally recalls the self-referential and self-organizing nature of legal systems as conceived by such writers as Kelsen and Hart.

For Kelsen, it will be remembered, the essential characteristic of law is that it '*regulates its own* creation and application'.[150] So far as this form of organization finds its ultimate principle in the existence of a basic norm, it seems that a legal system's identity depends on it possessing a *basic norm of its own* which both forms the basis of validity and ensures the unity of the set of norms belonging to it.[151] However, because of the monist postulate of the cognitive 'unity of all law',[152] Kelsen has to trace all legal norms to a *single* basic norm, whether that of state law or that of international law,[153] according to which one might recognize the primacy of the one or the other. In Kelsen, therefore, the conception of law as self-organizing leads necessarily to reducing the problem of a legal system's identity to its unicity.

Hart begins from a very similar hypothesis, since he stresses the self-referential nature of the legal rules that he terms 'secondary', explaining that they 'are all concerned with the primary rules themselves' and 'specify the ways in which the primary rules may be conclusively ascertained, introduced, eliminated, varied, and the fact of their violation conclusively determined'.[154] Now, it is precisely the introduction of this type of rule that, according to Hart, makes it possible to pass from a pre-legal to a legal world and leads to the view that the union of the three general categories of secondary rules that he distinguishes is 'enough to convert the régime of primary rules into what is indisputably a legal system'.[155] Among these secondary rules, there is however one which seems to acquire a privileged status: the 'rule of recognition', which, like Kelsen's basic

[149] Burdeau 1967: 407. [150] 1967: 71 (our emphasis), cf. 198.
[151] 1967: 195. [152] 1967: 328. [153] 1967: 332–3.
[154] Hart 1961: 92. [155] 1961: 91.

norm, specifies 'the criteria in terms of which the validity of laws' is 'ultimately assessed'[156] and by that token may be considered to form 'the foundations of a legal system'.[157] It can then be judged that the minimal condition on which a legal system possesses an identity in relation to another is that it is composed not only of rules of behaviour but also of a rule of recognition peculiar to it and making it possible for it to identify those rules as its own. As against Kelsen, however, Hart does not end by reducing the set of legal systems to unicity. Although he expresses serious doubts as to whether the rules of international law form a 'system'[158]—in the absence of a true rule of recognition—Hart readily admits explicitly the existence of a plurality of state legal systems,[159] each endowed with its own rule of recognition.

As with the concept of organic autonomy, however, it must be remembered that this faculty of self-organization of state legal systems is itself essentially relative. Although we would be inclined not to draw from this the same conclusions as he does, one could take up Kelsen's idea that 'The historical states, that is, the positive national legal orders, are neither entirely centralized nor entirely decentralized.'[160]

As concerns federated States, it can be said that their 'mode of organization . . . is not always autonomous' but 'sometimes imposed, whether totally or partially'.[161] It has also been pointed out that 'the "constitutional" function falling to federated communities boils down to very little: the faculty of providing themselves with rules of internal organization (usually by applying detailed and imperative prescriptions of the Constitution)'.[162]

Federal and unitary States themselves do not entirely escape from this principle of relativity, since 'in its internal constitutional structure, the State has exclusive competence—but, in exercising that competence, it ought to conform to the law of nations, for instance by adhering to such principles as that of State continuity, so that that competence, though exclusive, is regulated to some extent'.[163]

Lastly, it may be added that the configuration of some States, such as present-day Belgium, illustrates the possibility of conceiving degrees of autonomy which, in terms of the classical categories, lie 'sometimes within and sometimes outside the federal model'.[164]

[156] 1961: 110. [157] 1961: 97. [158] 1961: 231. [159] 1983: 337.
[160] Kelsen 1967: 314. [161] Rousseau 1974: 167.
[162] Delpérée 1980: 435.
[163] Rousseau 1974: 87. [164] See, especially, Delpéré 1972: 608.

It can therefore be seen that, while a legal system's identity seems to be logically tied to the existence of a certain autonomy, one cannot but observe the inevitable relativity of that autonomy, having regard as much to the diversity of the criteria in the light of which it is to be assessed as to the degree to which they are fulfilled. The result is a 'fuzzy image' rather like a 'badly adjusted and badly aimed telescope, which can only ever give a blurred picture'.[165] Any theoretical delimitation that means to deny or more simply ignore such relativity seems, however, arbitrary and must give way to a pluralist vision of law that accepts both the coexistence of a plurality of legal systems and the coexistence of identities with several faces.

4.6.2. *Diversity of Relations Between Legal Systems*

This plural conception, however, affects not only the problem of legal systems' *identity* but, equally, the *relations* that exist between those systems and which, themselves, may be of several different types.

In following the teaching of a writer such as Kelsen, it is tempting to think that relations between legal systems can end only in total integration or total indifference. In this regard, the theories developed first by Romano and further by writers such as Bobbio, Virally, and F. Rigaux seem to us plainly more fruitful and effective in describing legal reality in all its complexity. While one can accept the idea that the integration pure and simple of one legal system into another ends up dissolving their duality in the unity of the system thus enlarged, on the other hand there are several possible forms of relation between legal systems that are able to preserve their respective identities and, in doing so, their plurality.

A first distinction required here is that one legal system, with respect to another, may find itself in a relation of either 'relevance' or 'irrelevance', relevance being defined by Romano as the fact that 'an order's existence, content or efficacy conforms to conditions set by another order' and irrelevance as the fact 'that there is no relation between them'.[166]

Irrelevance, it must be stressed, has no effect on the existence of a legal system or on its internal efficacy; its only consequence is that that system will be ignored as such by another system and will not

[165] 1972: 660.

[166] Romano 1975: 106. ['Efficacy': in this context, production of legal effects. Tr.]

produce any legal effect with respect to that other system.[167] The possibility of such an absence of relations illustrates an extreme situation that may be called the 'watertightness' of a legal system[167] or the existence of a 'closed system' which 'functions naturally by closing itself up and accepting as valid only the norms that it secretes'.[169] Irrelevance consists sometimes of complete indifference[170] and sometimes of rejecting[171] a legal system's claims to existence—which is to treat it as a simple fact, possibly illicit,[172] such as a criminal gang or a terrorist movement.

Relevance can take various forms. There may be an extreme relation, whether of independence (as illustrated principally by relations between States or, possibly, between Church and State) or of subordination (as illustrated by relations between decentralized communities or private associations and the State). There may also, however, be an intermediate relation, whether of co-ordination (as illustrated very broadly by relations between the international legal order and state legal orders,[173] or similarly the linkages among several state legal orders in terms of private international law)[174] or of presupposition or 'dependence' (as is the case with the international legal order, which presupposes the existence of States and finds itself, in that sense, in a situation of dependence with regard to them).[175]

As Romano has very rightly said, it can also be added that these relations can themselves be viewed from different angles, since the legal relevance of one order to another can be considered from the standpoint of its existence, its content, or its effects.

Without being able to embark on a study of these relations here, it is sufficient to note that they amply manifest the diversity and complexity of the relations that can exist between different legal systems. For the idea of a single and closed legal system is substituted the idea of a plurality of systems that are more or less 'open'[176] in relation to

167 1975: 86.

168 François 1978: 171. We differ from François in taking this situation to be not characteristic of *all* legal orders but exceptional.

169 Virally 1960: 200. 170 Bobbio 1960: 195. 171 Ibid.

172 Romano 1975: 145.

173 See, especially, Virally 1960: 209, 'International or supranational organizations ... are still framed by an order of *co-ordination*, in that their organs' decisions are immediately applicable only within the international order.'

174 See also Batiffol 1956: 19, 'The modern development of private international law suggests that it is moving toward an order of systems, in the sense of working toward the *co-ordination* of separate, coexistent systems.'

175 Romano 1975: 114. 176 See Raz 1979: 119.

each other, where the frequency of relations of co-ordination, or even of total or partial subordination, means that complete independence of one system from another, and *a fortiori* its indifference, are relatively exceptional cases.

The resulting 'interpenetrations' of systems[177] have extremely important consequences, especially on the level of theory of validity and legal interpretation.

If the validity of a legal norm is defined as its membership of a legal system, it appears that this membership can be determined at least partially by rules belonging to another system. On the other hand, the problem of a rule's validity appears as a problem of a partly different kind from its applicability, in that a legal system can recognize the applicability of norms belonging exclusively to another legal system, that is, having no validity within the first system. Lastly, the problem of applicability appears in its turn to be separate from the problem of a norm's efficacy, in that one system can recognize the applicability of norms belonging to another legal system, at the same time as limiting its effects when asked to apply it within its own framework.

Similar problems arise with regard to interpretation, in that a norm belonging to one legal system can be interpreted by courts belonging to another system when the latter are asked to apply them. In this case, it can be imagined that the first legal system will in principle reserve to itself power to interpret them, be that in the course of proceedings or on final appeal; in other cases, the first system largely abandons such power to the other's courts. In that case, it is still for those courts to decide whether to conform generally to the interpretation given to these norms within the order to which they belong or to interpret those norms in complete autonomy.[178]

The study of relations between legal systems also gives rise to a second reflection. Kelsen's way of conceptualizing the unity of a legal system gives the impression that this problem is to be resolved exclusively in terms of validation 'from above' of legal norms occupying a hierarchically lower level. As Hart has rightly remarked, this relation seems not to depend only on one order's unilateral claim to include another order, or even subordinate that other order

[177] See Virally 1964: 491; F. Rigaux 1984: 175.
[178] On this point see, especially, F. Rigaux 1983: 1203ff.

to itself, but also on reciprocal recognition 'from below' of such a claim.[179] It seems possible, moreover, to extend this remark to all the other relations that we have mentioned between different legal systems, which appear not only as linear or hierarchical relations of grounding but also as tangled relations of reciprocal recognition.[180] M.-F. Rigaux has spoken similarly of 'network structuration of normativity', pointing thereby to 'the inability of any hierarchical perspective to express the reality of relations of interpenetration between separate normative orders'.[181]

This position of principle does not, however, exclude the existence of cases of non-reciprocity,[182] of tensions or even radical oppositions among the attitudes respectively adopted by the systems involved.[183] This divergence can lead to cases of unilateral relevance, where the existence of a relation produces legal effects only within the frame of the system that recognizes it. It can also end up with incompatible and even completely converse claims and find expression, at the extreme, in a will to pure and simple elimination.

In conclusion, it is still possible to assert that a pluralist conception of law dissolves the monist equation between legal space and territorial space, which maintains both that to a particular territory there can correspond only a single legal system—which, at the extreme, would coincide with the territory of the universal legal order[184]—and, reciprocally, that to every legal system there corresponds a particular territory. This equation seems wrong in two ways. On the one hand, because 'several legal spaces can be superimposed in the same place, which means that none of the systems involved has a territory of its own'.[185] On the other, because one can observe the existence of 'non-territorial legal orders',[186] such as Gypsy law, canon law, or the law peculiar to a transnational economic group exercising 'delocalized' powers.[187] To question such an

179 See Hart 1983: 337; 1961: 117, where Hart applies this idea to a colony whose courts no longer recognize the Westminster Parliament's competence to legislate for it.

180 On this, see Ost and van de Kerchove 1987: 244ff.

181 M.-F. Rigaux 1985: 270.

182 Romano 1975: 144–5.

183 Hart 1961: 118.

184 See also Kelsen 1967: 315, 'just as all states—so far as they are considered to be coordinated legal communities—must be regarded as members of a comprehensive international legal community, so also all state territories must be regarded as partial territorial spheres of validity of the universal legal order'.

185 Carbonnier 1972: 205.

186 F. Rigaux 1977*b*: 429.

187 1977*b*: 443.

equation fundamentally relativizes the notion of legal space: by dissociating it from its material and geographical substratum, it makes it a 'psychological construction',[188] a 'pure notion', an 'imaginary space' and even, at the extreme, a 'fiction'.[189]

This *spatial* relativity of a legal system is equalled only by its *temporal* relativity, as we shall see in the following chapter.

[188] Carbonnier 1972: 205. [189] F. Rigaux 1977*b*: 442.

5
Legal System and Temporality

The study of systems through time—their emergence, evolution, and equilibration, their way of handling the contradictory imperatives of adaptation and stability, their ability to alter their own rules of functioning, and their disappearance or possible entropy—is an important area of systems theory. After defining a system's state, or its situation of optimal equilibrium, one goes on to look at the various factors of alteration, both internal and external, that can affect its evolution; likewise, one uncovers the mechanisms (particularly of retroaction) that can restore the system's equilibrium or ensure it a higher level of integration, that is, a stronger capacity to adapt. Thus one gradually clarifies the phases of the system's transition and its laws of evolution. In this type of study, two approaches are often opposed: the structuralist method, which stresses the system's relatively stable elements, its invariant structures which define synchronic properties; and the genetic method, which emphasizes its variable elements, its factors of irreversible evolution which define diachronic properties.[1] The particular virtue of the systemic method is to link these two approaches: one arrives at a true understanding of change through taking account of a system's internal structures.

In order to pursue the question of the relations between legal system and time, we shall address the following questions in turn, bearing in mind that the problematic of legal change in its relation to social change has already been dealt with in the previous chapter, when studying the relations of legal systems to their environment. The first question, which is fundamental, concerns the relation between juridicity and systematicity: is law born in the form of a system? If, as we think, the answer to this question must be positive, it is still necessary to work out what kind of system is found in primitive forms of law (Section 5.1). The second question concerns the conditions of emergence of legal systems in the modern sense of

[1] Similarly, Walliser 1977: 225.

the term—systems that are largely formal and institutionalized. The theories of the union of primary and secondary norms (Hart) and of 'double institutionalization' (Bohannan), which will be used here for reference, will be explained and worked out further with the help of various other conceptions of legal evolution (Section 5.2). A third discussion will be devoted to the historical diversification of legal systems into several models that nowadays one tries to study under the rubrics of various 'families' of law (Section 5.3). A fourth section will then attempt, in a synchronic perspective, to pick out the minimal conditions necessary to the maintenance of a legal system (Section 5.4). Returning, next, to the diachronic approach, we shall try to show the diversity of legal temporalities and how systems of law, weighing these different rhythms of evolution, try to equilibrate change and conservation so as to resist entropy and increase their homeostatic capacities (Section 5.5). Finally, in a sixth section, we shall suggest a form of periodization of this legal evolution that will relate the levels of complexity of legal systems and the special features of the temporalities that emerge as dominant in them.

5.1. GENESIS OF JURIDICITY AND SYSTEMATICITY

The question whether law is born in the form of a system is fearsome. It seems to involve a decision on the natures of both law and system. Avoiding the kind of discussion that would have difficulty in escaping the metaphysical traps of the *a priori* determination of 'essences', we shall confine ourselves to observing, in the train of anthropologists and ethnologists, that the phenomena of primitive law certainly do not take the systematized forms with which we are familiar in our own part of the world. Social behaviour definitely exhibits regularities, but their legal specificity is far from sure. The rules are customary in nature and their content—as well as not being verbalized to any great extent—is hard to distinguish from the imperatives of morality, religion, taboos, and mores. There are no institutions formally authorized to state, alter, and apply the law; the community itself ensures respect for rules of which it does not imagine itself to be the author—tracing them, through tradition, to a sacred and immemorial origin. Thus there is no legal system in the modern sense, formalized and institutionalized: no codified rules, no concentrated political power, and no centralized administrative organization. Does that amount to saying that this kind of legal regulation does not form a system, at least in the basic sense given to the term by Arnaud: a consistent ordering of representations and practices emanating from a unitary and exclusive form of *legal reason* (a kind of ideology or world-view)?[2]

Understood in this sense, the idea of system does indeed apply to the forms of primitive law. Without a comparative anthropological study, which would exceed the limits of the present work, we shall confine ourselves to a single illustration taken from the investigation by Verdier and Le Roy of traditional African legal orders.[3]

'In traditional black Africa', Verdier writes,

> government is not exercised through statute and law is not laid down by an individual; cast back to the moment of society's foundation, the law is its basis; robed in myth, it is actualized in rites. Individuals' rights are joined to corresponding obligations with the status of laws and flow not from power belonging to individuals as such but from the concrete positions and real functions that they assume within society.[4]

Thus social life is arranged in three domains—kinship, territory, and religion—which Verdier calls 'particular legal orders' in the sense of 'systems of ideas, values and usages allocating to each person their condition of life'.[5] The 'fundamental law' that ensures the group's cohesion and co-ordinates these particular orders by connecting them to the order of the invisible and the sacred does not enjoy any logical pre-eminence like Kelsen's *Grundnorm* or Hart's 'rule of recognition'; nor is it an instrument of the power of the Prince.[6] The group's fundamental law is nothing other than its foundation myth, which simultaneously explains the society's position in the universe and utters the fundamental prohibitions. By reactivating this narrative, individuals learn that they participate in a 'nature of things', a cosmic order originally instituted by the gods and victorious over initial disorder, which still constantly threatens to win out. Also, the law maintaining this order has as much to do with prohibition as with natural necessity, and what is important in cases of transgression is probably less to punish the guilty than to restore the ruptured harmony between the visible and the invisible, to re-establish the compromised equilibrium deep in the nature of things.

Such a law is, of course, nobody's monopoly, not even that of a

[2] Arnaud 1981: 27. [3] Verdier 1984: 109 ff. [4] 1984: 109.
[5] 1984: 111. [6] 1984: 115.

God who, such as Yahweh on Sinai, gave it to his people. The foundation myth comes rather 'from below', emanating from the group and being traced back, immemorially, to the tradition of the ancestors. Let us note again this feature of African 'law', to which we shall return in a moment: 'Located in a time of before and return, the law is not of such a nature as to give rise to transformations for the future. Its plasticity certainly allows it to ratify an evolution of mores, but it is in no way created in order to innovate and to promote social changes.'[7]

The everyday manifestation of this kind of law is found in custom, which belongs as much to the socio-cosmic register as to the socio-political domain. First, it appears as a system of connections between the visible world and the invisible world of the ancestors and cosmic energies; secondly, it is the set of ways of doing things that are considered indispensable to the reproduction of social relations and to group survival. In these two functions, custom does not seem especially either judicial or legal. The very concept of 'rule' seems somewhat inadequate to describe it; it has rather to be understood as the moral of a tale. Moreover, its mode of transmission, by oral witness and periodic recitation, is revealing in this regard. Far from having the fixity of statute, the 'moral(ity)' of custom can be interpreted according to the particular needs of the moment. Customs also do not claim in any way to form a consistent system of rules, anything like a *corpus iuris*; the important thing in the spirit of custom is not so much its content, which lacks precision and is evidently variable, as the container, a particular way of approaching problems and resolving conflicts, which forms part of the transmission and reproduction, by palaver and conciliation, of the attitudes and values indispensable to group survival and community cohesion.[8]

This way of producing a social rule is connected with a mode of exercising power very different from that which will prevail later. In such a customary society, the exercise of power has two particular features: multiplicity and interdependence. As multiple, power seems not to belong to anybody since it is diffracted into different functions: the head of the family, district, or village responsible for initiation and the sacred wood; the smith protecting goods and persons; the hunter able to master energies and act as healer: everyone, according to their rôle and status, has one foot in the invisible and is recognized as 'herald' or 'spokesperson' of custom. This differenti-

[7] 1984: 117. [8] On all this, see Le Roy 1984: 210–40.

ation of responsibilities also requires an interaction of functions: that each person, at least in certain respects, is subject to the authority of another creates a reciprocity which, in its turn, reinforces the reproduction of the communitarian ideology, the 'spirit of custom'.[9]

Can this type of social control, conflict resolution, and exercise of power be classified as 'legal'—given that it is not moulded into a system of formal rules or arranged in a specific institutional set? Some anthropologists say not. Roberts, doubting that the concept of 'rule' even has any importance in some primitive societies, prefers to analyse their functioning in terms of 'order' and 'conflict'.[10] Others prefer a greatly enlarged concept of juridicity and reply to the question in the affirmative. Malinowski, for example, maintains that there is law when there appears a set of obligations considered as rights by some and as duties by others, and maintained in force by mechanisms of reciprocity and publicity inherent in the society under consideration.[11] This is also Gluckman's conception: when a society observes rules and penalizes those who break them, it lives under the régime of law, even if there is a lack of specific institutions.[12]

All told, this debate seems to be rather pointless, the respective positions being obviously functions of the *a priori* definition of juridicity adopted by the particular writer. What seems to be established, on any estimate, is that a traditional society does not possess a body of law in the same sense as that which reigns in a modern society. It is not impossible to suppose that this difference largely overlaps with that concerning the nature of normative systems in force in either model of society: in the first case, a substantive and implicit system of attitudes and values; in the second, a formal system of rules and institutions. Also, we will be able to get on with our enquiry by studying the passage from one social model to another with the help of, precisely, the concept of system.

5.2. DIACHRONIC PERSPECTIVE. THE EMERGENCE OF FORMAL AND INSTITUTIONAL SYSTEMS

In the anthropological literature, the threshold of juridicity is most often ascertained with the help of the criterion of 'double institutionalization' proposed by Bohannan, which fixes on the emergence

[9] 1984: 228–30. [10] Roberts 1979: 26–9. [11] Malinowski 1926: 58.
[12] Gluckman 1965: 182.

of a system of specific rules and institutions, supposing something like a break from the customary universe, an internal differentiation of the traditional ethic, and a division of community power. For Bohannan, any society has a certain number of primary institutions, such as the family; these institutions produce customary rules based on the idea of reciprocity. But such societies produce law only when new institutions—specifically legal and secondary—effect a re-institutionalization of the customary norms in force in a group: a legislative organ reformulates them, courts ensure their interpretation and executive agencies guarantee their application. This institutional duplication is also accompanied by a duplication of the norms produced: some are the more or less faithful transcription of customs in force in the group, while others are connected with secondary institutions and regulate the reformulation of the first kind of norm.[13]

Bohannan presumably has in mind the model developed by Hart: since a traditional society has only customary rules of behaviour (primary rules), the passage from a 'pre-legal' to a legal world is achieved when that society provides itself with secondary rules, conferring on both officials and individuals particular competences to identify, alter, and guarantee the application of primary rules. Such a union of primary and secondary rules achieves, according to Hart, 'what is indisputably a legal system', as opposed to the earlier situation classified as a 'régime of primary rules'[14] and which finds an equivalent in the body of rules of etiquette or those of public international law.[15] According to Hart, such a transformation would ensure a threefold progress with regard to the defects of uncertainty, rigidity, and inefficacy that characterize the customary régime. While some writers contest this last point,[16] custom seems in fact to be largely internalized by the group, hence known and applied simultaneously; moreover, as has been seen, its extremely simple structure ensures its adaptation to evolutionary changes—while in contrast the model preferred by Hart and Bohannan is today assuredly the central reference of the problematic that we are dealing with.

The emergence of specifically legal systems thus proceeds from a process of specification (the legal set, formerly a subset of the ethical set, gradually separates itself from it, in a passage from concentric to

[13] Bohannan 1967: 45–50. [14] Hart 1961: 91. [15] 1961: 228–31.
[16] Allott 1980: IX.

partially secant circles)[17] common to all systems: 'Every system', Chevallier writes, 'results from a process of differentiation within a physical, biological, or social context, until then undifferentiated and homogeneous'.[18] At the same time as there emerges a principle of differentiation of the legal from every other order, there is determined a criterion of system membership and there develop processes of mutual linkage between the norms of this system, which will no longer evolve autonomously but from now on will interact. With the secondary norms and the corresponding institutions there come into place techniques of self-regulation and a certain closedness of the set: what becomes manifest here is surely the sign of the emergence of a system.

This model, although extremely abstract and analytical, can be completed with the help of a variety of considerations drawn from several writers who have tried to conceptualize the evolution of legal systems; it can also be modulated into a succession of stages, since 'double institutionalization' obviously has not happened in a day.

The passage from 'law of the elders' to 'law of the chief', to use an expression current among the Diola of Senegal, may be explained first by considering the society's level of complexity. In the first model, characterized by a subsistence economy and domestic production, social rôles are only weakly differentiated, so that there is minimal division of tasks and the rules apply indifferently to all. On the other hand, once a society has reached a more developed stage, supposing the formation of surpluses and exchange of commodities, division of labour increases, tasks become specialized and, inevitably, the rules diversify, especially at the initiative of individuals. Durkheim conceived social evolution in these terms: in the first model, solidarity is mechanical, rules are simple, and their operation is ensured by the community as a whole; in the second case, solidarity is organic, rules are diverse and complex, and they are applied by specialized agencies.[19]

In the same order of ideas, such a writer as Maine has interpreted the transition from the traditional to the 'civilized' world as a passage from 'status' to 'contract'. While, in the first case, individuals are scarcely separated from the family, in which they assume various stereotyped 'statuses', rôles, or functions, at the very point where property relations are not differentiated from family relations his-

[17] 1980: 25. [18] Chevallier 1983: 14.

[19] Durkheim 1984; see also Chambliss and Seidman 1982: 25ff.

tory moves in the direction of a progressive autonomization of the individual, for whom contract will soon become the expression of the most efficacious legal will.[20] Here too, the explanation turns out to be complementary to Hart's: it appears in fact that the binding force of private contract is made possible only by the intervention of a secondary rule authorizing individuals to create law by the simple effect of their declarations of will (as in Article 1134 of the Civil Code).

Another aspect of this passage concerns the mode of conflict regulation prevailing in each of these types of society: while, within a communitarian framework, the major imperative is the restoration of solidarity, in a legalistic and statist framework resolving a conflict means applying a rule by sanctioning whoever has broken it. In the first case, the conflict will be stifled as far as possible and, if it gets to the light of day, it will be resolved by conciliation and arbitration, so that in the game of palaver not all the winnings will lie on one side ('not losing face'); on the other hand, in a society where bonds of solidarity are slackened conflict is resolved by the strict and unilateral application of a pre-established norm—one of the litigants must crush his or her adversary. In this logic of conflict, what appears in the end as the real stake is the rule's integrity rather than the group's cohesion.[21]

The emergence of modern, formal, and institutional legal systems also seems to go together with a process of differentiation of the community. We have already mentioned in this regard the progressive loosening of bonds within the family and the correlative individualization of its members. But it is also necessary to stress, following Marxist writers in particular, the splitting of the group into social classes with partially antagonistic interests and, in addition, the division of society against itself, so that it is then duplicated into civil society and State.[22] The writers who have stressed this reveal here a certain idealism inherent in the 'double institutionalization' thesis. Far from always constituting progress and operating with kid gloves, the passage from custom to law has often had to take the form of a violent process, related to deep social conflicts. Diamond, in particular, tries to show that secondary norms and specifically legal institutions have often been used to set up a tax system,

[20] Maine 1912: 26–9, 123–74.
[21] Similarly, Chambliss and Seidman 1982: 29 ff, 39 ff.
[22] See, especially, Engels 1902: 107 ff.

through which a central, bureaucratized, and militarized government could manage to impose itself on traditional communities and supplant their customs, tolerated only to the extent of their compatibility with the centralizing plans of the Prince.[23] Similarly, Seagle emphasizes that law originates in the pathology of social relations and that its development presupposes frequent disturbances of social equilibrium.[24] This argument resurrects the old theme of a 'collapse of the state of nature', so often invoked by modern iusnaturalists: is not the passage to civil society, to its constitution and institutions, explained here also by the uncertainties and dangers prevailing in the 'state of nature'? In their own vocabularies, Hobbes, Locke, Kant, and Rousseau have thus largely anticipated the ideas of Hart and Bohannan; certain pages of Locke in particular directly prefigure Hart's observations concerning the utility, in civil society, of secondary norms.[25]

The transition from the pre-legal to the legal world can be explained further with reference to a well-known feature on which Weber concentrated entirely: the form of rationality prevailing in each of the two models. As we know, on the basis of this criterion Weber was able to construct a typology of different legal systems and indicate the direction of their transformation. It will be recalled that the great German sociologist distinguished irrational systems (those that do not employ general norms), according either to their content (concrete and particular values which dictate solutions in the absence of *a priori* principles) or to their form (the use of irrational procedures such as oracles, ordeals, or duels), and rational systems (based on general rules), according either to their content (solutions grounded in the principles of a particular ideology) or to their form (the structuration of law in abstract and hierarchized concepts and categories).[26] Evolution, he suspected, proceeds in the direction of a progressive rationalization of legal systems:

> the formal qualities of the law emerge as follows: arising in primitive legal procedure from a combination of magically conditioned formalism and irrationality conditioned by revelation, they proceed to increasingly specialized juridical and logical rationality and systematization, sometimes passing through the detour of theocratically or patrimonially conditioned substantive and informal expediency. Finally, they assume, at least from an

[23] Diamond 1978: 241 ff. [24] Seagle 1946: 36.
[25] Locke 1960: ch. 9, especially sect. 131.
[26] Weber 1978: 656–7.

external viewpoint, an increasingly logical sublimation and deductive rigour and develop an increasingly rational technique in procedure.[27]

In questioning state interventionism and the accompanying legislative inflation, nowadays some writers, belonging to the neo-liberal tendency, seem to want to restore traditional spontaneous orders, in opposition to modern conventional orders, whose perverse effects can easily be shown. It will be sufficient here to mention the classification of legal and social orders proposed by Hayek, who distinguishes two opposed categories: *cosmos* and *taxis*.[28] The order understood as *cosmos* is spontaneous order, self-generated and ripened by time. Its equilibrium is endogenous: the result of the combined yet not intentional action of its innumerable agents, who, although they behave with particular kinds of regularity, nevertheless do not verbalize the rules that they in fact adopt. The social models referred to are those of custom, language, and the market (Adam Smith's 'invisible hand'). On the other hand, the order understood as *taxis* is planning and construction, organization rather than organism. An intentional product of human action, its equilibrium is exogenous; in the form of orders and commands, it operates entirely in the service of its creators' intentions. While law (*cosmos*), a set of customary and case-law principles of 'just behaviour', is not invented by anybody, legislation (*taxis*) expresses a devotion to social organization by the legislator, whose intervention the neo-liberals evidently want to reduce to a bare minimum.

The different theories just mentioned form a range of attempts to conceptualize the evolution of legal systems;[29] although developed independently of Hart's and Bohannan's ideas, they are broadly compatible with and clarify some important aspects of them. So it is possible to refine those ideas still further, by showing, following numerous writers, how the various secondary rules and the legal institutions corresponding to them are instituted by stages.

Thus MacCormick emphasizes that not all secondary norms are imposed at the same time. Very likely, rules of decision appeared first, followed much later by rules of change.[30] Bobbio systematizes this approach. Every normative system—law, grammar, the game of society, systems of technical rules, and moral doctrine—seeks its point of equilibrium, corresponding to its particular needs. Some

[27] 1978: 882. [28] Hayek 1982: 35 ff.
[29] On this question generally, see also Rottleuthner 1986*b*: 217 ff.
[30] MacCormick 1981: 103–20.

systems, called 'simple', like iusnaturalists' state of nature, are satisfied with norms whose addressees are simultaneously their authors and their judges. In other hypotheses, such systems are no longer able to direct behaviour efficiently. They then add to themselves either sanctioning rules or rules of change and form 'semi-complex' systems.

A game, such as football, whose rules are complete from the start, requires no procedure for change; however, its effective operation involves the intervention of referees applying sanctions to miscreant players. On the other hand, a system like that of technical rules requires constant updating—though it has no need of institutionalized sanctions, since not to adhere to the rules results in failure to obtain the result desired. These two types of semi-complex systems pursue, with a view to their survival and development, two opposite strategies: conservation in the first case, innovation in the second. Legal systems have employed both of these strategies in succession. International law is an example of a semi-complex system in search of its equilibrium, turning sometimes to an international court, sometimes to suprastate organizations, in order to supersede the merely customary régime of primary norms of which the States are both the authors and the addressees. On the other hand, national bodies of law, which may be called 'complex legal systems', generally manage to operate simultaneously techniques of stabilization and innovation, thus providing their rules with a sort of dynamic equilibrium.[31]

The transformations affecting the different concrete historical legal systems have, of course, led to a degree of differentiation among them. Study of the different forms that they take from a synchronic point of view—the 'families' of legal systems—belongs to comparative law, while the diachronic perspective, which we have used up to now, belonged to legal anthropology and sociology. The aim of the next section will be to review some results of this study of 'families' of legal systems.

5.3. SYNCHRONIC PERSPECTIVE. 'FAMILIES' OF LEGAL SYSTEMS

The diversity of the empirical legal systems to be found on the planet is considerable. However, common features, 'family resemblances', entitle comparatists to try to construct groupings in order to over-

[31] On all this, see Bobbio 1971: 114–22.

come local differences in forms of regulation, so as to be able to pick out the underlying structures. None the less, such classifications give rise to innumerable controversies: when the very concept of a 'family' of legal systems is not simply rejected, debates multiply over the criteria of classification and the ways of working out groupings on the basis of those criteria.[32]

It is therefore not surprising that the literature contains a great number of attempts at classification of this kind. Friedman, for example, proposes to group all legal systems by combining two criteria relating to the forms of legal reasoning developed in them: whether the system accepts or does not accept premisses of non-legal reasoning (the system will be called 'open' in the first case and 'closed' in the second); or whether the system accepts or does not accept that intentional changes may be made to it.[33]

Four types of legal system result from this matrix:

Type 1 *Sacred Law and Other Closed Systems*. In this case, the system is both closed and immutable. The holy book (Torah, Koran, and so on) is supposed to contain the whole of the law, so that decisions must refer only to it. In such a context, development of the system is conceivable only at the price of employing various fictions, which, with greater or lesser probability, attach new solutions to the letter of the text referred to. Friedman considers the Common Law to fit this model.

Type 2 *Legal Science*. In this case, rather paradoxically, the choice of premisses is given but the system accepts change. The reference model is drawn from the classical conception of science, which, although in constant progress, does not create new rules but limits itself to discovering them, to 'reading' them in nature. Friedman places Continental Law in this category.

Type 3 *Customary Law*. This model is the converse of the previous one: the system is open but rejects change. Judges largely find inspiration in solutions dictated by good sense, customs, and traditions, but no legal authority arrogates to itself the power to make intentional alterations to the system.

Type 4 *Revolutionary and Welfare Legality*. In these hypotheses, the system is both open and evolving; change is valued for itself and

[32] See, on this idea, Krislov 1985: 25ff; Podgórecki 1985: 1ff.

[33] Friedman 1977: 81ff.; 1975: 237ff.

various extra-legal knowledges are imposed on the judge and the legislator.

Although stimulating, classifications of this kind are obviously debatable. In his celebrated work, *Les grands systèmes de droit contemporains*,[34] David sticks to the more traditional groupings based on both legal technique (terminology, and rules of creation and application) and the conception of social order. The aim, which is purely didactic, is to group all legal systems in a number of families, as found in linguistics and in religious and natural sciences.[35] Four groups are retained: the Romano-Germanic family, the Common Law family, the family of socialist legal systems, and a fourth—as it were, 'residual'—category which groups under the label 'other systems' Islamic, Hindu, and Jewish law, and legal systems of the Far East and black Africa.

A few words on these four families, which form the usual chapters in teaching comparative law.

The Romano-Germanic systems have developed on the basis of Roman Law and the heritage of Germanic custom. The preponderant rôle is given to statute, generally in codified form. Civil law, law regulating private relations between citizens, forms the centre, the 'common law', of such a system, while the other branches of law, emerging later, appear only as 'exceptional law'.

The Common Law family, of English origin, has spread into many parts of the world that, at some moment in history, have been under the domination of England. This kind of law originates in case law, which explains why procedural rules rank in it at least equally with substantive rules. The Common Law norm, more concrete and individual than a norm in the Romano-Germanic family, aims to provide a solution to the particular case and not to formulate a general and abstract principle of behaviour.

The family of socialist legal systems was established first in the USSR, thanks to the 1917 Revolution, and then spread among the various régimes that adopted a constitution inspired by the principles of Marxism-Leninism. Although these systems have preserved many features drawn from earlier régimes (whether Romano-Germanic or Common Law), their specificity lies in the omnipotence accorded to the legislator, who is considered to represent the popular

[34] David 1982 (English version: David and Brierley 1985); Derrett 1968; Losano 1978.

[35] David 1982: 22.

will and to state the principles—the 'socialist legality'—guiding the Communist Party. Socialization of the means of production, a privileged measure aiming to ensure a collectivist and planned economy, is a salient characteristic of these régimes and evidently helps to ensure the pre-eminence of public over private law.

The group of 'other systems' comprises some, such as Islamic, Jewish, and Hindu law, that place a very high value on law but conceive it as an ideal order, a kind of 'natural law' representing an ideal of justice and order clearly distinct from purely factual effective law (customs and ordinances) and others, such as the kinds of 'law' found in China or black Africa, that are a very derived form of legal order, priority being given to justice, peace, and harmony arising from the social morality of the group.

Observation of concrete legal phenomena also reveals innumerable forms of hybridization among these different legal systems. Some are the result of forced imposition of legal régimes following upon colonization, while others result from voluntary reception (such as the adoption by Ataturk's Turkey, at the beginning of this century, of codes mainly inspired by Swiss law; or David's own drawing up of a Civil Code for Ethiopia; or, again, the adoption of 'socialist' constitutions by some Third World countries).

These phenomena pose the question of what is sometimes called 'legal development', in the same sense as economic or political development.[36] Is it appropriate and desirable for every country in the world to provide itself with a Western-style legal system? While such modernization can certainly serve the designs of current rulers by helping to wipe out local power-centres and traditional solidarity, on the other hand it is far from obvious that such acculturation favours the 'receiving' countries' harmonious and endogenous development. Moreover, on the hypothesis of a forced grafting of one legal order onto another, phenomena of rejection can be foreseen;[37] there is at least a danger that the real effectiveness of the official legal system will be rather weak, for, as has been seen, a legal order can develop durably only in osmosis with the social order that it is meant to regulate. This poses the question, to be discussed in the following section, of the necessary minimal conditions for maintaining a legal system.

[36] On this, see Friedman 1977: 45ff.; UNESCO 1980.

[37] See, especially, Carbonnier 1972: 240ff.; Papachristos 1975.

5.4. CONDITIONS OF SURVIVAL OF A LEGAL SYSTEM

Must a legal system have a certain structure or content if it is to stay alive, in 'force'?

This question may be treated as one of law or of fact. In law, the maintenance of a legal system worthy of the name supposes preserving the conditions of legitimacy obtaining when it was set up. For example, for a iusnaturalist writer such as Locke, a legal system exists only when the rulers use their powers to promote the public good; if they abandon that objective, the ruled are relieved of their duty of obedience.[38] Similarly, Fuller defines the criteria of the 'internal morality of law' (see above) to be adhered to by the good legislator on pain of breaking the 'social contract' which obtains the citizens' confidence, at the risk of thereby creating a form of official anomy.

We shall approach the question of the maintenance of legal systems as a question of fact, relating to the order of effectiveness, without thereby denying, however, the connections between a legal order's effectiveness and its legitimacy. According to Hart, for a legal system to be able to maintain itself two minimal, necessary and sufficient conditions must be combined: 'On the one hand those rules of behaviour which are valid according to the system's ultimate criteria of validity must be generally obeyed, and, on the other hand, its rules of recognition specifying the criteria of legal validity and its rules of change and adjudication must be effectively accepted as common public standards of official behaviour by its officials.'[39] This idea thus returns to the criterion of the union of primary and secondary norms—the condition for the emergence of legal systems—while this time giving it a temporal dimension, a pledge of their perpetuation. For a legal order to survive, the rules of behaviour must be generally obeyed (because of coercion or for any other reason), while the secondary rules must be seen as intrinsically binding by the officials, adopting what Hart calls the 'internal point of view'. Of course, a system will be the more stable, the more that the citizens' obedience too results from adopting an internal point of view—that is, from a freely given acceptance. As for the forms of 'pathology' that can affect legal systems, they arise from the absence

[38] Locke 1960: ch. 13, sect. 149.

[39] Hart 1961: 113. For a critical discussion of these ideas, see Raz 1970: 203–8. Raz particularly stresses the difficulty of measuring a legal system's effectiveness.

of one of the two remaining conditions, or even of them both: the question here is sometimes of revolution, sometimes of foreign occupation and sometimes of internal dissent. At the end of a longish and rather troubled period, these various disturbance factors can lead to the original system's disappearance, generally in favour of a new legal order. The questions arising from relations between these systems and from their identification were discussed in the previous chapter.

Elsewhere in his book, however, Hart offers some reflections on what he calls the 'minimum content of natural law', a content that can well appear as a supplementary condition for the maintenance of legal systems. Discarding iusnaturalist speculations on a necessary link between law and morality (see above), Hart nevertheless does not accept the positivist thesis that 'law may have any content': beginning from the idea that any human group aims at survival and taking as given a certain number of elementary substantive truths about human nature and the world surrounding us, one necessarily arrives at the conclusion that 'there are certain rules of conduct which any social organization must contain if it is to be viable'.[40] The result is that 'without such a content laws and morals could not forward the minimum purpose of survival which men have in associating with each other'.[41] What does this minimum content consist of? A number of rules relating to protection of persons, property, and promises and a number of sanctioning rules guaranteeing adherence to the former. Given that human beings are characterized by vulnerability, approximate equality, and limited altruism, a minimal protection of persons' physical integrity emerges as necessary to any form of life in society. Considering also the scarcity of available material resources, some division of labour is necessary and, with it, a minimal organization of property and exchange (keeping of promises). Finally, since human beings are endowed only with limited intelligence and will-power and therefore can easily cease to adhere to the first kind of rule, however well founded those rules may be, a system with sanctions proves indispensable if potential delinquents are to be deterred.[42]

The truisms that Hart maintains, as well as the conclusions he draws from them, are no doubt debatable; it is, however, indisputable that a legal system can attain its specific purpose—to maintain the group's coexistence and survival and to institute a minimum of

[40] 1961: 188. [41] 1961: 189. [42] See, generally, 1961: 189–95.

co-operation—only at the price of certain minimal achievements. On this count, Hart's ideas open up interesting perspectives on the necessary content of any legal order.

A legal system is not generally limited, however, to carrying out these elementary functions; it aims not only to maintain itself but also to develop. In managing its exchanges with the social environment (see above), it aims to equilibrate the needs for security and innovation in the most efficacious way possible. To do this, it plays not only with time itself in regulating the moment of its coming into force (transitional law) by accompanying its prescriptions with various time-scales, modes of prescription, amendment procedures, and provision for matters of urgency, but also modulates its own temporal constitution by harmonizing the multiple legal temporalities or rhythms by which it is characterized. The object of the following section will be to show the multiple temporalities that separately mark the rhythms of legal systems' development.[43]

5.5. THE MULTIPLE TEMPORALITIES OF LEGAL SYSTEMS

The different times of law can be related to the separate sources from which it is formed. In this way one can distinguish the time of foundation or time of constitution, the atemporal time of doctrine, the time of the *longue durée* or customary time, Promethean time or the time of legislation, and lastly the cyclical time of alternation between advance and lag or time of case law.[44] According to which of these sources predominates in a legal system, the corresponding temporality will necessarily be dominant; Section 5.6 will propose a new classification of legal systems on this basis.

The time of foundation appears as the description of a time of origin—fabulous, sacred, and mythical—referring back either to some founding event to which the group traces its birth (divine mandate, social contract, or revolution) or to some kind of human nature from which the individual draws unalterable rights. This time of foundation is *par excellence* the time of constitutions, which attempt to secure the foundations of political régimes on an unshakeable base and the intangible rights of individuals in a timeless, natural, or sacred register. While it is true that any national

43 On this, see Ost 1985: 115–53; see also Gurvitch 1963: 325ff.

44 Ost 1985: 115ff.

group forges its unity in some collective myth which it is for the constitutional text to translate into legal fact, there is mobilized a form of temporality which claims to escape from concrete historical time in order to shine forth in the eternal present of fable. What is completely lacking in this representation of time is an awareness of duration and the alterations it can make in the social body: hence the growing discrepancy which threatens to insinuate itself between constitutional fable and political reality.

Very close to this mythical time of foundation is the atemporal time of legal dogmatics. While the latter does not appeal explicitly to a fable of origin, it is none the less deployed in the form of an 'omnitemporal presence' designed to suggest the constant self-evidence of the principles appealed to and to shelter them from any historical context that could relativize their significance. The specific style of this doctrine is of course that of the commentary or gloss. Beginning from a fragment of text, as Legendre has clearly shown, a whole edifice of propositions is erected, whose compilation 'erases the trace of history' so that 'the text offers itself to the jurist not as a historical fragment, tied to particular circumstances, but in an atemporal and mathematical mode'.[45] Thus secured in the ether of purely logical thought, the legal text cannot disappear. As Pomian notes: 'Removed from the destructive action of time, texts appear to exist in a *durée* . . . within which no change occurs.'[46]

Customary time can be assimilated to this time of the *longue durée*, recently emphasized by the historians of the *Annales* School: this time, which is concerned more with mentalities than with events, is formed of 'layers of slow history shifting in the semi-immobility of a slowed-down time'.[47] This continuist temporality opens up a field to the gradual formation of custom, the accumulation of precedents, the formation of usages, the crystallization of practices, and the consolidation of factual situations (acquisitive prescription). Negatively, this *longue durée* destroys proof, weakens consents and legal titles, blurs the reasons behind laws, and erodes texts that are in force. Orientated to the past rather than to the future, this customary time is nevertheless not static. One might say that it brings the past to life in the present, while in return this heritage of the past insensibly modifies itself in contact with present realities. In legal thinking this social time, which refers back to

45 Legendre 1974: 91.
46 Pomian 1984: 257.
47 Vovelle 1978: 317–18.

popular culture (the seat of resistance to abrupt changes) and to 'vulgar' legal systems (see above) rather than to élite culture (the seat of innovation) and official legal systems, has hardly ever been appreciated, except by the Historical School of Law which developed in Germany during the first half of the nineteenth century. One of its leading representatives, Jacob Grimm, was able in this respect to compare the formation of law (understood as collective law issuing from popular consciousness, or from a *Volksgeist*) to that of language: law and language have in common 'their equal antiquity and equal youth. Each rests on an ancient and impenetrable fundament as well as on a tendency to regenerate themselves endlessly'.[48]

Then comes Promethean time, so called by reference to Prometheus, who as we know gave fire to men—a founding gesture which, defying the will of Zeus, revoked the time of the gods and inaugurated History, now marching to the rhythm of the progress of human reason. This Promethean time appears as a conscious and even voluntary time, controlled by reason with the aim of realizing the objectives that it sets. Just as customary time was oriented to the past, Promethean time is oriented to the future, polarized by the description of the future which it constantly brings alive in the present. In law, its privileged translation takes the form of statute and codification. As has been seen, the phenomenon of codification is inspired directly by the great eschatological descriptions which affirm progress through history. It may be noticed that putting law in writing creates a movement which, far from favouring fixity of solutions, as might be expected, on the contrary engenders their continuous transformation. While custom reflects an existing state of affairs, statute, at least to all intents, anticipates a possible state of affairs. And, in this logic, a higher value is given to change itself; modern iusnaturalism, as well as positivism, contribute to that effect.

Lastly, one can distinguish a fifth form of temporality, probably the most representative of legal rationality. It may be called the time of 'alternation between advance and lag', to take up one of Gurvitch's categories: a time oscillating between tradition and anticipation, memory and prediction, *longue durée* custom and Promethean laws. One can get still closer to reality by conceiving this time in the form of a spiral: a cumulative evolution progressing without ever denying itself. We shall therefore speak of cumulative time, charac-

[48] Grimm, *Kleinere Schriften*, viii. 547, cited by Dufour 1982: 101.

terizing a kind of change within continuity, of progress superimposing itself on the achievements of the past without ever substituting itself totally for them. This time is, *par excellence*, that of the judge, whose task is now to bring tradition up to date, to modernize customs and usages, and now, in the opposite direction, to moderate burning desires to transform the law. But the converse position can equally be maintained: as a sort of temporal differential charged with harmonizing the variations in legal rhythms, the judge is sometimes called upon to anticipate legislative developments that social evolution renders absolutely necessary.

It is not difficult to imagine the countless combinations that all these legal temporalities can make up: now one can observe movements of acceleration, in 'hot' historical periods of social upset, and now processes of stabilization, in 'cool' historical periods. Thus, after the explosion of revolutionary time in 1789 and the great codifications that it produced, there was a period of halt in legal creativity, witnessed by exegetical and atemporal forms of doctrine and case law—albeit that soon an innovative movement insensibly recommenced, first at the initiative of judges and later at that of legislators.

These last comments open the way to attempting to express legal temporalities diachronically. For, to grasp the relations between them it is not sufficient to juxtapose them; it should be possible, without thereby falling once again into the traps of historicism, which supposes the existence of a sort of 'meaning of history' necessarily marking social evolution, to make sense of the movement which, historically, runs through legal systems. A remark by Pomian sheds a lot of light here: 'The history of time', he writes, 'thus reveals itself to be closely akin to that of levels of organization'.[49] This outlines the programme of the diachronic presentation that will be offered in the following section: we shall try to link up the succession of legal temporalities with transformations of levels of organization of the corresponding systems.

5.6. LEGAL TEMPORALITIES AND LEVELS OF ORGANIZATION OF SYSTEMS

A convenient point of departure for this discussion is Gustav Husserl's essay on legal time.[50] He suggests that one must distinguish the

[49] Pomian 1984: 354. [50] Husserl 1955: 63ff.

past-orientated time of the judge, the future-orientated time of the legislator and the present-orientated time of the executive. On this basis, the following periodization is proposed: while a community is anchored in its past, tradition is the source of law and it is the judge who, quite naturally, makes him- or herself its interpreter. The example given is that of the gradual development of the Common Law. On the other hand, when the community turns towards the future, statute comes to be the predominant source of law and, with it, a temporality pointing towards the future. Finally, when the great value systems attaching human beings to their past weaken, or project them into the future, the reign of the present installs itself and, with it, the domination of the executive over the two other powers: legislation is scarcely any longer demarcated from regulation, while, in judicial decision making, considerations of appropriateness now argue the toss with submissions in terms of law.

Although one might accept this description overall, it can nevertheless be sharpened up by relating it precisely to the levels of increasing complexity that characterize the different legal systems. Referring once again to Hart's conception of the union of primary and secondary norms, we propose the following: the time specific to simple normative systems, which are composed exclusively of primary norms, is the customary time of the *longue durée*; complex legal systems, however, suppose a time intentionally controlled by legal agents: this will therefore be a Promethean time, although often tempered by cumulative time, alternating between advance and lag. Finally, if we may take the risk of offering an up-to-the-minute interpretation of our own legal systems, we shall advance the hypothesis that they, affected by a rupture of equilibrium that intervenes in the established relation between primary and secondary norms, have today become committed to a new—precarious or random—variety of temporality which may well entail a decisive alteration of the legal form itself.

Of the first two levels of organization (simple and complex legal systems) we shall say little more, since they have been described at length in earlier sections. We shall only observe that complex legal orders are characterized by a kind of dynamic equilibrium resulting from an adequate dose of norms of transformation and sanction. A conscious control of legal time is thus established, accompanied by an attempt to regulate social time. The general direction of movement is definitely orientated toward the future, which one now claims to regulate intentionally; but, at the same time, it is important to consolidate one's position, so that Promethean time is tempered by cumulative or alternational time. The variety of functions performed by secondary norms well expresses the arbitration thus accomplished between past and future. Being self-regulated, complex legal systems seem able to control the duration of their rules' validity and the rhythm of change with which it is appropriate to mark them; their degree of homeostasis appears to be optimal.

Today, however, this equilibrium seems to be compromised in the framework of 'hyper-complex' legal systems, which accompany the establishment of what is conventionally called the 'Welfare State'. From the moment when law is not limited to arbitrating social relations but desires to become an agent of social change, it ceases to refer to a general interest conceived in abstract and static terms; it now determines itself with respect to dynamic objectives, outlining the future. In these conditions, the stability and rigidity of the classical legal rule constitute obstacles to overcome: the norm has to take a supple and adaptive form calling itself 'plan', 'authorizing law' (conferring substantial discretion on administrative or para-administrative officials) or 'orientating law' (setting general objectives for public authorities). A legal form then becomes the object of an instrumentalization in the service of objectives defined by disciplines external to law: economics, management science, medicine, psychiatry and so on.[51] This time, the mutability of principle lying at the heart of complex legal systems is itself placed in the service of a radically evolutionary social normativity. There result a variety of dysfunctionalities that are generally identified under the name of 'crisis of the *État de droit*', whose principal features are legislative inflation, ineffectiveness of criminal sanctions, and erosion of the very normativity of law. It appears, very significantly, that these defects are intimately linked to the functions believed to be performed by secondary norms in complex legal systems: the functions of identifying specifically legal and genuinely obligatory rules, adapting rules to change and guaranteeing rules when they are broken. It is as if, in the present situation, secondary norms are no longer doing their job.

It is thus possible to formulate the following hypothesis: although, in a customary context, one can record a quasi-absence of secondary rules, corresponding to a static temporality, in a modern context one

[51] Similarly, Chevallier and Loschak 1978: 446–7.

finds a form of equilibrium between primary and secondary norms, corresponding to a cumulative temporality, alternating tradition and anticipation, while, in a post-modern context, one is on track to an inflation of secondary rules, corresponding to bureaucratization of the State and the gradual dissolution of primary norms. Not that the primary rules, imposing duties and specifying prohibitions, disappear; on the contrary, they abound. But, precisely because they proliferate, are altered more and more frequently, and their content is most often determined *a posteriori*, these rules are now less and less known and interiorized. Such therefore is the disequilibrium gradually established: an intense recourse to rules of change is not made good by largely ineffective sanctioning rules or excessively complex rules of identification. After the predictability of the *État de droit* gives way to the Welfare State's more flexibly programmatic approach, a form of regulation emerges that is characterized by a temporality that is not only accelerated but, far more, hazardous. Condemned to manage the unpredictable, the Welfare State's law loses its homeostatic capacities.

To conclude by way of a query: it will be seen that it is only in cases where these homeostatic mechanisms function efficiently that legal systems appear with a degree of autonomy; before thus becoming at least partially self-regulated, law is difficult to separate off from mores, morality, and religion, while today unreasonable recourse to rules of change and sanction can easily have the effect of denaturing law by enslaving it to norms defined by the interpreters of technoscience. In a primitive society, law is barely identifiable, since it is only one content immersed in others; in a post-modern society, law is in danger of losing its specificity, through having it reduced to a game of forms animated by a heterogeneous, technical kind of reason. As if a legal system required a minimum equilibrium between form and content, rigidity and dynamism, openness and closedness, self- and hetero-regulation ...

Conclusions

> A book neither begins nor finishes:
> at most, it pretends to.
>
> Mallarmé

How does one begin a book devoted to the legal system? How does one end it?

This was touched on in the Preface: the conception of law in the form of a system seems intrinsically tied up with the emergence of the image of modern Western law. Our discussion, despite its borrowings from the most recent developments in systems theory, is located in that intellectual tradition. None the less, how can one claim to conclude a study of this kind? After investigating the various dimensions of a legal system—its elements, its structures, the relations that it maintains with its environment, and its rhythms of evolution—should one not also combine these 'systematically', in order to arrive at a description of its effective operation? To state, for example, the processes through which a change in public opinion can produce a reversal in the trend of case law, which in its turn can lead doctrine to adopt a new classification? Or, conversely, to show how the legislator's instituting a new principle can generate a new form of social morality or influence the case law of a supra-national court? To distinguish, in short, the countless circuits taken by legal systematicity in order to reorganize itself continuously, to restore its ever compromised equilibria and, if possible, to improve its performance so as to combat the entropy menacing it?

Although our discussions of this have been essentially incomplete, it has seemed to us at least necessary to supersede two opposed descriptions of legal phenomena that can easily be seen to be both unrealistic and pernicious. The first may be illustrated cartoon-fashion by the figure of Ubu Roi, in which law is reduced to a succession of *ad hoc* and arbitrary decisions lacking any principle of cohesion. The second is expressed symptomatically in Bentham's utopia of a legal order that is perfectly systematized, transparent, consistent, and complete, and uniformly pursues the realization of the greatest interest of the greatest number.

Although, in the history of legal thought, these two descriptions no doubt play very different rôles, both quantitatively and qualitatively, in our view they are subject to what Bachelard has called the law of the 'bipolarity of error', which is that 'obstacles to scientific culture always come in pairs'.[1]

Since it is possible to show this for many other antinomic conceptions of legal phenomena,[2] it has seemed to us that the opposition between a description of law in terms exclusively either of order or of disorder can only be an obstacle to a satisfactory knowledge of law. It appears, however, that in each of the two cases the obstacles are not strictly of the same kind. The dogmatism inherent in an entirely systematic conception of law often attests to an excessive complacency with regard to the descriptions that the actors in a legal system give of their own discipline.

In so doing, it sticks firmly to a point of view internal to the object studied, depriving reflection of the epistemological break indispensable to developing a scientific theory. Conversely, the scepticism inherent in an 'anti-systematic' conception of law often witnesses to a excessive desire to break with descriptions internal to the object studied. Such adoption of what we have called a radical external point of view can now be seen to amount to ignoring an essential dimension of legal phenomena and to mistaking their specificity. The adoption of a 'moderate' external point of view has accordingly seemed to us the only path able to overcome this twofold doubt, by leading us to develop a critical theory of legal systematicity that will account not only for the phenomenon's reality and its recurrent place in jurists' thinking but also for its diversity and relativity. It is in this sense that a critical theory should lead on to a both plural and relativistic conception of systematicity in law, situating it resolutely between order and disorder.

From the moment that order and disorder appear less as avowedly antinomic givens than as separate poles of the legal field, between which range the discourses and practices of jurists and legal subjects, it can also be understood that incessant exchanges take place between them: disorder can give rise to order and order can induce disorder. Our enquiries have provided many illustrations of these

[1] Bachelard 1977: 20. [2] See, especially, Ost and van de Kerchove 1988.

propositions. Those enquiries have made it possible, firstly, to relativize the claims of legal thought to produce a system that is perfectly ordered according to a unitary logic and have shown instead, by marking off the limits of any unilateral form of systematicity, that systematization of law is produced and reproduced *between* order and disorder.

Thus it was seen, in the chapter on the elements of a system, that for the monism of an exclusively normativist conception must be substituted the pluralism of a conception able to demonstrate the heterogeneity of these components: norms, of course, but also concepts, institutions, branches, principles, and values.

Likewise, in the chapter on relations between elements of a system, it was concluded that none of the 'pure' types of systematicity imagined by legal thought could withstand the evidence of facts. Rather than speaking of a system as static *or* dynamic, one has to settle for a hybrid paradigm, at least if one wants to describe the observable legal systems that appear to be *simultaneously* static and dynamic, in that general rules cannot be so perfect that they would rein in any faculty of interpretation in the mind of each organ of application, while, conversely, those organs cannot be so creative that they can dispense with all general rules. In the same sense, one can speak of a 'partially deductive' system or a 'quasi-axiomatic' model, so as to reduce some writers' ambitions in the area of formal systematization of law to more correct proportions. Here too, syllogism has to compromise with intuition; the work of systematization borrows both from logical inferences and from axiological and teleological considerations, nor is it ever quite finalized. Lastly, it has also been discovered that the image of a perfectly linear or hierarchical systematicity was opposed not so much by the model of an acephalous circularity, which in fact is utopian, as by that of 'tangled hierarchies', which supposes that, for the vertical relations of authority or authorization to be incontestably effective within the legal field, they have nevertheless to be constantly frustrated by processes of retroaction. The ordering of law is thus not only one-way: while the movement from top to bottom (the relation of authority) is certainly the mostly readily associated with the image of law, none the less the converse movement, from bottom to top (a relation of recognition or opposition), turns out to be equally constitutive.

The work of the judge seems to be the most significant form of this constant arbitration between order and disorder: between the casuistics produced in grasping the many and varying conflicts of interest and the systematics that appear to demand conformity to the legislator's codifications and to doctrinal syntheses, the production of case law attempts to reconcile the requirement of individualization which equity demands and that of generalization which is involved in any form of rational justice.

If, then, a legal system is thus partially 'disordered', it cannot claim absolute autonomy with regard to its environment. Against the radical idea of autopoiesis, we have been able to offer the paradigm of 'relative self-organization', in order to give its due to the dialectic of law and society. This dialectic appears in a variety of forms: the intertwining of law and infra-law, the phenomenon of 'internormativity' or a legal order's capacity to incorporate rules from other normative registers, and the relative autonomy of law with regard to ethics and politics—so many indications of the permeability of legal systems. Systems, moreover, that in many ways are related reciprocally, which obviously reinforces proportionately their openness towards the outside.

Finally, in the chapter on forms of legal temporality, it also appeared that it is important to describe the evolution of systems of law, at least from the moment when they have reached a minimal threshold of complexity, in terms of unstable equilibrium between conservation and change, homeostasis and break, and immobility and movement.

But it is probably necessary to go still further; legal systematicity does not develop solely *between* order and disorder, as if it kept to a prudent middle way between two irreducibly opposed extremes. Its progression seems rather to take now the paths of order and now those of disorder, as if the two kinds of path secretly exchanged their positions and the tension running through the legal field, between the poles of organization and disorganization, were inverted.

It can be shown, firstly, that order may emerge from disorder. This idea has been established by biologists and information theorists: noise can create information, a chance event or exogenous shock can produce an organizational innovation in the heart of a system, provided that the system possesses a sufficient degree of indeterminacy to ensure its adaptation to these unprecedented conditions. A work of art, in Eco's view, 'introduces forms of organized disorder into a system' (a system of language or of conventions) 'to increase its capacity to convey information'.[3] It has likewise been suggested that, unless a certain number of factors of disorder are present, a legal system will not be able to fulfil the functions of ordering and regulation expected of it. In this respect, one must cease to think of the inevitable ambiguities, redundancies, gaps, ineffectivenesses, and antinomies affecting a legal system as necessarily deficiencies.

Who cannot see that the ambiguity of certain 'confused notions' favours the adaptation of texts to unforeseen circumstances, at the same time as making compromise easier to achieve? Who is not aware that the pedagogical function of law requires a certain amount of repetition? Who can ignore the virtue of some of those gaps that, proceeding from the legislator's wisdom rather than lack of foresight, leave to the organ of application an indispensable margin of manœuvre demanded by the diversity of fact situations? And how can one not welcome certain forms of intentional ineffectiveness of a legal rule, foreshadowing the repeal of superseded laws or indicating a concern, particularly by repressive authorities, to force themselves into beneficial self-limitation? Is it necessary to recall here Carbonnier's quite recent and penetrating enquiries into the beneficent spaces of non-law that law has been able to leave?[4] Finally, we are happy to push paradox so far as to stress the positive effect, particularly in terms of peace or social order, of certain axiological tensions running through the legal field. For instance, the development, in the course of the twentieth century, of social law (*droit social*: primarily labour law, together with social welfare law), whose absence of directive principles as well as the contradiction it produces with regard to civil law presented as 'common law' have of course been jealously exposed. Yet, are we aware that the emergence of this new form of law, beyond contributing decisively to establishing social peace, has permitted the survival and even extension of the legal order overall? There has been the price, of course, of a number of internal disturbances, but these are absorbed in so far as the logic of the law as a whole is able to reorganize itself. And, to generalize that idea, can one not see in the recurrent opposition between natural law and positive law the paradigmatic image of this 'creative disorder'?

Agents who are, as it were, sources of scandal are also to be found in a legal system. We shall mention here only the case of the 'rebel' judge, whose decisions, at first isolated, may end by establishing a

[3] Eco 1989: 60. [4] Carbonnier 1971: 3–58.

new direction in case law and leading higher courts to revise their position.

While a certain form of disorder may be creative of order, it is not difficult to see that the reverse is equally true and that, beyond certain limits, order almost ineluctably produces disorder. Albeit that that can, in its turn, favour the creation of new order ...

We shall support this idea simply by returning to a number of questions raised earlier. First: the impossibility of a legal order achieving the formal properties of decidability, independence, consistency, and completeness beyond a certain degree without producing serious dysfunctions, of a kind that could eventually endanger its very existence. Extreme precision in the formulation of legal norms has the logical consequence of freezing law into an rigidity from which it can escape only at the price of constant legislative alteration, in the same way as the adoption of exhaustive criteria for identifying norms deprives law of any chance of adapting to crisis situations or to an unpredictable novelty. The desire to remove any form of redundancy between different norms is both a factor of unpredictability and an obstacle to communication. Spontaneous consistency of a legal system can be achieved only at the price of an impracticable unification of normative authorities, a harmful rigidity and a degree of uniformity of the applicable legal régimes that is hard to accept. Completeness of a legal order, finally, can be realized spontaneously only by excluding the possibility of resolving any legal question that is unforeseeable or even simply not foreseen. Unconditional acceptance and long-term maintenance of such dysfunctions would make it difficult for a legal order to ensure its survival.

Comparable, if not still graver, perils indubitably threaten a 'hyper-complex' legal system, which at the extreme would develop the kind of metasystem that can be formed by secondary rules designed to perfect its systematicity.

As is revealed by some signs already discernible in the framework of the Welfare State, one can imagine some kinds of dysfunction flowing from a hypertrophy of such rules. The multiplication and diversification of identification criteria or modes of formation of legal norms can only increase the possibilities of conflict between them and the dangers of slowness and, indeed, paralysis in their application. The inflation of sanctioning rules—and rules providing criminal sanctions in particular—is a factor of ineffectiveness, uncertainty, and discrimination which cannot go beyond a certain threshold of tolerance on the part as much of the organs of application as of citizens themselves. Finally, it has been seen that for rules of change to become extremely flexible introduces in the heart of a legal order a random temporality which deprives it of its homeostatic qualities and prevents any form of reasonable interiorization of norms by the citizens.

The disorder that flows from this—and which is particularly likely to take the form of what we have called a veritable 'decodification'—is therefore not a purely imaginary danger.

Even if such a hypothesis goes beyond the limits of the present work and confirms it as uncompleted, can one not accept the idea that these various observations are only particular manifestations of a much more basic relation between order and disorder, in terms of which any order can be established only at the price of some disorder? And that may be so, whether it consists in the abolition of an old order for which it means to substitute itself—as civilization means to supplant barbarism, statute means to abolish custom, or law claims to substitute itself for mores; in a desire to treat as disorder whatever does not fit into its own order, as every norm sets up as deviant whatever does not conform to it; or, lastly, through excess of order, in engendering its own disorder.

References

AARNIO, A., 1986, 'On Changes in the Systematics of Law', *Rechtstheorie*, Beiheft 10, p. 161.

ALCHOURRÓN, C. E., 1986, 'Systematization and Change in the Science of Law', *Rechtstheorie*, Beiheft 10, p. 171.

—— and BULYGIN, E., 1971, *Normative Systems* (New York: Springer).

ALLOTT, A., 1980, *The Limits of Law* (London: Butterworths).

AMSELEK, P., 1964, *Méthode phénoménologique et théorie du droit* (Paris: Librairie Générale de Droit et de Jurisprudence).

—— 1978, 'Réflexions critiques autour de la conception kelsénienne de l'ordre juridique', 94 *Revue du droit public et de la science politique en France et à l'étranger* 5.

—— 1986, 'Philosophie du droit et théorie des actes de langage' in P. Amselek (ed.), *Théorie des actes de langage, éthique et droit* (Paris: Presses Universitaires de France).

APEL, K. O., 1987, *Sur le problème d'une fondation rationnelle de l'éthique à l'âge de la science: l'*a priori *de la communauté communicationnelle et les fondements de l'éthique*, trans. R. Lellouche and I. Mittmann (Lille: Presses Universitaires de Lille).

ARNAUD, A.-J., 1969, *Les origines doctrinales du Code civil français* (Paris: Librairie Générale de Droit et de Jurisprudence).

—— 1975, *Les juristes face à la société du XIXe siècle à nos jours* (Paris: Presses Universitaires de France).

—— 1981, *Critique de la raison juridique*, i, 'Où va la sociologie du droit?' (Paris: Librairie Générale de Droit et de Jurisprudence).

ATIAS, C., 1987, *Théorie contre arbitraire: éléments pour une théorie des théories juridiques* (Paris: Presses Universitaires de France).

ATLAN, H., 1974, 'Discussion', in *L'unité de l'homme*, ii, 'Le cerveau humain' (Paris: Seuil).

—— 1979, *Entre le cristal et la fumée: essai sur l'organisation du vivant* (Paris: Seuil).

—— 1983, 'L'émergence du nouveau et du sens', in P. Dumouchel and J.-P. Dupuy (eds.), *L'auto-organisation: de la physique au politique* (Paris: Seuil).

BACHELARD, G., 1977, *La formation de l'esprit scientifique* (Paris: Vrin).

BAREL, Y., 1979, *Le paradoxe et le système* (Grenoble: Presses Universitaires de Grenoble).

BATIFFOL, H., 1956, *Aspects philosophiques du droit international privé* (Paris: Dalloz).

BATIFFOL, H., 1981, 'La responsabilité de la doctrine dans la création du droit', 6 *Revue de la recherche juridique: droit prospectif* 175.

BAUER-BERNET, H., 1986, 'Représentation des connaissances et systèmes experts en droit', in *Ordre juridique et ordre technologique* (Paris: Centre National de Recherche Scientifique).

BECCARIA, C., 1979, *Des délits et des peines* (1764) (Paris: Flammarion).

BELAID, S., 1974. *Essai sur le pouvoir créateur et normatif du juge* (Paris: Librairie Générale de Droit et de Jurisprudence).

BELLET, P., 1980, 'Rapport de synthèse', in *La réaction de la doctrine à la création du droit par les juges, 31 Travaux de l'Association Henri Capitant* (Paris: Economica, 1982).

BELLEY, J. G., 1986, 'L'État et la régulation juridique des sociétés globales: pour une problématique du pluralisme juridique', 18 *Sociologie et sociétés* 11.

BELVÉDÈRE, A., JORI, M. and LANTELLA, L., 1979, *Definizioni giuridiche e ideologie* (Milan: Giuffré).

BENTHAM, J., 1829*a*, 'De la codification', in E. Dumont (ed.), *Œuvres de Jeremy Bentham, jurisconsulte anglais* (Brussels: Hauman), iii. 87.

—— 1829*b*, 'Traités de législation civile et pénale', in E. Dumont (ed.), *Œuvres de Jeremy Bentham, jurisconsulte anglais* (Brussels: Hauman), i. 1.

—— 1829*c*, 'Vue générale d'un corps complet de législation', in E. Dumont (ed.), *Œuvres de Jeremy Bentham, jurisconsulte anglais* (Brussels: Hauman), i. 305.

—— 1970, *Of Laws in General*, in H. L. A. Hart (ed.), *The Collected Works of Jeremy Bentham* (London: Athlone Press; New York: Oxford University Press).

BERGEL, J.-L., 1985, *Théorie générale du droit* (Paris: Dalloz).

BERTALANFFY, L. VON, 1973, *General System Theory* (Harmondsworth: Penguin).

BLANCHÉ, R., 1967, 'L'évolution de la logique mathématique contemporaine', in *La logique juridique* (Travaux du IIe Colloque de Philosophie du Droit Comparée) (Paris: Pedone).

—— 1970, *L'axiomatique* (Paris: Presses Universitaires de France).

BOBBIO, N., 1960, *Teoria dell' ordinamento giuridico* (Turin: Giappichelli).

—— 1965, 'Des critères pour résoudre les antinomies', in C. Perelman (ed.), *Les antinomies en droit* (Brussels: Bruylant).

—— 1971, 'Nouvelles réflexions sur les normes primaires et secondaires', in C. Perelman (ed.), *La règle de droit* (Brussels: Bruylant).

—— 1977, *Dalla struttura alla funzione: nuovi studi di teoria del diritto* (Milan: Comunita).

BOHANNAN, P., 1967, 'The Differing Realms of the Law', in *Law and Warfare* (Austin, Texas: University of Texas Press).

BOURCIER, D., 1986, 'Le droit médiatisé, réflexion sur quelques enjeux', in *Ordre juridique et ordre technologique* (Paris: Centre National de Recherche Scientifique).
BOURDIEU, P., 1986, 'Habitus, code et codification', 64 *Actes de la recherche en sciences sociales* 40.
—— 1987, 'The Force of Law: Toward a Sociology of the Juridical Field', trans. R. Terdiman, 38 *Hastings Law Journal* 805.
—— 1988, *Homo Academicus*, trans. P. Collier (Cambridge: Polity Press).
BREDIN, J. D., 1981, 'Remarques sur la doctrine', in *Mélanges offerts à Pierre Hébraud* (Toulouse: Université des Sciences Sociales de Toulouse).
BRITO, J. S., 1972, 'Relire Bentham: A propos de l'édition de *Of laws in general* de Bentham par Hart', 17 *Archives de philosophie du droit* 451.
BULYGIN, E., 1976, 'Sobra la regla de reconocimiento', in *Derecho, filosofia y lenguaje* (Bueños Aires: Astrea).
—— 1982, 'Time and Validity', in A. A. Martino (ed.), *Deontic Logic, Computational Linguistics and Legal Information Systems*, ii (New York: North-Holland).
—— 1986, 'Legal Dogmatics and the Systematization of Law', *Rechtstheorie*, Beiheft 10, p. 193.
BURDEAU, G., 1967, *Traité de science politique*, 3rd edn., ii. 'L'État' (Paris: Librairie Générale de Droit et de Jurisprudence).
BUTTGENBACH, A., 1966, *Manuel de droit administratif*, 3rd edn., pt. 1, 'Théorie générale du droit administratif belge' (Brussels: Larcier).
CANARIS, C. W., 1968, 'De la manière de constater et de combler les lacunes de la loi en droit allemand', in C. Perelman (ed.), *Le problème des lacunes en droit* (Brussels: Bruylant).
—— 1969, *Systemdenken und Systembegriff in der Jurisprudenz entwickelt am Beispiel des deutschen Privatrechts* (Berlin: Duncker & Humblot).
CARBONNIER, J., 1967, *Droit civil*, i, 7th edn. (Paris: Presses Universitaires de France).
—— 1971, *Flexible droit: textes pour une sociologie du droit sans rigueur* (Paris: Librairie Générale de Droit et de Jurisprudence).
—— 1972, *Sociologie juridique* (Paris: Presses Universitaires de France).
—— 1979, 'Les phénomènes d'inter-normativité', in *Essais sur les lois* (Paris: Répertoire de Notariat Defrénois).
CARRÉ DE MALBERG, R., 1920, *Contribution à la théorie générale de l'État*, i (Paris: Sirey).
—— 1931, *La loi, expression de la volonté générale* (reprint of 1931 edn., Paris: Economica, 1984).
CASTORIADIS, C., 1984, *Crossroads in the Labyrinth*, trans. K. Soper and M. H. Ryle (Brighton: Harvester).
—— 1987, *The Imaginary Institution of Society*, trans. K. Blamey (Cambridge: Polity Press).

CHAMBLISS, W., and SEIDMAN, R., 1982, *Law, Order, and Power*, 2nd edn. (Reading, Mass.: Addison-Wesley).

CHEVALLIER, J., 1983, 'L'ordre juridique', in J. Chevallier *et al.* (eds.), *Le droit en procès* (Paris: Presses Universitaires de France).

—— and LOSCHAK, D., 1978, *Science administrative*, ii (Paris: Librairie Générale de Droit et de Jurisprudence).

CHURCHMAN, C. W., 1968, *The Systems Approach* (New York: Dell).

COIPEL, M., 1980, 'Les réactions de la doctrine à la création du droit par les juges en droit civil', in (1980) 31 *Travaux de l'Association Henri Capitant* (Paris: Economica, 1982).

COMBACAU, J., 1986, 'Le droit international: bric-à-brac ou système?', 31 *Archives de philosophie du droit* 85.

COMMAILLE, J., 1982, 'Esquisse d'analyse des rapports entre droit et sociologie: les sociologies juridiques', 8 *Revue interdisciplinaire d'études juridiques* 9.

COTTA, S., 1982, 'La coexistencialidad ontologica como fundamento del derecho', in 9 *Persona y derecho* 13.

—— 1983, 'Six thèses sur les rapports entre droit naturel et droit positif', in *Naturrechtsdenken heute und morgen, Gedächtnisschrift für René Marcic* (Berlin: Duncker & Humblot).

COUSY, H., 1983, 'Rechtssysteem en Onderwijsmethode', in *Liber Amicorum Frédéric Dumon* (Antwerp: Kluwer).

CROZIER, M., and FRIEDBERG, E., 1977, *L'acteur et le système: les contraintes de l'action collective* (Paris: Seuil).

DABIN, J., 1935, *La technique de l'élaboration du droit positif spécialement du droit privé* (Brussels: Bruylant; Paris: Sirey).

—— 1950, *General Theory of Law*, in *The Legal Philosophies of Lask, Rabruch, and Dabin*, trans. K. Wilk (Cambridge, Mass.: Harvard University Press).

—— 1969, *Théorie générale du droit*, new edn. (Paris: Dalloz).

DALLOZ, *Répertoire de droit civil*, iv, at 'Doctrine'.

DAVID, R., 1971, *Les grands systèmes de droit contemporains*, 4th edn. (Paris: Dalloz).

—— 1982, *Les grands systèmes de droit contemporains*, 8th edn. (Paris: Dalloz).

—— and BRIERLEY, J. E. C., 1985, *Major Legal Systems in the World Today: An Introduction to the Comparative Study of Law*, 3rd edn. (London: Stevens).

DELMAS-MARTY, M., 1986, *Le flou du droit: du Code pénal aux droits de l'homme* (Paris: Presses Universitaires de France).

DELPÉRÉE, F., 1972, 'La Belgique, État fédéral?', 88 *Revue du droit public et de la science politique en France et à l'étranger* 607.

—— 1980, *Droit constitutionnel* (Brussels: Larcier).

Derrett, J. D. M. (ed.), 1968, *An Introduction to Legal Systems* (London: Sweet & Maxwell).

Desmet, J., 1984, 'De Invloed van de Doctrine op de Wetgeving', in *De Invloed van de Doctrine, Feestbundel 20 jaar T.P.R.* (Ghent: Story Scientia).

Diamond, S., 1978, 'The Rule of Law versus the Order of Custom', in C. E. Reasons and R. M. Rich (eds.), *The Sociology of Law: A Conflict Perspective* (Toronto: Butterworths).

Diederichsen, U., 1966, 'Topisches und systematisches Denken in der Jurisprudenz' 16 *Neue juristische Wochenschrift* 697.

Ducrot, O., 1972, *Dire et ne pas dire: principes de sémantique linguistique* (Paris: Hermann).

Dufour, A., 1982, 'La théorie des sources du droit dans l'École du droit historique', 27 *Archives de philosophie du droit* 85.

Dumouchel, P. and Dupuy, J.-P. (eds.), 1983, *L'auto-organisation: de la physique au politique* (Paris: Seuil).

Du Pasquier, C., 1967, *Introduction à la théorie générale et à la philosophie du droit*, 4th edn. (Neuchâtel: Delachaux & Niestlé).

Duport, M., 1790, *Principes et plan sur l'établissement de l'ordre judiciaire* (Paris: Imprimerie Nationale).

Dupuy, J.-P., 1982, *Ordres et désordres: enquête sur un nouveau paradigme* (Paris: Seuil).

Durkheim, E., 1984, *The Division of Labour in Society*, trans. W. D. Halls (London: Macmillan).

Dworkin, R., 1978, *Taking Rights Seriously: New Impression with a Reply to Critics* (London: Duckworth).

—— 1986, *Law's Empire* (London: Fontana).

Eco, U., 1989, *The Open Work*, trans. A. Cancogni (Cambridge, Mass.: Harvard University Press).

Eisenmann, C., 1966, 'Quelques problèmes de méthodologie des définitions et des classifications en science juridique', 11 *Archives de philosophie du droit* 25.

Engels, F., 1902, *The Origin of the Family, Private Property and the State*, trans. E. Untermann (Chicago: Kerr).

Engisch, K., 1956, *Einführung in das juristische Denken*, 4th edn. (Stuttgart: Kohlhammer).

—— 1957, 'Sinn und Tragweite juristischer Systematik', 10 *Studium Generale* 173.

Esmein, A., 1902, 'La jurisprudence et la doctrine', 1 *Revue trimestrielle de droit civil* 5.

Febbrajo, A., 1984, 'Legittimazione e teoria dei sistemi', 1 *Sociologia del diritto* 30.

Fenet, P.-A., 1827, *Recueil complet des travaux préparatoires du Code civil*, 15 vols. (reprint of 1827 edn., Osnabrück: Zeller, 1968).

Foriers, P., 1965, 'Les antinomies en droit', in C. Perelman (ed.), *Les antinomies en droit* (Brussels: Bruylant).

—— 1967, 'L'état des recherches de la logique juridique en Belgique', 37 *Logique et analyse* 30.

——1968, 'Les lacunes du droit', in C. Perelman (ed.), *Le problème des lacunes en droit* (Brussels: Bruylant).

Fourré, J., 1986, 'Les codifications récentes et l'unité du droit en France', 3–4 *La codification et l'évolution du droit, revue juridique et politique: indépendance et coopération* 724.

François, L., 1978, *Le problème de la définition du droit*. (Liège: Faculté de Droit, d'Économie et de Sciences Sociales de Liège).

Frank, J., 1932, 'Mr. Justice Holmes and Non-Euclidian Legal Thinking', 17 *Cornell Law Quarterly* 568.

Friedman, L., 1975, *The Legal System: A Social Science Perspective* (New York: Sage).

—— 1977, *Law and Society: An Introduction* (Englewood Cliffs, NJ: Prentice-Hall).

—— 1986, 'Law as a System: Some Comments', *Rechtstheorie*, Beiheft 10, p. 311.

Fromont, M., 1984, 'République Fédérale d'Allemagne: l'État de droit', 100 *Revue du droit public et de la science politique en France et à l'étranger* 1203.

Fuller, L. L., 1958, 'Positivism and Fidelity to Law—a Reply to Professor Hart', 71 *Harvard Law Review* 630.

—— 1964, *The Morality of Law* (New Haven, Conn.: Yale University Press).

—— 1969, *The Morality of Law*, revised edn. (New Haven, Conn.: Yale University Press).

Gardies, J.-L., 1974, 'Système normatif et système de normes', 19 *Archives de philosophie du droit* 75.

—— 1979, 'En quel sens un droit, un système de dispositions juridiques peut-il être dit complet?', 24 *Archives de philosophie du droit* 285.

—— 1987, 'Système juridique et système logique', in W. Krawietz and W. Ott (eds.), *Formalismus und Phänomenologie im Rechtsdenken der Gegenwart: Festgabe für Aloïs Troller zum 80. Geburtstag*.

Gassin, R., 1981, 'Système et droit', *Revue de la recherche juridique: droit prospectif* 353.

Gaudemet, J., 1986, 'Tentatives de systématisation du droit à Rome', 31 *Archives de philosophie du droit* 11.

Geny, F., 1919, *Méthode d'interprétation et sources en droit privé positif:*

essai critique, 2 vols., 2nd edn. (Paris: Librairie Générale de Droit et de Jurisprudence).

GÉRARD, P., 1981, *Droit, égalité et idéologie: contribution à l'étude critique des principes généraux du droit* (Brussels: Facultés Universitaires Saint-Louis).

—— 1987, 'Validité juridique et souveraineté', in F. Rigaux *et al.* (eds.), *Droit et pouvoir*, i. 'La validité' (Brussels: Story Scientia).

GLUCKMAN, M., 1965, *Politics, Law and Ritual in Tribal Society* (Oxford: Blackwell).

GOLDING, M. P., 1971, 'Kelsen and the Concept of "Legal System"', in R. S. Summers (ed.), *More Essays in Legal Philosophy: General Assessments of Legal Philosophies* (Oxford: Blackwell).

GOYARD-FABRE, J., 1986, 'L'idée d'ordre dans la théorie juridique de Kelsen', 9 *Cahiers de philosophie politique et juridique* 25.

GRZEGORCZYK, C., 1986, 'Évaluation critique du paradigme systémique dans la science du droit', in 31 *Archives de philosophie du droit* 281.

GURVITCH, G., 1963, 'La multiplicité des temps sociaux', in G. Gurvitch, *La vocation actuelle de la sociologie*, ii, 2nd edn. (Paris: Presses Universitaires de France).

HABERMAS, J., 1972, 'Knowledge and Human Interests: a General Perspective', in J. Habermas, *Knowledge and Human Interests*, trans. J. J. Shapiro (London: Heinemann).

HAESAERT, J., 1948, *Théorie générale du droit* (Brussels: Bruylant).

HART, H. L. A., 1958, 'Positivism and the Separation of Law and Morals', 71 *Harvard Law Review* 593.

—— 1961, *The Concept of Law* (Oxford: Clarendon Press).

—— 1965, Review of L. L. Fuller, *The Morality of Law*, 78 *Harvard Law Review* 1281.

—— 1982, 'Bentham's *Of Laws in General*', in H. L. A. Hart, *Essays on Bentham* (Oxford: Clarendon Press).

—— 1983, 'Kelsen's Doctrine of the Unity of Law', in H. L. A. Hart, *Essays in Jurisprudence and Philosophy* (Oxford: Clarendon Press).

HAYEK, F. A., 1982, *Law, Legislation and Liberty* (3 vols. in 1), i, 'Rules and Order' (London: Routledge & Kegan Paul).

HÉBRAUD, P., 1968, 'Rapport introductif', in *La logique judiciaire* (Paris: Presses Universitaires de France).

HECK, P., 1948, 'The Formation of Concepts and the Jurisprudence of Interests', in M. M. Schoch (trans. and ed.), *The Jurisprudence of Interests* (Cambridge, Mass.: Harvard University Press).

HOFSTADTER, D. R., 1980, *Gödel, Escher, Bach: An Eternal Golden Braid* (Harmondsworth: Penguin).

HOLMES, O. W., 1897, 'The Path of the Law' 10 *Harvard Law Review* 457.

HUBERLANT, C., 1965, 'Antinomies et recours aux principes généraux', in C. Perelman (ed.), *Les antinomies en droit* (Brussels: Bruylant).

HUSSERL, G., 1955, *Recht und Zeit* (Frankfurt am Main: Klostermann).

HUSSON, L., 1972, 'Analyse critique de la méthode de l'exégèse', 17 *Archives de Philosophie du Droit* 115.

INGBER, L., 1972, 'Le pluralisme juridique dans l'œuvre des philosophes du droit', in J. Gilissen (ed.), *Le pluralisme juridique* (Brussels: Université de Bruxelles).

JEANNEAU, B., 1954, *Les principes généraux du droit dans la jurisprudence administrative* (Paris: Librairie Générale de Droit et de Jurisprudence).

JHERING, R. VON, 1969, *L'esprit du droit romain dans les diverses phases de son développement*, trans. O. de Meulenaere, 3rd edn., i (reprint of 1886–8 edn.) (Bologna: Forni).

JORI, M., 1984, 'Ordre juridique', 29 *Archives de philosophie du droit* 347.

KALINOWSKI, G., 1965, *Introduction à la logique juridique: éléments de sémiotique juridique, logique des normes et logique juridique* (Paris: Librairie Générale de Droit et de Jurisprudence).

—— 1967, *Le problème de la vérité en morale et en droit* (Lyon: Vitte).

—— 1969, *Querelle de la science normative (une contribution à la théorie de la science)* (Paris: Librairie Générale de Droit et de Jurisprudence).

KELSEN, H., 1925, *Allgemeine Staatslehre* (Berlin: Springer).

—— 1926, 'Les rapports de système entre le droit interne et le droit international public', 4 *Recueil des Cours de La Haye* 263.

—— 1946, *General Theory of Law and State*, trans. A. Wedberg (Cambridge, Mass.: Harvard University Press).

—— 1959, 'Justice et droit naturel', 3 *Annales de Philosophie Politique* 1.

—— 1967, *Pure Theory of Law*, trans. M. Knight (Berkeley, Calif.: University of California Press).

—— 1991, *General Theory of Norms*, trans. M. Hartney (Oxford: Clarendon Press).

KLUG, U., 1966, *Juristische Logik*, 3rd edn. (Berlin: Springer).

—— 1981, 'Rechtssystem und Rationalität in der juristischen Dogmatik', *Rechtstheorie*, Beiheft 2, p. 299.

—— 1984*a*, 'Die Lehre von Stufenbau des Rechts: Eine säkularisierte politische Theologie?', *Rechtstheorie*, 5, p. 255.

—— 1984*b*, *Recht als Regelsystem* (Wiesbaden: Steiner).

KRAWIETZ, W., 1986, 'Recht und moderne Systemtheorie', *Rechstheorie*, Beiheft 10, p. 282.

KRISLOV, S., 1985, 'The Concept of Families of Law', in A. Podgórecki *et al.* (eds.), *Legal Systems and Social Systems* (London: Croom Helm).

LACHMAYER, F., 1975, 'Struktur der Rechtsinstitution', in G. Winkler (ed.), *Rechtstheorie und Rechtsinformatik* (Vienna: Springer).

Ladrière, J., 1984, 'Droit naturel, droit, éthique', 13 *Revue interdisciplinaire d'études juridiques* 90.

—— 1985, 'Système (épistémologie)', in *Encyclopaedia universalis*, (Paris: Encyclopaedia Universalis), xvii. 586.

Lalande, A., 1962, *Vocabulaire technique et critique de la philosophie*, 9th edn. (Paris: Presses Universitaires de France).

Larenz, K., 1969, *Methodenlehre der Rechtswissenschaft*, 2nd edn. (Berlin: Springer).

Laszlo, E., 1972, *Introduction to Systems Philosophy: Toward a New Paradigm of Contemporary Thought* (New York: Gordon & Breach).

Laurent, F., 1881, *Cours élémentaire de droit civil*, i (Brussels: Bruylant; Paris: Chevalier-Maresq).

Lebrun, A., 1932, *La coutume: ses sources: son autorité en droit privé: contribution à l'étude des sources du droit positif à i'époque contemporaine* (Paris: Librairie Générale de Droit et de Jurisprudence).

Lefort, C., 1984, 'Les droits de l'homme en question', 13 *Revue interdisciplinaire d'études juridiques* 11.

Legendre, P., 1974, *L'amour du censeur: essai sur l'ordre dogmatique* (Paris: Seuil).

Le Moigne, J.-L., 1977, *La théorie du système général: théorie de la modélisation* (Paris: Presses Universitaires de France).

—— 1978, *La théorie génerale des systèmes* (Paris: Presses Universitaires de France).

—— 1985, 'Les systèmes juridiques sont-ils passibles d'une représentation systémique?', 10 *Revue de la recherche juridique: droit prospectif* 155.

Lenoble, J., 1984, *Introduction aux sources et aux notions générales du droit: la relativité des ordres juridiques* (Louvain-la-Neuve: mimeo.).

—— and Ost F., 1980, *Droit, mythe et raison: essai sur la dérive mythologique de la rationalité juridique* (Brussels: Facultés Universitaires Saint-Louis).

Le Roy, É., 1984, 'L'esprit de la coutume et l'idéologie de la loi', in *La connaissance du droit en Afrique* (Brussels: Académie Royale des Sciences d'Outre-mer).

Leurquin-De Visscher, F., and Simonart, H., 1980, *Documentation et méthodologie juridiques* (Louvain-la-Neuve: Faculté de Droit de l'Université Catholique de Louvain).

Llewellyn, K. N., 1941, 'My Philosophy of Law', in (various authors) *My Philosophy of Law* (Boston: Boston Law Book Co.).

Locke, J., 1960, *Second Treatise of Government* (1690), in J. Locke, *Two Treatises of Government,* ed. P. Laslett (New York: Mentor).

Losano, L., 1978, *I grandi sistemi giuridici* (Turin: Einaudi).

Loschak, D., 1981, 'Le principe de légalité: mythes et mystifications', in 37 *L'actualité juridique: droit administratif* 387.

Luhmann, N., 1974, *Rechtssystem und Rechtsdogmatik* (Stuttgart: Kohlhammer).

—— 1988, 'The Unity of the Legal System', trans. P. Knight, in G. Teubner (ed.), *Autopoietic Law: A New Approach to Law and Society* (Berlin: de Gruyter).

—— 1989, 'Le droit comme système social', 11/12 *Droit et société: revue internationale de théorie du droit et de sociologie juridique* 53.

MacCormick, N., 1981, *H. L. A. Hart* (London: Arnold).

Maine, H. S., 1912, *Ancient Law* (London: Murray).

Malaurie, P., 1980, 'Rapport français', in *La réaction de la doctrine à la création du droit par les juges* (1980) 31 *Travaux de l'Association Henri Capitant* (Paris: Economica, 1982).

Malgaud, W., 1965, 'Les antinomies en droit: à propos de l'étude de G. Gavazzi', in C. Perelman (ed.), *Les antinomies en droit* (Brussels: Bruylant).

Malinowski, B., 1926, *Crime and Custom in Savage Society* (London: Routledge & Kegan Paul).

Marnierre, E. S. de la, 1976, *Éléments de méthodologie juridique* (Paris: Librairie du Journal des Notaires et des Avocats).

Maturana, H., and Varela, F., 1980, *Autopoiesis and Cognition: the Realization of the Living* (Dordrecht: Reidel).

Mazeaud, H., L., and J., 1972, *Leçons de droit civil*, i (Paris: Montchrestien).

Miaille, M., 1976, *Une introduction critique au droit* (Paris: Maspero).

Michaut, F., 1985, *L'École de la 'sociological jurisprudence' et le mouvement réaliste américain: le rôle du juge et la théorie du droit* (Lille: Atelier National de Reproduction des Thèses, Université de Lille III).

Montesquieu, 1989, *The Spirit of the Laws* (1748), trans. and ed. A. M. Cohler *et al.* (Cambridge: Cambridge University Press).

Opałek, K., and Woleński, J., 1975, 'Das Problem der Axiomatisierung des Rechts', in G. Winkler (ed.), *Rechtstheorie und Rechtsinformatik* (Vienna: Springer).

Orianne, P., 1982, *Introduction au système juridique* (Brussels: Bruylant).

Ost, F., 1978, 'L'interprétation logique et systématique et le postulat de rationalité du législateur', in M. van de Kerchove (ed.), *L'interprétation en droit: approche pluridisciplinaire* (Brussels: Facultés Universitaires Saint-Louis).

—— 1983, 'Juge-pacificateur, juge-arbitre, juge-entraîneur: trois modèles de justice', in P. Gérard *et al.* (eds.), *Fonction de juger et pouvoir judiciaire: transformations et déplacements* (Brussels: Facultés Universitaires Saint-Louis).

OST, F., 1985, 'Les multiples temps du droit', in *Le droit et le futur* (Paris: Presses Universitaires de France).

—— 1987, 'Essai de définition et de caractérisation de la validité juridique', in F. Rigaux *et al.* (eds.), *Droit et pouvoir*, i, 'La Validité' (Brussels: Story Scientia).

—— 1988, 'Between Order and Disorder: the Game of Law', trans. I. Fraser, in G. Teubner (ed.), *Autopoietic Law: A New Approach to Law and Society* (Berlin: de Gruyter).

—— and VAN DE KERCHOVE, M., 1987, *Jalons pour une théorie critique du droit* (Brussels: Facultés Universitaires Saint-Louis).

—— 1988, 'De la "bipolarité des erreurs" ou de quelques paradigmes de la science du droit', 33 *Archives de Philosophie du Droit* 177.

PAPACHRISTOS, A. C., 1975, *La réception des droits privés étrangers comme phénomène de sociologie juridique* (Paris: Librairie Générale de Droit et de Jurisprudence).

PEINE, F. J., 1983, *Das Recht als System* (Berlin: Duncker & Humblot).

PERELMAN, C., 1961, 'La distinction du fait et du droit: le point de vue du logicien', in *Le fait et le droit: études de logique juridique* (Brussels: Bruylant).

—— 1962, 'Ce qu'une réflexion sur le droit peut apporter au philosophe', 7 *Archives de philosophie du droit* 35.

—— 1963*a*, *Justice et raison* (Brussels: Presses Universitaires de Bruxelles).

—— 1963*b*, 'La spécificité de la preuve juridique', in *Justice et raison* (Brussels: Presses Universitaires de Bruxelles).

—— 1965, 'Les antinomies en droit: essai de synthèse', in C. Perelman (ed.), *Les antinomies en droit* (Brussels: Bruylant).

—— 1968, 'Le problème des lacunes en droit: essai de synthèse', in C. Perelman (ed.), *Le problème des lacunes en droit* (Brussels: Bruylant).

—— 1971, 'A propos de la règle de droit, réflexions de méthode', in C. Perelman (ed.), *La règle de droit* (Brussels: Bruylant).

—— 1976, *Logique juridique: nouvelle rhétorique* (Paris: Dalloz).

—— 1984, 'À propos de l'idée d'un système de droit', in *Le raisonnable et le déraisonnable en droit* (Paris: Librairie Générale de Droit et de Jurisprudence).

—— and OLBRECHTS-TYTECA, L. 1970, *Traité de l'argumentation: la nouvelle rhétorique*, 2nd edn. (Brussels: Éditions de l'Université de Bruxelles).

—— and VANDER ELST, R. (eds.) 1984, *Les notions à contenu variable en droit* (Brussels: Bruylant).

PERRIN, J.-F., 1987, 'Qu'est-ce que la dogmatique juridique?', in *Formalismus und Phänomenologie im Rechtsdenken der Gegenwart: Festgabe für Alois Troller zum 80. Geburtstag* (Berlin: Duncker & Humblot).

PESCATORE, P., 1978, *Introduction à la science du droit* (Luxembourg: Office des Imprimés de l'État, 1960; updated reprint, Centre Universitaire de l'État, 1978).
PLESZKA, K., and GIZBERT-STUDNICKI, T., 1986, 'Le système du droit dans la dogmatique juridique', 31 *Archives de philosophie du droit* 107.
PODGÓRECKI, A., 1985, 'Social Systems and Legal Systems: Criteria for Classification', in A. Podgórecki *et al.* (eds.), *Legal Systems and Social Systems* (London: Croom Helm).
POLAK, J. M., 1984, 'De Invloed van de Doctrine op de Wetgeving', in *De Invloed van de Doctrine, Feestbundel 20 Jaar T.P.R.* (Ghent: Story Scientia).
POMIAN, K., 1984, *L'ordre du temps* (Paris: Gallimard).
PORTALIS, J.-É.-M., 1844, *Discours, rapports et travaux inédits sur le Code civil* (Paris: Joubert).
POULANTZAS, N. A., 1965, *Nature des choses et droit: essai sur la dialectique du fait et de la valeur* (Paris: Librairie Générale de Droit et de Jurisprudence).
Pour une critique du droit: du juridique au politique (Paris: Maspero; Grenoble: Presses Universitaires de Grenoble; 1978).
RAY, J., 1926, *Essai sur la structure logique du Code civil français* (Paris: Alcan).
RAZ, J., 1970, *The Concept of a Legal System* (Oxford: Clarendon Press).
—— 1972, 'Legal Principles and the Limits of Law', 81 *Yale Law Journal* 823.
—— 1979, *The Authority of Law* (Oxford: Clarendon Press).
REISINGER, L., 1975, 'Probleme der Symbolisierung und Formalisierung im Recht', in G. Winkler (ed.), *Rechtstheorie und Rechtsinformatik* (Vienna: Springer).
RENAULD, J., 1958, 'La systématisation dans le raisonnement juridique', 1 *Logique et analyse* (NS) 168.
RIALS, S., 1986, 'Supraconstitutionnalité et systématicité du droit', 31 *Archives de philosophie du droit* 57.
RICŒUR, P., 1976, *Interpretation Theory: Discourse and the Surplus of Meaning* (Fort Worth, Texas: Texas Christian University Press).
—— 1985, 'Éthique et politique', 101 *Esprit* (May 1985) 1.
RIGAUX, F., 1966, *La nature du contrôle de la Cour de Cassation* (Brussels: Bruylant).
—— 1974, *Introduction à la science du droit* (Brussels: Vie Ouvrière).
—— 1977*a*, *Droit international privé*, i. 'Théorie générale' (Brussels: Larcier).
—— 1977*b*, *Droit public et droit privé dans les relations internationales* (Paris: Pedone).
—— 1983, 'L'interprétation judiciaire d'une norme empruntée à un autre

ordre juridique: à propos des arrêts du 21 janvier 1982', in *Liber Amicorum Frédéric Dumon*, ii (Antwerp: Kluwer).

—— 1984, 'Quelques réflexions sur l'évolution constitutionnelle de la Belgique et les relations internationales', in *Évolution constitutionnelle en Belgique et relations internationales: hommage à Paul de Visscher* (Paris: Pedone).

RIGAUX, M.-F., 1985, *La théorie des limites matérielles à l'exercice de la fonction constituante* (Brussels: Larcier).

RIVERO, J., 1951, 'Apologie pour les "faiseurs de systèmes"', in *Dalloz*, Chronique 23.

ROBERTS, S., 1979, *Order and Dispute: an Introduction to Legal Anthropology* (Harmondsworth: Penguin).

ROMANO, S., 1975, *L'ordre juridique*, trans. L. François and P. Gothot (Paris: Dalloz).

ROSS, A., 1958, 'Definition in Legal Language', 1 *Logique et analyse* (NS) 139.

—— 1968, *Directives and Norms* (London: Routledge & Kegan Paul; New York: Humanities Press).

ROTTLEUTHNER, H., 1986*a*, 'Les métaphores biologiques dans la pensée juridique', 31 *Archives de philosophie du droit* 215.

—— 1986*b*, 'Theories of Legal Evolution: Between Empiricism and Philosophy of History', *Rechtstheorie*, Beiheft 9, p. 217.

ROUBIER, P., 1951, *Théorie générale du droit*, 2nd edn. (Paris: Sirey).

ROUSSEAU, C., 1974, *Droit international public*, ii. 'Les sujets du droit' (Paris: Sirey).

SARTORIUS, R., 1971, 'Hart's Concept of Law', in R. S. Summers (ed.), *More Essays in Legal Philosophy: General Assessments of Legal Philosophies* (Oxford: Blackwell).

SCALFI, G., and ROMAGNOLI, E., 1980, 'Rapport général', in *La réaction de la doctrine à la création du droit par les juges* (1980), 31 *Travaux de l'Association Henri Capitant* (Paris: Economica, 1982).

SCARPELLI, U., 1958, 'La définition en droit', 1 *Logique et analyse* (NS) 127.

SEAGLE, W., 1946, *The History of Law* (New York: Tudor).

SERVERIN, E., 1985, *De la jurisprudence en droit privé: théorie d'une pratique* (Lyon: Presses Universitaires de Lyon).

—— 1986, 'La technique comme analyseur institutionnel: les définitions de la jurisprudence à l'épreuve des banques de données juridiques', in *Ordre juridique et ordre technologique* (Paris: Centre National de Recherche Scientifique).

SÈVE, R., 1986, 'Système et code', 31 *Archives de philosophie du droit* 77.

SILANCE, L., 1965, 'Quelques exemples d'antinomies et essai de classement', in C. Perelman (ed.), *Les antinomies en droit* (Brussels: Bruylant).

—— 1968, 'Un moyen de combler les lacunes en droit: l'induction amplifiante', in C. Perelman (ed.), *Le problème des lacunes en droit* (Brussels: Bruylant).

SUMMERS, R., and HOWARD, C., 1975, *Law: Its Nature, Functions, and Limits*, 2nd edn. (Englewood Cliffs, NJ: Prentice Hall).

TAPPER, C. F. H., 1973, 'Powers and Secondary Rules of Change', in A. W. B. Simpson (ed.), *Oxford Essays in Jurisprudence* (Oxford: Clarendon Press).

TARELLO, G., 1979, '"Sistema giuridico", "ordinamento giuridico'', in S. Castignone *et al., Introduzione teorica allo studio del diritto: lezioni* (Geneva: Ecig).

TEUBNER, G., 1988, 'Evolution of Autopoietic Law', in G. Teubner (ed.), *Autopoietic Law: a New Approach to Law and Society* (Berlin: de Gruyter).

THINÈS, G., and LEMPEREUR, A. (eds.), 1975, *Dictionnaire général des sciences humaines* (Paris: Éditions Universitaires).

TIMSIT, G., 1986, *Thèmes et systèmes de droit* (Paris: Presses Universitaires de France).

TREVES, R., 1987, *Sociologia del diritto* (Turin: Einaudi).

TROPER, M., 1981, 'Kelsen, la théorie de l'interprétation et la structure de l'ordre juridique', 138 *Revue internationale de philosophie* 518.

—— 1986, 'Système juridique et État', 31 *Archives de philosophie du droit* 29.

'Un thème de recherche: l'itinéraire législatif' (1981) 6 *Revue de la recherche juridique: droit prospectif* 57.

UNESCO 1980, *Domination ou partage? développement endogène et transfert des connaissances* (Paris: UNESCO).

VAN DE KERCHOVE, M., 1985, 'Jurisprudence et rationalité juridique', 30 *Archives de philosophie du droit* 2.

—— 1986, 'Fondement et limites du pouvoir discretionnaire du ministère public: aux confins de la légalité', 18 *Sociologie et Sociétés* 77.

—— 1987, *Le droit sans peines: aspects de la dépénalisation en Belgique et aux États-Unis* (Brussels: Facultés Universitaires Saint-Louis).

VANDERLINDEN, J., 1967, *Le concept de code en Europe occidentale du XIIIe au XIXe siècle: essai de définition* (Brussels: Éditions de l'Université de Bruxelles).

—— 1972, 'Le pluralisme juridique: essai de synthèse', in J. Gilissen (ed.), *Le pluralisme juridique* (Brussels: Éditions de l'Université de Bruxelles).

VAN HOECKE, M., 1986, 'La systématisation dans la dogmatique juridique', *Rechtstheorie*, Beiheft 10, p. 217.

VAN QUICKENBORNE, M., 1971, 'La structure de la notion d'égalité en droit', in *L'égalite*, i (Brussels: Bruylant).

VARELA, F., 1979, *Principles of Biological Autonomy* (New York: North Holland).

VARGA, C., 1977, 'Types of Codification in Codificational Development', 19 *Acta Juridica Academiae Scientiarum Hungaricae* 31.

VARGA, C., 1979, 'Law and its Approach as a System', 21 *Acta Juridica Academiae Scientiarum Hungaricae* 297.

VERDIER, R., 1984, 'Ordres juridiques, loi et société politique en Afrique noire', 7 *Droit et cultures* 109.

VERHOEVEN, J., 1978, 'L'État et l'ordre juridique international: remarques', in *Rapports belges au Xe Congrès international de droit comparé* (Brussels: Bruylant).

VEROUGSTRAETE, I., 1984, 'De Invloed van de Doctrine op de Rechtspraak', in *De Invloed van de Doctrine, Feestbundel 20 Jaar T.P.R.* (Ghent: Story Scientia).

VIANDIER, A., 1986, 'La crise de la technique législative', 4 *Droits: revue française de théorie juridique* 75.

VIEHWEG, T., 1969, *Topik und Jurisprudenz*, 4th edn. (Munich: Beck).

VILLEY, M., 1968, 'Les fondateurs de l'École du droit naturel moderne', 13 *Archives de philosophie du droit* 99.

—— 1978, 'Préface historique', 23 *Archives de philosophie du droit* 1.

VIRALLY, M., 1960, *La pensée juridique* (Paris: Librairie Générale de Droit et de Jurisprudence).

—— 1964, 'Sur un pont aux ânes: les rapports entre droit international et droits internes', in *Mélanges offerts à Henri Rolin* (Paris: Pedone).

VOVELLE, M., 1978, 'L'histoire et la longue durée', in *La nouvelle histoire* (Paris: Retz-CEPL).

VULLIERME, J.-L., 1986, 'Système politique/système juridique', *Rechtstheorie*, Beiheft 10, p. 353.

WALLISER, B., 1977, *Systèmes et modèles: introduction critique à l'analyse des systèmes: essai* (Paris: Seuil).

WEBER, M., 1978, *Economy and Society: An Outline of Interpretive Sociology*, ed. G. Roth and C. Wittich, in 2 vols. (Berkeley, Calif.: University of California Press).

WEINBERGER, O., 1970, *Rechtslogik* (Vienna: Springer).

WINKLER, G., 1969, *Wertbetrachtung im Recht und ihre Grenzen* (Vienna: Springer).

WRIGHT, G. VON, 1963, *Norm and Action* (London: Routledge & Kegan Paul).

WRÓBLEWSKI, J., 1972, 'Systems of Norms and Legal System', 49 *Rivista internazionale di filosofia del diritto* (4th series) 224.

—— 1981, 'Law as an Instrument of Social Homeostasis', 67 *Archiv für Rechts- und Sozialphilosophie* 1.

—— 1983*a*, 'Change of Law and Social Change', 60 *Rivista internazionale di filosofia del diritto* 293.

—— 1983*b*, 'Fuzziness of Legal System', in *Essays in Legal Theory in Honor of Kaarle Makkonen*, 16 *Oikeustiede Jurisprudentia*.

Wróblewski, J., 1984, 'Dilemmas of the Normativistic Concept of Legal System', *Rechtstheorie*, Beiheft 5, p. 319.

—— 1985, 'Systemic Validity and Limits of the Dogmatic Approach to a Legal System', 1 *Studies in the Theory and Philosophy of Law* 85.

—— 1986, 'Concepts of Legal System and Conceptions of Validity', 24 *Acta Universitatis Lodsiensis* 3.

—— 1987, 'Validité des normes juridiques: approche analytique', in F. Rigaux *et al.* (eds.), *Droit et pouvoir*, i. 'La Validité' (Brussels: Story Scientia).

Ziembiński, Z., 1969, 'Lawyers' Reasonings Based on the Instrumental Nexus of Legal Norms', 12 *Logique et analyse* (NS) 112.

—— 1986, 'La doctrine, source d'unification internationale du droit', in *Rapports polonais présentés au douzième Congrès international de droit comparé* (Wrocław: Ossolineum).

Subject Index

Name Index